'This book is about building the social health of organisations and how to recognise, achieve and maintain it. I recommend this book not only to those who are responsible for man[...]who are part of an organisation. There ar[...]k, backed up by live examples which giv[...]nking about business and which will hel[...]the business world. More importantly, it [...]ecome more self-fulfilled in their lives thr[...]

William O. Walker Jr,
*board member of European Baha'i Business Forum and
Managing Director of DuPont de Nemours (Luxembourg)*

'A truly trail-blazing book, full of excellent advice for making work a better place for all of us. Very reflective and deeply spiritual.'

Alan Harpham, first chairman of MODEM

'Many non-profits have grown on the basis of "a cause to die for". In *The Spirited Business* the author shows that companies who encourage soul-driven work practices produce the ultimate social benefits of profitable growth and employable people.'

*Professor Brian Henshall,
Co-founder, Knowledge Communities International*

'I read Georgeanne's book while on holiday in Namibia, a country that awakens your soul. Both experiences did just that. The book is an inspiration to those of us who believe that companies that have a culture of caring for and developing their people are the ones that will succeed against those that do not care or do not know how to care.

'Georgeanne has researched the area and has some wonderful case studies. She then continues to give a selection of interesting ways to find and develop a company's soul. Many of them I intend to share with members of the Academy for Chief Executives.'

Brian Chernett, CEO of the Academy of Chief Executives

'I read the first chapter of *The Spirited Business* on the tube and I was enjoying it so much that I passed my stop! It is really well-written – fluent and fluid, eloquent and inspirational.'

Roger Darlington, Strategy Adviser, Communication Workers Union

'Superb research and insightful writing about seven soul-friendly companies. Georgeanne Lamont presents very readable and convincing cases and stories which characterise the many facets of spirituality in the workplace. An inspired, practical and compelling addition to the literature about spirit in business.'

*George Starcher, Secretary General,
European Baha'i Business Forum*

'Refreshing to read a book that recognises spirituality as something shared by all faith groups and a multi-cultural phenomenon.'

Ram Gidoomal, Chairman, South Asian Development Partnership

'A wonderful tonic for the tortured soul of people who work in life-draining organisations. Georgeanne Lamont has served up a great antidote for the rampant cynicism and widespread resignation that is found throughout so many companies in these stress-filled days of 24/7 work.'

John Renesch, business futurist, author of
Getting to the Better Future, New Traditions in Business
and Leadership in a New Era, *and co-editor of*
Learning Organizations, Rediscovering the Soul of Business
and other collections

'The great value of this book is the concrete proof it gives that spiritual values can actually work in organisational life. This is a wonderful antidote to that deadly enemy of corporate transformation: cynicism.'

David Welbourn, Industrial Chaplain

'Companies worldwide are coming to realise that conducting themselves properly towards their employees, their customers, their suppliers and the environment in the broadest sense is good business as well as good citizenship. As they start to wonder how to put this understanding into practice, *The Spirited Business* offers just the right sort of practical guidance. For the best of motives, enlightened self-interest, it is a must-read.'

Tony Stoller, 2001 Swarthmore lecturer and author of
Wrestling with the Angel

'In her soul-mining activity Georgeanne Lamont has exposed the lode called "respect" which yields the nuggets of innovation and the dedication that makes good companies great. This book should be read by every director.'

John Carlisle, Director, John Carlisle Partnerships

'Over the last few years there have been a large number of books published on aspects of socially responsible business practice. However, Georgeanne Lamont's book stands out from many of the other books. She clearly understands the concept of spirituality in business and makes no apologies for the fact that spirituality is illogical, irrational and comes from the heart rather than from the head. This makes her book refreshing and uplifting as well as informative. Reading her book made me rededicate myself to both the understanding of and the practising of spirited business practice.'

Dick Hubbard, Managing Director of Hubbard Foods, New Zealand

THE SPIRITED BUSINESS

SUCCESS STORIES
OF SOUL-FRIENDLY
COMPANIES

Georgeanne Lamont

Hodder & Stoughton

British Library Cataloguing in Publication Data
A record for this book is available from the British Library

ISBN 0 340 78637 X

Typeset by Avon Dataset Ltd, Bidford-on-Avon, Warks

Printed and bound in Great Britain by
Clays Ltd, St Ives plc

Hodder & Stoughton
A Division of Hodder Headline Ltd
338 Euston Road
London NW1 3BH

www.madaboutbooks.com

To my husband,
Andy Rickford

CONTENTS

PREFACE

MANY WORKPLACES DESTROY people; they drain them of hope, deaden enthusiasm, sap energy and leave people disheartened, quietly defeated and in dull despair. It does not need to be like this.

I grew up longing for something I could not name. The nearest word I could find when a teenager was 'integrity', that wholeness, goodness and oneness that underpins life. I was convinced that this was far removed from the world of business, which I regarded with suspicion and scepticism. It has therefore been with surprise that I have found within the corporate world the unnameable quality I was looking for. I call it 'spirit'.

I have found that there are a growing number of highly successful businesses that are passionately committed to people, wisdom and service. Here in the muddy, messy field of commerce are these remarkable, joyful enterprises. And what is exciting to me is that some are exceptionally high-performing companies whose outstanding commercial success grows out of their commitment to values and to the human spirit. They are a quantum leap ahead of other bodies and are tapping into something that makes them different. They are able to ride the waves of overwhelming change while the old-style companies are crushed by them.

This book takes you inside these soul-friendly companies. I introduce you to the people there: the managing directors and financial directors; the receptionist; the packer; the health and safety officer. They are ordinary people, like yourself, who find themselves creating an environment in which some of the best things, like courage and integrity, can flourish and where destructive habits can wither away.

I believe these companies are those of the future and that your work-place can be one of them. I hope that this book will help make it so.

The book involves spirituality but it is not about religion nor is it an esoteric practice meant only for a few. It is a robust spirituality that is relevant to those of all faiths as well as those of no faith, and is based upon our contemporary understanding of how the natural universe works. As such it is full of paradoxes and questions, some of them imponderable.

It is a practical spirituality that can help people find paths through confusion; it breathes life into business; it frees individuals and com-panies to be the force for good that they want to be. The stories that you will find in this book are part of the astonishing evolutionary force that is transforming the relationship between business and the rest of the world.

ACKNOWLEDGEMENTS

T<small>O BE ABLE TO SPEND</small> three years learning about the soul of companies and then to write that up and share it has been an enormous luxury afforded by the generosity of others to whom I am very indebted.

This work grew out of the Values and Visions project born in 1989 in Manchester. Thank you to those early pioneers who joined me then in creating rigorous and joyful ways of developing spiritual and global awareness in organisations. We were building on the earlier World Studies work of Dave Hicks and Robin Richardson. I am particularly grateful to Andrew Burns, Sally Burns and all those in the twentieth-century Values and Visions development group. Later, in New Zealand, Rachel Lawrence and Anne Wicks helped the work to evolve into business.

Thank you to the twenty-first-century Values and Visions development group, which over the last two years has encouraged this book into being:

- to Anne Yarwood, for her sisterly care and for her love of justice
- to Denise Russell, for her compassion, business sense and good heart
- to Sue Jones, for passionately caring about theology at work
- to Nick Parrish, for his great enthusiasm for this project
- to Yin Wong, for his practical critique and broad experience
- to Geoffrey Court, for always taking our thinking one level further and deeper
- to Gordon Dunkerley, for his inspiring commitment to the earth and those who come after us
- to Dermot Fitzpatrick, for his wisdom and generous kindness
- to David Yarwood, for his hospitality and warm welcome.

I am thankful to all the people in the companies with whom I spoke. The book is theirs: it is their courage and their willingness to speak from their soul to a stranger that made the book. There are over a hundred of you – some of your stories are in the book; others surround the book – and I thank each of you, in particular my first interviewee, Roger Gundry.

The process of writing required a strangely high investment. How can one little book require so much? I am deeply indebted to:

- my husband, Andy Rickford, who gave sound advice, coaching and encouragement. He provided the back up and the patience that gets things done. He worked alongside me
- The Joseph Rowntree Charitable Trust, who provided faith and financial support at the vital moment
- my mother and father, Jean and Gordon Rowe, for their selfless support, leaving me free to get on with the work single-mindedly
- the Russell family, who helped in countless, mindful ways
- Jonquil Florentin and Julian Friedman, who made sure that the stories found a publisher, giving plenty of advice on the process
- my daughters, Marie and Beth, both in their twenties, who brought young eyes to look at the work
- Edward Milligan, for being my mentor and for illuminating the astonishing link between seventeenth-century Quaker businesses and contemporary developments in the corporate world
- Sheila Ross, for the early editing; Hilary Hosier and Caroline Taylor, for the audio-typing that made the process flow; and Robert Wallace, for painstaking work on the bibliography
- Douai Abbey, especially Father Tredget and Father Gervase, for providing a re-fuelling station
- Judith Longman at Hodder & Stoughton, who brought clarity, great suggestions and completion to the venture
- Pauline Wilde and Miriam Steiner, for their constant encouragement
- Karen Szulakowska, a remarkable coach, and Soleira Green, a fine guide
- all those people who, for some reason that they cannot quite explain, care passionately about transforming our world of business and who serve spirituality in the workplace in whatever way they can. Thank you.

CHAPTER 1

INTRODUCTION

A MAN GOES TO HIS office and is told he is to fly off on a business trip. The ticket is waiting for him at the airport and he is to leave straight away. His mind leaps to his wife: they had agreed to spend the evening thinking through an issue she is concerned about. He hopelessly recalls his children's school where he is a governor and the meeting coming up the next night. 'I can't go just like that', is his shorthand reply. Casting around for something to hang on to, he says limply, 'I have nothing with me'. 'We've packed the work documents you need, and there's the Duty Free shop – that's what they are there for. You can get what you need there and ring your wife on the way to the airport.'

Six months earlier he would have refused, explaining why. But six months in the company have been highly corrosive. His own reality, his own values and priorities, his relationships with his wife, family and community, have been overlaid with the commandment that the company comes first. The harshness and immorality of this are hidden behind words such as dedication, commitment, getting results, going the extra mile, quality and customer satisfaction. Masquerading as virtues, such words have eaten away at the relationships that give meaning to the man's life, and relationships, like rusted pipes, begin to flake and crumble.

Six months earlier he would have refused, but now he knows the cost. He saw a colleague refuse and then watched him being sidelined out of the company: 'He didn't really belong.'

There are companies that quietly but firmly take away your soul. Those things that you prize most are laid to one side, ignored and

Spirituality is not religion; it is not about beliefs, creeds or dogmas. It is about being fully alive, relationships and that which gives meaning and purpose to life.

**Georgeanne Lamont and
Sally Burns**

● ●

denied. Gradually, as you conform to the company's culture of dedication, all that really gave meaning to your life fades away. Graham has a three-year-old child whose life is threatened by kidney failure. He is still expected to work sixty hours a week for six weeks in order to get the testing schedule in on time. Caroline has not been able to have a Christmas celebration with her staff for the past two years because they are too busy. The fabric, woven from families, friendships, care and celebration, that holds us together is treated as if it did not exist.

The companies we are considering in this book do not destroy people and ignore what is important to them. On the contrary, they encourage people to grow by allowing their souls to breathe and live. I call these soul-friendly companies. They have always existed, but it is now, in this time of stress and turbulent change, that they are emerging as leaders with something extraordinary to offer the world, a way of working that uses spiritual principles to achieve success.

WHO THE BOOK IS FOR

I have written this book for employees who are disheartened, for managers who are concerned about performance but know that they cannot push any harder, for leaders who want to find ways of carrying their workforce forwards with vision, and for all those who are weary and wish that there were a better way. And I have written it for the many people who want more from work than stress, strain and mediocrity.

I have written it for organisations that are going through rapid change. People are being required to live with constantly accelerating chaos that breeds disillusionment, absenteeism, increased staff turnover and defeatism. The old ways of working are failing to prevent the exhaustion of the workplace; a radical response is now needed, to dig deeper and tap into the wellspring of the spirit. The resource that most organisations have not yet acknowledged and which releases fresh strength and reduces waste is that of the spirit. It clears away low morale, conflict and resentment and in their place provides trust, vision, courage, creativity, patience, integrity, connectivity and community.

WHAT DOES SOUL LOOK LIKE IN PRACTICE?

In this book we will look at the ways in which a variety of companies put these principles into everyday practice in their offices and factories, at the soul qualities that people use in these companies. The soul perceives those things that our physical senses alone cannot grasp: courage, truth, goodness, beauty, forgiveness, kindness, trust and joy. It needs soul to see these qualities, and in a cynical environment that destroys the soul, these qualities cannot be recognised. Courage is then seen as foolhardiness, truth as naivety; goodness is plain daft, beauty is completely irrelevant, forgiveness does not exist, patience is tested and fails, compassion is alien, kindness is soft-in-the-head, trust is foolishness, and joy is not a word to be used.

In *The Spirited Business* managing directors talk about how they drew on spirit in setting up their companies, and how these values continue to nourish their organisations. Receptionists, the newest recruits and others tell of how it all works in the humdrum of daily life. Their stories offer positive ways of addressing many of the major concerns of current business-disillusionment, burnout, sickness, high staff turnover, lack of loyalty, low performance, cynicism, work/life imbalance and resistance to change. These stories demonstrate that spirituality in the workplace is about everyday practice and common sense, and that it offers radical and pioneering ways

3

forward. They show new ways of seeing and running hard-pressed organisations, and of creating working environments where both business and the human spirit can thrive. Here, soul and clear business objectives work side by side in mutual support.

This is not a theoretical study, and there are many aspects of spirituality on which I have not touched: the related disciplines of psychology, sociology, physics, theology and economics, for example, bear significantly on this area. There are many facts and figures that I have not included. What I have set out to do is simply to listen to people, listen to the soul of these companies and tell you their story.

WHAT YOU WILL FIND

- Stories of how successful companies, both large and small, are working in new soul-friendly ways.
- Ideas on how to deal with practical work problems and simple activities to help transform working environments so that you can thrive rather than survive.
- Soul paths that have integrity for those who are hungry for something more than dry materialism but do not want to return to exclusive religion.
- A coherent and unique, tried-and-tested theoretical framework that supports people through the process of global and local change.
- Tools and strategies for individuals, teams and whole companies.
- An insight into some of the tough issues that spirit at work brings with it.
- Practical examples of what successful companies are doing to incorporate spirit into the workplace.
- A twenty-one day programme to begin the process of making your company soul-friendly.
- A questionnaire to help evaluate the spirit of your company so you can find out where you are flourishing and where you can make improvements.

HOW TO USE THIS BOOK: THE DYNAMIC CYCLE

This book is practical; it is about looking at soul at work, what this really means in practice and how one goes about developing it. What we are looking at are not static facts but an experience that is dynamic and evolutionary. In order to work with this process of transformation we use a particular cycle developed in 1992 and used since with countless groups. It is adapted from the widely used learning cycle of experience, reflection and action (Figure 1). We start from our own experience, at the heart of which, inextricably linked, lie suffering and joy. We then reflect on our experience, using one or more of the eight spiritual tools listed below. Through reflection, we come

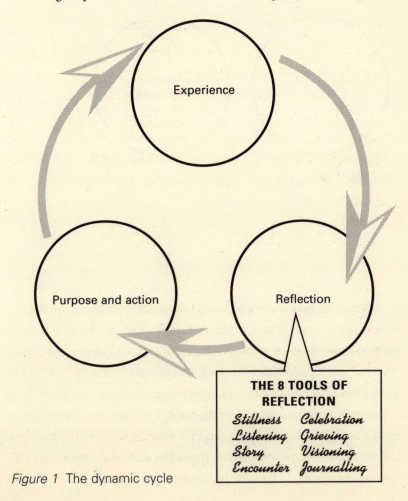

Experience

Purpose and action

Reflection

THE 8 TOOLS OF REFLECTION

Stillness   Celebration
Listening   Grieving
Story   Visioning
Encounter   Journalling

Figure 1 The dynamic cycle

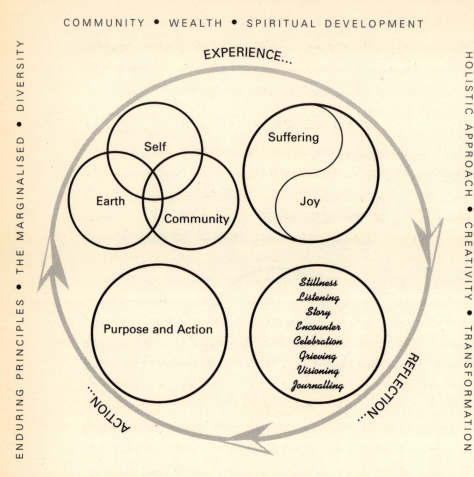

COMMUNITY • WEALTH • SPIRITUAL DEVELOPMENT

EXPERIENCE...

Self

Earth

Community

Suffering

Joy

Purpose and Action

Stillness
Listening
Story
Encounter
Celebration
Grieving
Visioning
Journalling

ACTION...

REFLECTION...

ENDURING PRINCIPLES • THE MARGINALISED • DIVERSITY

HOLISTIC APPROACH • CREATIVITY • TRANSFORMATION

HERE AND NOW • VALUES AND VISIONS • HUMAN BEINGS

Figure 2 Framework for transformation

to a deeper understanding of our purpose and can therefore decide how to act – inner change leading to outer change. This action then gives us new experiences on which we reflect, and so the cycle continues (Figure 2, above). Each part of this cycle is crucial if action is to be grounded in wisdom and experience.

For each of the companies in the book, I will describe their experience, then reflect on their story and provide ideas for action that you can take into your own workplace. If you just want inspiration, read the stories and skip the reflection and action. If you want to change your work experience, use the points of reflection and the activities that follow – you will swiftly begin to see a transformation of your workplace.

WHEN THE CRUNCH COMES

It is when the bottom line meets the principles, when financial necessity encounters ideals, it is then, at that very moment that it is crucial not to sacrifice one to the other. You *can* have both *if* you pass the material difficulty through the prism of your values and your vision. This will show you the most powerful way of dealing with it, by enabling you to tap into your core motivating forces. In doing this, in the moment of embracing both the material constraint and the higher ideal, there will be spiritual growth. It will become possible to jettison resentment, gossip and negativity in favour of forgiveness and humour. The retreat into the safety of *either* this *or* that will be replaced by *we* shall have it all. The blockage of energy that comes from prejudice and fear, and the tendency to look for someone to blame, will be replaced by a feeling of shared responsibility: we are all in this together. This will take strength, faith and the will to move away from egoism into altruism. At the very moment when you refuse to choose between the bottom line and the values, and insist instead that the company can have both, at that moment of ridiculous belief, then all else follows, and the company takes on a soul force. There is no guarantee, and at times there will be disappointment; but the companies in this book share a quality of resilience. Whatever hits them, and however hard, they spring back, and are willing to go forwards through the confusion and trust the adventure.

● ● ● ● ● ● ● ● ● ● ● ● ● ● ●

*In the next century, a company will stand or fall
on its values.*

Robert Haas, Levi Strauss

WHERE THE BOOK COMES FROM

Throughout the 1980s I worked on developing global awareness in public sector organisations. Whenever I was working with a group, I found that a process of transformation took place: people who had arrived tired and dispirited left energised and with an appetite for life. I recognised that what was happening was in fact related to spirituality. It was about people getting back in touch with their hope and remembering their vision. I decided to set up a national project, Values and Visions, to work on spiritual awareness. Originally the work was aimed at the educational world, it has since been used in many contexts, including war-torn areas of the world. I then became concerned that workplaces were becoming soul-destroying, and I wanted to use the knowledge I had gained from the Values and Visions work. I have therefore spent the past three years going into successful thriving organisations to see what spirit looks like in practice in the corporate world, listening to their experiences and distilling the lessons they have on how to have success with soul.

The small and medium-sized companies were not hard to find. I suspect that there are many small companies out there where people work with passion and soul. Locating the large multinationals was, however, more of a challenge. The companies were to some degree self-selecting. I rang dozens of multinationals and explained that I was writing a book on companies in which values and soul were important. Some companies understood these words, others did not; the former invited me in, the latter did not return my call.

I chose seven of the companies I visited to cover aspects of the corporate world that touch all our lives. For each company, there are just a few glimpses of the people and facets of highly complex organisations. Each company could have a whole book written about it, but what I hope emerges is the spirit of these companies – how they make money, run a business and do something far more astonishing, create a company that generates soul.

CHAPTER 2

PRINCIPLES INTO PRACTICE

IN THE LATE EIGHTIES I set out to explore spirit at work in organisations and founded Values and Visions, one of the first national projects to work on spirituality and global awareness. When we looked at what spirituality was like in practice, and what principles were at work, we saw that spirituality is not something brought in from outside; it is already there, latent in every situation. The question is what needs to happen to clear the ground so that spirit can become visible and vibrant. We found that when this clearing took place, twelve interrelated principles were at work.

The first three principles form a BASELINE.

PRINCIPLE 1: BE IN THE HERE AND NOW

The most important moment in our life is right now; it is not in our memories and regrets, nor in our fears and hopes for the future, but in the here and now. Not one of us can guarantee that we will be alive tomorrow. All that we know is that we are alive right now. Each of us has the freedom to make of the present moment what we will. As individuals, the more time we can spend alive to the present moment, the more we can experience our power. As part of a company, we are at our most powerful when we are alert to what is happening now, to the signals that are being given to us from both within the company and the age in which we live.

One large computer company was so wrapped up in hype about the markets it wanted to storm that it failed to note that a third of its staff had resigned over the previous six months and that yet another member of staff was that day handing in their notice. Lost in the future, they were allowing the present to fester. The resignations were a sign of the staff's unease and unhappiness, the unhappiness in turn a sign that the staff were being asked to operate unworkable systems that would, over the next two years, lead to a collapse in the edifice. Managers had ignored the fact that the key to what needed to be done lay in the present moment.

At Peach Personnel, one of the soul-friendly companies described in this book, the receptionist makes herself fully available to any person who walks through the door, her current task being momentarily suspended while she greets the person who has just arrived. This ability to be fully present and engaged is a hallmark of the company, from the odd-job man to the senior partner.

In an age that has given great weight to the rational, it is easy for people to overlook what is confronting them now and to escape into a world of ideas divorced from reality. Flow charts and schedules skate over the fact that yet another member of staff rang in sick this morning, concealing burn out, or that another old-timer is incredulous at the flood of new-fangled bureaucracy.

The companies in this book are here-and-now companies. They are responsive and alert, enjoying being alive and in the present.

PRINCIPLE 2: STAND IN YOUR VALUES AND VISIONS

Held in tension with being in the here and now is the capacity to be, moment by moment, in touch with our values and visions, and this is the paradox characterising soul-friendly companies. The exigencies of the present are passed through the prism of their values and their vision. The vision acts as an energised magnet of desire that draws people away from the past and makes the present a source of hope in that it faces and leads to a positive future. The values provide a template for decision-making. When an organisation loses its vision, it loses a powerhouse. Part of our fundamental need as human beings is to have a vision that helps make sense of the present. Without a vision, people are like cars without petrol; they simply do not get very far. They can be pushed and pulled into doing things, but the energy that enables then to run spontaneously – not because of guidelines and directives, but because this is what they want to do; this energy comes from their vision.

In a soul-friendly company, the vision exists to inspire and enlighten everyone within the company and those it comes into contact with. Values, clearly stated, are pointers towards the vision, stepping-stones on the path of aspiration. The industrial maintenance group, IMG, uses values very explicitly. Relationships, honesty, forgiveness, tolerance, patience, kindness, humility and awareness are the values that a visitor will see listed on people's computer terminals. These values are consciously practised hundreds of times a day as decisions are made on how to increase sales, how to handle redundancies, how to work with a difficult colleague. And the single value that was expressed over and over in our seven companies was that of respect for others: do to others what you would like them to do to you.

When a company sacrifices its values to short-term expediency, allowing profit to overrule any other human consideration, its capacity to make sound judgments will be severely impaired. Decision-making becomes crude as it fails to take into account the human factors that are, in the end, what guarantee success. Many companies have balanced budgets and cut costs brilliantly only to find that the goodwill, experience, trust and teamwork are in tatters.

The role that values and vision can play in an individual's capacity to create the 'impossible' is embodied in Nelson Mandela. Whether in a court room facing the death sentence or in prison hacking rock from a quarry, he stood in his vision and daily practised his values, and did so for decades. This made him invulnerable to the threats,

11

discouragement, despair and helplessness of a lifetime of apparent failure, so that he was enabled, in a way unique to himself, to begin to heal a nation. People of Nelson Mandela's calibre are rare, but what I have seen in soul-friendly companies is a similar capacity of people to hold to their values and vision, unshaken by some of the overwhelming misfortunes that confront any organisation. They have a steadiness that enables them to survive some crushing blows. When Microsoft's shares fell from $120 to $40 overnight it was the passion with which they believed in their vision – a vision of a world in which people connect – that helped staff to move through the discouragement and disappointment.

Visionaries can at times be dangerous people as their vision may be out of touch with reality and fuelled by prejudice or psychosis. It is therefore important, first that the vision is fully grounded in current reality, in everyday needs and experience, and second that the vision is compatible with a respect for human beings, for the needs and rights of all peoples, individuals and groups. Although all the individuals within a company will have their own personal values and vision, there is often much shared ground, and when staff are aligned behind a shared vision and are able to practise their values, their combined effect can move mountains.

PRINCIPLE 3: HUMAN BEINGS MATTER

Perhaps the most radical question one can ask is 'What is a human being?' – the answer to this is likely to colour all one's relationships and transactions. A human being is a bundle of almost infinite possibilities. As humans we are capable of compassion, creativity, fun and love beyond imagination, but we are also capable of destruction, hatred, ugliness and despair almost unbearable to imagine. The creature that created the music of Mozart also created Auschwitz and apartheid, watching while billions of people have died for want of food and water. Our ability as human beings is immense. The task facing any company is how to create an environment that minimises

Do the action that is required of you; action is better than inaction.

Baghavad Gita

● ●

the growth of the destructive seeds while maximising the germination and development of the creative, positive ones.

A company that fails to do this will be dogged with pettiness, envy, anxiety, stress, internal competitiveness and all the waste this entails. The consequent lack of clear communication will lead to misunderstandings, resentments, frustrations and personality clashes. Grievances and divisive disciplinary proceedings may well follow, the end result being low morale and poor performance. Given that people generally enjoy a sense of achievement, this low performance further decreases morale. This quite swiftly affects the bottom line, and as profits are threatened, cost-cutting comes in, further increasing anxiety, fear and isolation, which then pushes the whole spiral further downward. You now have an unhappy, inefficient and eventually unprofitable business.

The amount of human unhappiness here is immeasurable. As companies place more and more demands on staff in a vain attempt to produce better results in environments inherently inimical to productivity, people suffer stress and burnout. Families feel the strain, and marriages break down. At work itself, human beings feel forced to give up their integrity, their vision, their hopes of fulfilment. These become meaningless words. People become instead cynical and defeated.

If on the other hand a company maximises the human capacity for creativity and compassion, the results are seen in increased excitement, satisfaction and happiness. People experience parts of themselves that may have lain dormant for years, and they feel fulfilled. This can lead to a sense of thankfulness, well-being and loyalty that enables people to work with high energy, trust and openness. The results are teams that work with the grace and ease of a fit and healthy organism. This increases creativity which in turn augments satisfaction, so the whole company is propelled forward. Absenteeism, staff turnover, recruitment costs, sickness and burnout are greatly reduced, and performance is high. The benefits can be seen in the bottom line. In this scenario, where seeds of creativity and compassion are nurtured, the enthusiasm created affects countless people as it spills out from individual employees into their families and the wider community. It is no coincidence that the original meaning of 'enthusiasm' is 'filled with god'.

The soul-friendly companies in this book regard human beings as all-important. They treat each person, regardless of status, as an individual of unique worth with great potential, and they offer people the opportunity to grow and develop. They pay attention to meeting people's physical, emotional, mental and soul needs, creating environments within which the positive aspects of our humanness can thrive and in which the negative elements are acknowledged but given little ground to flourish or fester. In each company there are many stories of people who have arrived perhaps with little experience, low self-esteem, few skills, and not much hope. These same people have gone on to become confident and fulfilled people able to offer leadership. The companies know how to grow people, how to bring the very best out of them, benefiting not only the individuals themselves, but also the lives of many others around them.

**The next three principles provide the SOURCES
on which companies draw.**

PRINCIPLE 4: ENDURING PRINCIPLES

The information age has flooded us with facts and opinions, and change is tumultuous and sudden. In order to handle this deluge of information, we can draw on some enduring principles that have weathered centuries, if not millennia, of evolution, providing stability in shifting sands. The reservoirs of this old wisdom tend to be the sacred texts. It is very unfashionable to quote these, and they have too often been used out of context to justify self-interest. Religion has indeed been used by so many rogues to justify inhumanity that many spiritual people will have nothing to do with it.

The leaders of some soul-friendly companies have an explicit faith but the majority do not. Nevertheless, these companies put into practice the principles that lie at the core of all the world faiths, emphasising the profound dignity of human life. In Judaism lies the teaching that we are called to be involved in co-creating with the creator; in Sikhism each is seen as having a part of the divine; in Christianity each is potentially a child of God; and in Islam we are stewards of creation who hold life as sacred. Translated into the company situations, this plays out in people who, with great humility, dare to generate incredible situations, services and products, and who enable each other to transform and grow in unlimited and creative ways.

Another enduring principle is the importance of discernment, of taking time to reflect on what is of real importance. In soul-friendly companies, time and space are set aside for reflection: at Microsoft the leading management team take one day off a month for this purpose. At IMG's factory the factory workers and administrative staff stop each morning for their own thought for the day. Time is taken for solitude, silence and stillness.

* * * * * * * * * * * * * * * *

You shall love your neighbour as yourself.

Mark 12:33

May I treat others as I would be treated. What I like
not for myself may I dispense not to others.

A Sufi prayer

● ●

PRINCIPLE 5: THE MARGINALISED

When one is snug in the middle of an organisation, possessing power and comfort, one cannot always see what change is needed; it is often those on the margins who first experience changing conditions and the necessity for a new response. When the Titanic went down, the wealthy, cosseted and shielded on the top deck, were the last to understand what was going on; they found it easy to delude themselves that everything was all right. Those in third class, in the hold, realised, however, that something had gone drastically wrong. Globally, the richest country in the world, the USA, has been the last to recognise the problem of climate change. Protected by its wealth, it has not experienced the effects of drought and flood in the same way as the people of Madagascar and Bangladesh. The powerful may be cocooned against reality, but those working at the coal face are certainly not.

These soul-friendly companies listen to the newest recruit, the youngest, the least powerful. Those who in traditional companies would be on the margins are brought into the centre. Instead of a company running with a few leaders and lots of followers, all are encouraged into taking on leadership. The work of those 'on the margins' is valued as highly as any other contribution. At Peach Personnel, the odd-job man, Greg, clears the car park of rubbish and does whatever sorting needs to be done. No member of staff is more highly prized than Greg. He speaks with an understanding of the vision that only someone who has seen and known the margins can have. At Bayer UK/Ireland, Millie spends each day tending and watering the multitude of plants that cascade over the balconies of the atrium, her valued work reflecting the authenticity of this company.

The marginalised, often the first to experience change, are also the most likely to know how to use scarce resources and are most experienced in adapting to tough times. They are the gold within a company. Imagine if all their knowledge, experience and wisdom were brought into the heart of the organisation. Soul-friendly companies *do* bring every person right into the body of the company, valuing each person's contribution as a vital part of the whole. And the managing director and financial director do not sit in splendid isolation out on their own margin but are there in the thick of it, working, listening, laughing, learning and sometimes making the tea with everyone else.

PRINCIPLE 6: DRAWING ON DIVERSITY

The tribal human being looks at difference and feels fear. For millennia the response to difference was flight or fight: 'They are different from me; there is not room for both of us, one of us must be superior and it had better be me.' In the soul-friendly company difference is seen as necessary to success and something to be embraced and enjoyed. No one type of person or perspective is adequate to respond to the complexity of today's world, and a company that wants to be fully creative must draw on the diversity of people. Women, men, young, old, black, white, disabled, able-bodied, left-brain thinkers and right-brain thinkers – the full range of personality types – all are needed if the many different aspects of the company are to be covered. The days of monolithic macho culture, hopelessly ill-equipped to deal with the current multicultural market, are passing; such a culture is too limited and inflexible to compete with the liveliness and flexibility of a company in which there is diversity. For the soul-friendly company, however, this desire for diversity is more than simple practical business sense. It is part of the nature of these companies to reach beyond the confines and comfort of their own limited experience as individuals and be open to respecting and learning from that which is different.

17

*This is what Yahweh asks of you, to act justly, to love
tenderly, and to walk humbly with your god.*

Micah 6:8

● ● ● ● ● ● ● ● ● ● ● ● ●

**The following three principles are about the WAY in
which we work.**

PRINCIPLE 7: CREATIVITY

Human beings are bursting with creativity but often spend much of
their lives acting as if they were robots. Soul-friendly companies,
however, delight in and thrive on creativity; it is almost their life
blood. When a difficulty arises, they think, 'What an opportunity to
find new ways of working'. They ask the unthinkable, they experiment, they venture, they fail, they try something different, they play,
they create.

The old way was to emphasise the use of the left brain, the linear,
logical, rational part of our minds. Soul-friendly companies accept this
as vital but add to it in equal part the right-brain thinking that involves
drawing, visioning, imagination, poetry, fun, games, invention and
creation. If getting the desired result requires a song and dance, so be
it. In other words, these companies not only double up brain power by
drawing on the other side of the brain, but also release unquantifiable
creativity by combining the two sides. When this is combined with
trusting team work the results are the stuff of life. Such companies
have been responsible for some of the life-transforming inventions we
have seen over the past fifteen years – drugs that fight lethal diseases,
software that brings instant global communication. Along with these
obvious results comes a change in consciousness, an excitement and a

reduction in robotic, stagnant behaviour. When a restless dissatisfaction crept into the administration office at Happy Computers, the staff threw everything up in the air and found new ways to bring life to their work. When the telesales team at IMG wanted to bring more energy into their sales that day, they stood together and chanted a Maori-style Haka that they had invented.

Creativity that is unbounded by enduring principles and a respect for individuals including the marginalised can be nothing but the idle prattle and tinkerings of a management divorced from reality. Too many companies and people have suffered from bright ideas that have disastrous results. But where creativity is practised within the context of these enduring principles and is channelled into the service of people, it leads to breakthroughs.

The creativity of human beings is limited largely by self-inflicted fear. Many companies expend enormous energy on ensuring that this creativity does not come out. Guidelines and procedures are designed to eliminate the excesses of creativity, to ensure standardised quality. People have to swallow their almost irresistible urge to create until finally they forget how to do it and, like an unused muscle that becomes lifeless, their creativity dies. Structured, left-brain working is necessary. A large hotel chain, for example, has very clear procedures to guard basic standards but it also invites staff to use their freedom to work creatively. When I was running a training session at their Cardiff hotel, I needed some flowers for the group I was working with, but there was nowhere close by to purchase them. The receptionist looked at the huge vase of daffodils that graced the reception and straight away sent it down to the training room.

The companies in this book revel in creativity. It is not reserved for brainstorming sessions in meetings; it emerges at any moment of the day when it can contribute. People enjoy difficulties because these provide the problems that they can solve. Work becomes play. Some of these companies are creating something that has never before been done. Although they can draw on principles, there are no precedents available. Turning a division within NatWest bank into a caring/mentoring division was unknown territory for the managing

19

director. When Ernest Bader gave away his company Scott Bader for it to become a Commonwealth, there were no existing guidelines on how to do it. The people in such companies are often stepping out into emptiness and creating what without them would not come into existence. This is the essential act of creation.

PRINCIPLE 8: A HOLISTIC APPROACH

The old Newtonian way of looking at the world broke everything down into component parts, each part being treated as discrete, and this old model is reflected in a style of management that attempts to deal with problems as being isolated from the whole. The soul-friendly company recognises the interdependence of all parts and thinks systemically and holistically. It acknowledges that each person and task is part of the whole and that the whole is greater and more powerful than the sum of its parts. The company takes on board the entire person, his or her mind, body, heart and spirit. Each part of the company is aware of itself as a part of the larger whole, and the company in turn thinks of itself as part of the greater whole of society.

In the seventeenth and eighteenth centuries, a disproportionate number of Quakers became, against harsh odds, highly successful industrialists, playing key roles in the inventions and development of the Industrial Revolution. Part of the secret of their success was that they 'lived in an ever present certainty of the unity of life and all its multifarious activities'. Compartmentalisation and the separation of business and finance from science, friendship, civic responsibilities and nature was precluded by this inner knowledge of the interconnectedness of all facets of life. This enabled them to make connections and discoveries that escaped those who categorised work as being separate from the rest of life. Similarly, these soul-friendly companies look at life as a whole. People bring the whole of themselves to work, and the experience of work enriches people's lives both within and outside of the company. The unity of life is implicitly recognised.

PRINCIPLE 9: TRANSFORMATION

If you add one drop of cochineal to a glass of water, all the water turns red – something quite small transforms the entire contents. When Rosa Parkes refused to move from her seat in a Southern states bus, it was a small action but one that was the catalyst for the complete transformation of race relations in the USA. The task for companies is therefore not to find large solutions that require many resources but to find those tiny pivotal actions which can lead to a qualitative shift rather than a quantitative increase. This is the sort of transformational way of working that soul-friendly companies use. When IMG telesales staff members choose to see all clients as people with whom they have a relationship rather than as clients with whom they make a transaction, the entire quality of their business changes. When the managing director of an organisation asks for forgiveness from an employee, huge blocks of resentment can evaporate.

Transformation often occurs as the result of a change in perception or a change of heart. One of the greatest sources of transformation is silence – the gap, the emptiness, the hiatus between what is and what may be. This gap allows the possibility of choice and of doing it differently, of breaking with perhaps millennia of conditioned responses and finding a new response that springs from creativity and compassion.

**The following three principles are about the
OUTCOMES of this way of working.**

PRINCIPLE 10: COMMUNITY

Soul-friendly companies build a strong sense of community, of belonging, even when harsh economic exigencies lead to painful change. Community occurs when there is a sense of well-being, when each person and group feels valued and part of a whole, and when each is able to be most fully themselves while, paradoxically, being one with another. Community is ideally characterised by individuals being valued and diversity being celebrated. There is inclusiveness with a door open to the wider world, reaching out to include others. There are shared resources, responsibilities, endeavours, values, visions, history and culture. A community is a living, growing organism in which individuals themselves evolve. It is both a safe place and a challenging place in which people can be fulfilled.

The old tribal community defined itself in terms of opposition to another, drawing its identity from a sense of superiority over some other community. Such pseudo-communities create division and lead to disastrous conflict. The companies in this book have, however, a strong sense of community at its best, each possessing a distinctive, unique culture that is both delicate and robust, subtle and simple.

PRINCIPLE 11: WEALTH

Each of the companies described is successful and makes a profit, for some a very large profit. Wealth and profit may be a thorny issue for some readers: just as faith has been discredited by some who abuse religion, so the business of making money has been discredited by those who have used it for greed. However, generating wealth, when this occurs within ethical boundaries, is vital to the well-being of all. Without wealth, companies cannot exist. These companies take the business of generating money very seriously and do so successfully.

Over the past few years business has been demonised, the many problems of our world having been laid at the feet of the corporates. This is convenient as it means that the remainder of us can rest easy. We do not have to change; 'It is not our responsibility; business has caused our problems, and business needs to take responsibility' we say and then we return to our lives. The pharmaceutical companies are charged with not curing AIDS, the high-tech companies are accused of dehumanising life, and anyone who makes a profit is suspect. But this is at best a partial view and at worst one that is irresponsible and escapist. Whilst there are businesses that grossly abuse their power there are many others that do not. The greed of a few companies does not invalidate the business of generating wealth. It is not the sole responsibility of companies that we, as human beings, have not yet devised an economic system that is humane or just.

The soul-friendly companies described here are successful profit-making businesses; if they did not make a profit, they would be unable to provide the jobs and services they do. The large multinationals in this book work within global markets and function within the harsh discipline of capitalism. That within such demanding, unforgiving economic constraints they manage to achieve soul qualities is an extraordinary achievement.

Paradoxically, it may be that such relentless economic demands will themselves prove to engender soul. As people are being asked to deliver more than is 'humanly' possible, they find that it is only by returning to the basic principle of compassion that they can break through into a new way of working that is creative, satisfying and successful. The old ways of working cannot deliver what the present requires. Evolution itself is demanding a quantum leap.

The companies we will visit perceive wealth in terms of not only money and share price, but also the richness that they contribute to one another's lives. Wealth without health and balance has little value, and these companies seek to ensure that, both individually and corporately, they are balanced and healthy. The issue this book does not tackle, however, is the degree to which they contribute to the wealth of the wider global community and to the earth.

PRINCIPLE 12: SPIRITUALITY

Spirituality has something to do with breath, with life and with that which is life-giving. It eludes definition or containment. It makes the heart light when all is bleak, it brings peace when there is distress, it stays constant when all else changes, it takes the dross and transforms it into something of beauty. It is often known at birth and at death. It is what makes the everday worthwhile. It lives around courage, forgiveness, vulnerability, perseverance, persistence, patience and humility. It is bound up in the interdependence of all life and matter. It expresses itself through care. It is understood by ordinary people and is often lost on the erudite and powerful. It goes by many names. It tells of itself through people's lives, through their stories and is understood in metaphor rather than description. It is transcendent and yet everyday, intangible and yet incarnate. It changes everything and yet everything may appear the same. It grows only in freedom, and it flourishes where there is truth, beauty and equality. It is stifled by fear, lies, pretence, inauthenticity, constraint, autocracy, pride, self-deception, envy, lack of forgiveness and harshness. It requires each human being to take complete responsibility, to acknowledge their freedom and to practise choice. It offers moments of happiness.

It is very like our breath in that it is light and much of the time it is imperceptible, yet nevertheless, like the breath, it is crucial to life. Just like the breath, it is observable only when we stop to pay attention to it. And like the breath, when it stops there is a crisis.

As spirit has something to do with life-giving movement, soul has something to do with stillness. It is like the place that does not change, the place where knowledge is held, the place where the bottom line concerning human life resides. It is here that we know there is more to life than meets the eye, more to life than the mortgage, mere survival and material comfort. The soul hungers for good relationships, for freedom, goodness and a sense of peace.

The companies in this book are filled with spirit and full of soul. This is seen in the quality of their relationships, in the way in which people treat each other as they want to be treated, in their trust, warmth, creativity and fun. It is seen in happiness and the ability to sleep at night. All is not always calm and easy – there are plenty of stresses and strains, crises and losses, there are redundancies and despair – but these are handled in ways that do not attack the integrity of individuals or the soul and spirit of the company.

Spirituality is not ethereal and disembodied; it is incarnate, seen in everyday, practical actions. It is not esoteric and peripheral; it is ordinary and everywhere since everyone has a soul and they either express it or suppress it. It is not the preserve of erudite practition-ers; it is often, but not always, well understood by the young and the marginalised. It is not airy-fairy and vague; it is very concrete and requires specific disciplines. It is not an optional extra; it is central to how we as individuals and organisations live and work. It is not reli-gion; it is common to every single human being, whether or not they are religious, and often it is non-religious people, free from dogma or creed, who are more open to it. It is not complex; in some ways it is very simple – it is about treating others as we want to be treated. It is not a soft option for softies; it requires courage and discipline. It is full of paradox and goes beyond words.

EIGHT TOOLS OF REFLECTION

Many workplaces are awash with experience and action. Between the crevices is anxiety about the past and worry about the future, but lit-tle real reflection on the experience and action itself.

There are many spiritual tools to help human beings make sense of their experience, to reflect on it and to integrate it into their lives. The eight tools outlined here are particularly useful in organisations. It is time that they came out of the closet, no longer the monopoly of priests, rabbis and imams, but there to be used by all who wanted to transform their experience of life positively. They are tools that have been used over millennia by all cultures and that have a place in companies.

- **Stillness:** simply be present, be still, be empty.
- **Listening:** listen with your whole person, your ears, your eyes, your heart, and hear the meaning behind the words.
- **Story:** experience events as part of a story that has meaning, a past, a present and a future.
- **Encounter:** be prepared to meet others with openness to change and to be changed.
- **Celebration:** enjoy, be thankful, have fun, make a song and dance about life.

- **Grieving:** be open about suffering; empathise with others and share losses.
- **Visioning:** picture the future and allow it to help to shape and create the present.
- **Journalling:** use a notebook to take time to reflect on and explore some of your experience.

We will explore these further when telling the stories of our seven companies.

CHAPTER 3

HAPPY COMPUTERS:

CREATING THE ENVIRONMENT
FOR SUCCESS

*How to make companies more human – how to unleash
the potential of their people by creating environments
in which they thrive.*

Henry Stewart

HAPPY COMPUTERS is one of the largest independent computer training facilities in the country, training some 25,000 delegates every year and employing 40 people. It was set up 11 years ago by Henry Stewart with very little capital and only one trainer – Henry himself. Today it is a leading, prize-winning company whose achievements are nationally recognised. Based in London, it specialises in serving the charitable sector and making computer literacy accessible to all, including the disadvantaged. It has doubled in size every three years and is both financially and professionally successful. Perhaps even more significantly, it is a source of great happiness for the delegates who go there, those who work there and those within the wider community who benefit from its generosity.

Happy Computers has as its priority a commitment to happiness, not fluffy, ephemeral happiness but a light, deep happiness that is grounded in courage and compassion. It recognises that if people are happy, they will learn better, work better and live better. The litmus test for whether or not something should be done is whether it generates happiness.

Happiness is a much underestimated state. Although we work and make tremendous sacrifices to learn, to earn, to achieve, to establish homes and relationships, most of this is really done in order to reach that simple state of happiness. Although we may dress our efforts in grand terms of vision, art, excellence and service, do we not pursue these because we believe them to be sources of true happiness? But despite all our daily endeavours, happiness tends to elude very many people, especially in our Western world.

What characterises each of the soul-friendly companies in this book is the high degree of happiness experienced by the majority of people who work there, and this tends to spread out into the wider community. At Happy Computers, the focus on happiness ensures that this is not something that is pursued but something that is enjoyed by everyone who comes into contact with the company – if you need a dose of energising happiness, you will find it when you visit this company.

Twelve aspects of life at Happy Computers show how it creates an environment of happiness.

1 **An exuberant environment** – Happy Computers has created a reception area that expresses warmth, welcome and a sense of home-coming. *Happy Computers practises hospitality.*

2 **Henry's story** – The company grew out of experiencing a failure, learning from it and using the experience to develop something new and bold. *It practises going through and beyond failure.*

3 **Management structures** – Management is carefully structured to enable people to make mistakes, have phenomenal successes, reflect, learn from them and go forward. The management style invites celebration, offers friendship and serves colleagues. *It practises mutuality and care one for another.*

4 **Action groups** – The company is action focused; it identifies areas for development and acts on these, paying careful attention to detail. *It practises what it preaches.*

5 **Feedback** – Happy Computers places great store on constant feedback and builds this into its systems and management. The feedback is given in a spirit of friendship, of wanting the very best for the other. This requires courage, honesty and vulnerability. *It practises undefendedness.*

6 **Dealing with difficult people** – If someone is unable to enter into the caring ethos of Happy Computers, the company perseveres in inviting that person to reflect, learn and develop. If after a long period this person is unable to change, he or she leaves the company. *It practises perseverance with limits.*

7 **Howlers that bloom** – One of the achievements of the company is that it has created a no-blame culture. Mistakes are literally celebrated as great advances grow out of mistakes. People feel safe and open; unfettered by anxiety and fear, they are able to take risks and grow very fast. *It practises detachment and non-judgment.*

8 **Emotional literacy** – The founder is a co-counsellor and has incorporated many counselling principles into the company. This involves acknowledging, accepting and expressing all emotions, both the dark and the light of who we are as human beings. *It practises facing the shadow.*

9 **Throwing everything up in the air** – The company is open to thinking anew, to experimenting, to daring to do it differently and seeing what will emerge. *It practises trusting the process.*

10 **Understanding the finances** – Happiness is supported by material success, and all staff are involved in taking financial responsibility, understanding what they cost and what they generate for the business. *It practises stewardship of resources.*

11 **Having a life** – The company is a beguiling place in which to be, but it does not absorb people in such a way that they have no life outside. The company has received the Parents at Work Best Boss Award for its commitment to flexible working that enables people to have a full life with their families, friends and communities. *It practises passion without addiction.*

12 **Delights, generosity and balancing the books** – Happy Computers has woven a rich, intricate culture of giving and receiving. It brings generosity into daily life and in turn benefits from high performance and balanced books. It makes a healthy, but not vast, profit, the wealth of the company being more than just profit. *It practises the principle that in giving we receive.*

The hidden treasure is wherever you try to leave the world
a better place than you found it.

Liz Straton

● ●

EVERYDAY PRACTICE

AN EXUBERANT ENVIRONMENT

It was a cold, grey, rainy January day, but when I arrived at Happy Computers, I found myself in a room that gave a general impression of sunshine. This café-lounge area, a heart-warmingly cheerful room, is unlike any other I have known.

Large, original modern art canvasses with masses of yellows, reds and blues hang on the walls. At the foot of the tall windows that make up one side of the room are boxes crowded with healthy plants, which a woman is watering, carefully and unhurriedly. Even on this dull day there is plenty of natural light. Between the windows are hung inspirational quotations, each drawn up and framed in its own style, and perched on the window sill is a Dilbert cartoon desk calendar. The tables are covered with richly coloured PVC cloths. Comfortable sofas house satin cushions in the shape of gleaming fish, echoing the well-maintained aquarium by the entrance.

The café is laden with appetising goodies. A tray of coloured mugs sits next to a rack of herb teas, flasks of hot water, freshly ground coffee, hot milky chocolate, jars of chocolate biscuits and a range of pure fruit juices ready for people to help themselves. Everything is clean, the mugs unchipped, the tables shining. Lunch comprises freshly prepared, simple home cooking with piles of vegetable rice, golden chicken, veggie samosas, crispy salad and sandwiches bulging with smoked salmon. Abundance.

Nearby is a shelf of leaflets that outline in clear and orderly fashion the 20 or so training courses available, each brochure stating crisply the specific outcomes trainees will receive from the course. They promise a great deal and make me feel that I might at last manage painlessly to get to grips with computers. A six-foot high poster declares:

> Tell me and I will forget
> Show me and I will remember
> Involve me and I will
> understand

These little details indicate that this company understands what it takes to coax a person into efficiently learning something technologically new.

EVERYDAY PRACTICE

• • • *Reflection* • • •

Providing welcome and hospitality is integral to most spiritual traditions. Far from spirituality being some disembodied, ethereal happening, it is very much about food and drink, warmth and shelter, and taking care of people's physical needs. Only when these have been met can the work get underway. The Benedictine monks offer a beautiful model of this holistic way of working one with another.

• • • • • • • • • • • • • • •

HENRY'S STORY

I have come to meet Henry Stewart, the founder and MD of this award-winning company. For some reason – probably his full, relaxed and expansive voice on the phone – I am expecting a large, rotund man. I had initially phoned Henry out of the blue to say I was writing a book on company soul and could I come and see him, perhaps on the following Tuesday. He had warmly replied, without hesitation, 'Yes, I'm doing nothing that day.' I have an image of a portly individual leaning comfortably back with all the time in the world, so I am slightly surprised when a slender, wiry, man approaches me, arms wide open to greet me in a welcoming hug. He immediately leads me through the premises, giving me a brisk overview of everything. There are the training rooms, each in its own colour, with room for six delegates and a trainer. But no overhead projectors in sight:

> We ban overhead projection because the basic principle is 'tell me and I will forget; show me and I may remember; involve me and I will understand.' It's a very old quote but that's what we live by: everything is about involvement.

Henry leads me into a vast room soon to be turned into five more training rooms. Stacks of unpacked computers and keypads are waiting to be installed, witness to the ongoing expansion of the company. Another large area is being converted into a chill-out area for staff to relax and play pool. We go swiftly through to the bustling room housing the smoothies, the name chosen by the administrative staff for themselves

· ·

A good mind, a good heart, warm feelings – these are the most important things. If you don't have such a good mind, you yourself cannot function. You cannot be happy, and so also your kin, your mate or children or neighbours and so forth won't be happy either.

Fourteenth Dalai Lama

because it encapsulates the smooth way in which they operate. Nearby, screened off from all the hubbub, is the quiet help desk, and further along the new online learning zone of the separate company Learnfish. As we pass through, Henry swiftly introduces me and announces that I am writing a book on soul and have come to find out more about the company. He asks whether anyone can help: hands go up and smiles of welcome look over to me. We then return round to the lounge where we began, and Henry tucks his feet under him on the sofa.

He explains how Happy Computers grew out of a very difficult experience. In 1986 he and others had set out on an extraordinary venture, raising £6.5 million to set up a radical Sunday newspaper, the *News on Sunday*. This was when Thatcherism was at its height and this different perspective was eagerly awaited. But within a few days of its launch, Henry realised it was doomed. The ideas, the intentions, the values were all very fine, but the environment itself was disastrous, fraught with egotistical personality clashes, and as a result the product was poor. The paper ran out of money after four weeks, staggering on for a further six months with outside funding. Henry went away, licked his wounds and then set out to create a business in which the environment itself would be the key to success. His goal was to create an environment in which people could work as effectively as possible:

> The principle is that people work best when they feel good about themselves. What's important is to create a really great place to work, to create a place that gives back to the community, to deliver a truly great service and to make an impact and be an example to others.

Henry emphasised that it was the failure of the *News on Sunday* that had provided his motivation:

> that drove me to find better ways of managing better places to work. I was left with the desire to create something that combined principle with effectiveness.

So he set up Happy Computers, now one of the largest independent IT training facilities in the UK.

Your happiness depends on three things, all of which are within your power; your will, your ideas concerning the events in which you are involved, and the use you make of your ideas.

Epicetus

● ●

It was the beginning of 1991 when we set up the first training centre in a little place with one training room with me and a half-time member of staff. In ten years we have grown from that to fourteen training rooms and forty staff.

The choice of name was significant:

People said at the time that you couldn't have a silly name like Happy Computers; nobody would book with you, and you had to tell people what to do and you couldn't really create nice places to work as you had to make a profit and all this kind of thing. What has become very clear to me over the ten years is that that is all rubbish, that a distinctive name is great. The thing about the name is that you can't answer the phone without a smile on your face; you can't say, 'This is Happy Computers' in a grumpy voice, it doesn't work; so that name actually set it up the whole way along.

Despite people's scepticism, Henry went ahead with his goal to create a whole new standard of quality for computer training as well as happiness, not a superficial happiness but one based on honesty, openness, kindness, feedback, team spirit, fun, creativity, appreciation of diversity and commitment to excellence and to people. Numerous top national awards, the staff and clients' stories and an ever-expanding company all testify to the fact that Henry is daily achieving his goal.

For Henry the most important thing about Happy Computers is that:

It has changed the lives of the people who have been involved with it; they have become more powerful, more in control of their lives, more able to achieve their dreams than they were before they came into contact with the company, and not just the staff but the clients. One client wrote after a Quattro Pro course, 'I felt better about life generally for days afterwards.' That's the sort of impact we want to have. I want to see a world where humans don't harm other humans any more. I believe that people are basically good so when you look at bullying you don't just throw the kids out of school, you look at a human solution; when you look at criminal justice you don't just throw more people in prison; you look at these humans – these people are human beings and what can we do, what can we do to make it work? That there are real human solutions, that's what inspires and drives me, the belief that it is possible to create a more human society.

MANAGEMENT STRUCTURES

Henry's philosophy is underpinned by a system of management that weaves in constant support and challenge. Management in the company is both complex and simple. Its backbone is that each staff member has a coordinator and a buddy; these people, along with team spirit, provide the support and challenge around which the company is structured.

The management is headed by Cathy, a trainer whom I first met as I sat in on a trouble-shooting meeting. As it ended, I asked Cathy if I could interview her. She had that morning returned from holiday and, being a pivotal person in the company, was clearly inundated with work. For a fleeting moment she looked anxious, but by the time we reached her desk a minute later she had relaxed, the mental clock had disappeared. Cathy explained that:

> The most important thing is that everything is set up around making people feel good about themselves, so everything we do should be with that in mind; whether it is as a peer, as a manager, as a trainer or as somebody on the phone to a client . . . whoever we are in contact with, that's our aim and that's something that is very clear to people from the very beginning. If we have that right, then everything else should follow from it.

The coordinator meets fortnightly with his or her staff member to affirm what is going well, to identify what could go better, to find positive ways forward and for both to let off steam. Every six months they have a two-hour long appraisal meeting. In between, coordinators take care of their staff members, getting to really know them and tuning in to when they need encouragement or help.

This relationship with the coordinator does not fit into the standard management model. Nicky, a smoothie who had been depressed, describes how the coordinator role works in practice:

> When I first started here, I was amazed by so many things. I think that the thing that is most amazing still is the relationship I've got with my coordinator. She is someone who looks out for you and notices. It was she, Cathy, who said to me, 'What's going on?' when I wasn't happy. She knew; she could tell by the way I was – and for your manager to say, 'Well, what can we do to make you more happy at work?', I never had a manager who said anything like that to me before.

With that sort of support and modelling, Nicky finds it easy to deal with issues openly. Every two weeks she meets her coordinator to let off steam, raise issues and work on solutions:

> So if there was something that was bothering you, you could deal with it and we would all look for a way to sort it out in a supportive way. In this way no difficulty you may be having with another staff member becomes personal.

The coordinators are there to help people towards their targets through structured meetings, appraisals and spontaneous caring. They help staff members to accept, process and learn from the feedback they receive from clients or peers. Every three months all staff

● ● ● ● ● ● ● ● ● ● ● ● ● ● ● ● ● ● ●

Some day, after we have mastered the winds, the waves, the tides and gravity, we shall harness . . . the energies of love. Then for the second time in the history of the world, man (sic) will have discovered fire.

Teilhard de Chardin

members evaluate each other, this being shared with the coordinator. Feedback is both affirming and challenging; people do not hesitate to give constructive criticism wherever they can see scope for another to reach greater achievement or happiness.

The combination of coordinator, buddy and teamwork structures ensures that many of the usual tasks of management are forestalled. The inventiveness and meticulous care invested by coordinators means that rows, misunderstandings, resentments, overload, missed targets, high staff turnover and low performance are regularly eased away before they surface. Moreover, the process ensures daily staff development so that maximum results are achieved.

The coordinators' work is supported by strong teamwork, which is itself prioritised and regularly appraised, the combination of management and teamwork providing structure and constancy to the support available at Happy Computers. Jenny, the finance manager, describes her experience of that support:

> There is a commitment to each other and to supporting each other. From day one, it's always been, 'What can I do to help you?', and even when people are up to their eyes in their own work, they will still find time to help you if you need it. It's that sort of personal care that makes it fine; even when you're really tired and you've got too much work, it still makes it a pleasure to come to work. It's feeling absolutely cared for.

Jenny is overloaded at the moment because it is a particularly busy time in the financial year, and the teamwork considerably eases the situation:

> It's a priority, valuing each other and you value supporting each other so you will actually make time. If you've got an extra ten minutes, you will offer it. Last week Natalie was working flat out yet she had ten minutes off, and she said, 'Look Jen, what can I do to support you?' Even if you've only got ten minutes, it'll be offered to somebody who is just that little bit more overloaded . . . there's always little gaps. So it is about prioritising each other, and it's good to know that you are a priority.

The measure of mental health is the disposition to find good everywhere.

Ralph Waldo Emerson

● ●

Cathy has overall responsibility for coordinating management, and it is her views on human nature that determine her management style and provide her with the confidence to believe that there is always a way through a problem. People at Happy Computers develop very fast, taking on ambitious projects and reaching tightly timetabled targets. Cathy attributes this partly to the fact that:

> I constantly reinforce the fact that people need support and people need to be believed in – if you believe in someone, anything is possible; they will believe themselves that anything is possible, so for all the coordinators it is that constant thing of giving positive feedback, believing in people. If someone is not well, instead of thinking, 'I bet they're taking a false sicky', it's 'I hope they're OK.' It's coming at it from the real belief that nobody is intentionally going to try and let us down, and if you start every conversation, every thought, with that belief, then you will react completely differently from if you think, 'I bet they're taking advantage behind my back.'

While I was working on this book, Cathy continued to win accolades and national awards. Cathy would be the first to say that anything she achieves is thanks to her colleagues, all of whom make an unforgettable difference to the lives of others, seeing the very best in people, ensuring their happiness and fighting for them to achieve the very highest they can in all areas of their life. Management structures are there to provide support for Cathy and for others in this process.

● ● ● *Reflection* ● ● ●

The purpose of structures and the law is to serve something higher than those structures and law: management structures are only there to serve the highest purpose of the company. The company must first, however, be clear what that purpose is and then ensure that the structures do indeed serve the purpose rather than impede it. This sounds very obvious but the majority of organisations work the other way around, structures and rules binding and throttling the work rather than enabling it.

Spiritual traditions have a great deal to say about this weakness we human beings have for putting the cart before the horse, for hiding behind procedures in order to evade having to live fully. An outstanding example comes in Christian teachings, in which there is an insistence that we should honour the spirit of the Jewish law rather than the 'law' itself; there is an equal insistence on not getting caught up in the trappings of the law and the hypocrisies that accompany them. This teaching is given with passion, not just because the false use of law and structures hampers effectiveness, but, far worse, because it kills off people's enthusiasm and ability to be fully who they are meant to be and so creates misery.

● ● ● ● ● ● ● ● ● ● ● ● ● ● ● ● ● ● ●

ACTION GROUPS

The work of the coordinators is supplemented by that of action groups made up of people from across the company. These groups include the business plan group, the equal access group, the having fun at work group, and the group that looks at the little things like who fits the clocks around the building and makes sure that there are towels in the bathrooms and poems on the walls. Michael, a smoothie, describes how this works:

Every six months you get to choose which group you want to go into it. I'm in the equal access one. We have our plan of what we are going to do, everyone knows which area they are supposed to be looking into and it's something to do on top of the everyday work but also it gives you that relationship, the chance to get to know people who you wouldn't normally perhaps deal with from other departments.

One of the groups is called the culture club. This is a group important to many because staff are concerned that, as the company rapidly expands, the unique quality of the culture does not get lost. Cathy explains:

My highest vision would be that we continue to grow at the rate that we are growing but that we still have the culture that we have now and that's the hardest thing. Everyone says when you get bigger you can't stay the same, and we're determined to stay the same. We felt so strongly about it as a team that we set up the culture club, which meets on a weekly basis to talk about things that can affect the culture and come up with solutions.

When large contracts took trainers away from Happy Computers for days on end, this had an impact:

Obviously what people love about Happy Computers is being at Happy Computers, and if you're not here for long periods of time, you start feeling unenthusiastic, and we realised it was an issue.

- -

This is the true joy of life, that of being used for a purpose recognised by yourself as a mighty one, being a force of nature instead of a feverish, selfish little clod of ailments and grievances, complaining that the world will not devote itself to making you happy. I am of the opinion that my life belongs to the whole community and as long as I live it is my privilege to do for it whatever I can. I want to be thoroughly used up when I die, for the harder I work the more I live. I rejoice in life for its own sake . . .

George Bernard Shaw

The culture club thought through how trainers could take with them something of the company culture to enjoy wherever they were. Ideas included paying for tickets to the cinema and posting off presents and cards. So the good things at Happy Computers – the fine coffee, the ice cream – were in the end packed along with the training manuals for trips away. Income generated by the trainers increased, and consequently trainers working away increased their salaries.

Another issue the culture club looked at was the mess. Happy Computers is an exuberant place, with books and papers everywhere and desks and windowsills filled with flowers and papers. There are no private offices; everyone works in a fairly small space, and these sometimes overflow. Henry is apparently the worst (but not the only) culprit, and some people complained. The solution they came up with was that everyone would in turn be part of a group that would have a full-scale tidy-up four times a year.

Another concern was that the different teams – the administrators, the trainers and the online team – were growing too far apart, so the club organised job shadowing to build up empathy:

> New trainers come in to the smoothie office and spend a day in here learning how to answer the phones, get an understanding of what the smoothies do. And we're just about to do job shadowing with Learnfish, the online department, so that smoothies have an understanding of their jobs and vice versa. So it's very much that, although you may not have to do the job yet, you have more appreciation of what stress may be involved in doing that job if yourself have had a go at doing it.

The smoothies undertake a basic training day as trainers and are videoed, receiving feedback before having another go. This is all part of taking care of the culture, breaking down barriers and dispelling prejudice and lack of respect. People come to realise how complex and demanding other people's work is:

> It's interesting to hear people as they shadow saying, 'This is stressful, I couldn't do this, I really appreciate it.' When we had trainers in the smoothie's section answering the phones, phones were ringing off the

*Let every word be the fruit of action and reflection.
Reflection alone without action or tending towards it is
mere theory, adding its weight when we are overloaded with it already . . . Action alone without reflection is being busy pointlessly. Honour the word eternal
and speak to make a new world possible.*

Helder Camara

● ●

hook and people are asking you for help; it is really hard work. And it's that sense of appreciation that we feel for each other that breaks down the barriers that are often there between different teams.

I ask Cathy about the cost:

I think you can't afford not to do it – because it all comes back to if you have an unhappy staff force; it doesn't matter how hard you're going to make them work, they are not going to work hard because they won't want to do it. But here people want to work hard because they know that if they don't, it's going to affect somebody else, and that person's their team member. We all have a laugh and a joke, but nobody takes advantage because they wouldn't be told off by me, they'd be told off by one of their peers – it isn't acceptable behaviour.

Knowing that the stresses and demands of one's job are understood and appreciated by colleagues lessens the load and increases the sense of being valued. It is energising to know that your hard work makes a difference not only to yourself, but also to other people for whom you care.

FEEDBACK

The happiness within Happy Computers rests partly on the exhilaration of constantly achieving ever-higher results. Receiving plenty of authentic, rapid feedback is crucial to this process as it provides the mirror that gives people clear information on which to base their decisions. Its purpose is not to test, check up on, rank or intimidate but to help people to get results and become who they want to be. It is given in a spirit of support and with zealous commitment to excellence. Henry explains the importance of getting fast, regular feedback:

> We are very lucky in training: we get feedback at the end of each day, and the key thing about feedback is it must not come through the manager because that's then just what the manager thinks of something.

Henry makes a graphic analogy with football. He points out how hard it would be to play the game if you only learnt whether or not you had scored a goal three months after the event:

> You can imagine how effective footballers would be if they didn't actually know whether the ball had gone in the net. And in fact, at work it is not even that; most people's experience is their manager's interpretation of whether they scored three months later – so they still don't know if they scored or not.

At Happy Computers they set up direct feedback mechanisms so that, just as in the training room, you find out straight away whether or not you are being effective:

> For training we have a built in monitoring system whereby if the evaluation hits a particular threshold we would ring everyone on the course and we'd say, 'We got it wrong; do you want your money back or a new course?' We'd know from the evaluations. The possible evaluations are very poor to poor, average, good, excellent, and on a class of six there are basically thirty scores. If two of these fall in the 'average' category, we ring everyone on the course since the evaluations are anonymous.

The problem may just be that one of the participants was feeling off-colour that day but still thought that the trainer was great. If, however, Happy Computers find any dissatisfied customers, they ask why and offer them a free course. The company is uncompromising on excellence:

> A fundamental principle of our evaluations it that everyone is capable of putting 'excellent', and if at any time as a trainer you start to

*We have no more right to consume happiness
without producing it than to consume wealth
without producing it.*

George Bernard Shaw

● ● ● ● ● ● ● ● ● ● ● ● ●

aim for anything else than excellent, your training goes downhill. It may be that there are one or two people out there who are sick of life and always put 'average', but if you act on that assumption you create that result. If you act on the assumption that every single person in this class was capable of putting 'excellent' – and I know from our best trainers that they are – then . . .

Henry recalls the trainer who, over her entire training career involving thousands of delegates, has received an 'average' only once, and that for some minor detail. This track record is the kind of response the company wants and expects:

So don't anybody in this organisation dare have a vision that anything less than that is possible. That's the one thing in the first few months we have to get through to people. It isn't about 'Four delegates put excellent, the other put average, it must be their problem.' It's your responsibility as a trainer to get excellent, and that is crucial. I had a trainer who said, 'I don't necessarily believe what you are saying here but I know that my training improves if I act as though I believe it.' And that's what we ask of people, that they act as though they believe it.

Outside the training, there are 360 degree appraisals for all the staff. Cathy is about to hand out the forms for the quarterly peer appraisal, so she explains how it works, how everyone is appraised three times a year by everyone else. The forms vary according to how closely a person works with a colleague, the questions including:

- How supportive are they of you?
- Do they recognise when you've done good work?
- Is this person visibly or verbally stressed?
- How much of a positive person are they?
- How approachable are they?
- Do you feel appreciated by them?
- Does this person leave you feeling good about yourself?
- Is this person willing to help?
- A real team player?
- Overall verdict.

> So you can't go around not doing those things because when your peer appraisal comes in, if you're not doing well it will reflect through your entire appraisal process.

Every six months staff members have an appraisal meeting with their coordinator, looking at what has gone well in their work, where there is room for improvement and what action they should take in order to move forwards. The meetings are rigorous, and difficult issues are not avoided. If a trainer is not achieving the consistent 'excellent' rating required, the trainer him- or herself chooses a coordinator to meet with weekly, and together they set a few focused targets, consolidate, review and give plenty of positive feedback, reflecting on where things could be done better. The company has always managed to turn such situations round: 'I guess we have done it by giving them feedback, setting clear targets, making the targets achievable, step by step.'

Debbie, who has been at the company a year and is Cathy's support person, describes how she experiences appraisals: 'I love them because they are a two way thing.' She recalls how formal and hollow appraisals were in her last company, her boss making notes and talking while Debbie was just left sitting passively:

> Whereas here I write my appraisals; I put down what I want and then my coordinator writes things next to it, so it's a shared experience. It makes it a much more open process.

45

The process is two-way:

> I appraise my coordinator, tell them what they're doing that is good and maybe what they are not doing so good, and the same with the MD. The MD's one is a lot longer; he takes it on board. They are all anonymous when it comes to the MD and the upward appraisals.

Henry points out that self-evaluation and reflection is integral:

> Half way through every day trainers ask delegates, 'What's going well, what's not going well, what do you want from the afternoon?' At first trainers found it difficult to ask what was going well, it felt as though they were asking for praise and people weren't used to that.

This whole process of feedback and appraisal is integral to the company's overarching objectives – to generate happiness, contribute to the community, provide the best training in the country and succeed as a business:

> We are very demanding and staff have to meet amazing targets, but we very rarely have people failing because we support them to reach them; it's exhilarating.

• • • *Reflection* • • •

Spiritual traditions teach that awareness determines whether we go through life blindly or with the light of truth. Without awareness, we are like the eagle in the fable who, brought up by hens, loses all awareness of his ability to fly. When old, he looks up one day to see a golden eagle soaring through the sky, and laments, 'Oh, if only I had been an eagle.'

As human beings, we have a tremendous capacity to delude ourselves. It is feedback, given with care by others, that can enable us to begin to see with awareness. And if we trust them, we will hear.

Exuberance is beauty.

William Blake

● ●

DEALING WITH DIFFICULT PEOPLE

Cathy states something that is overlooked in some companies:

> No one, maybe only a tiny percentage, comes into work thinking 'I'm going to try and hack everyone off today' . . . or 'I'm going to make as many mistakes as possible.' We don't wake up in the morning and go ahead like that. So if you actually believe that people are doing their best and you work on that basis, then you can turn anything around.

People at Happy Computers are ordinary people in an extraordinary environment: all have bad days, and the occasional staff member remains intractable and very difficult to work with. Such employees receive feedback from all their colleagues every three months, but instead of giving a six-monthly appraisal, Cathy will meet with the member of staff every month and look at the feedback. Every support is given to help that person find ways of making a positive change in how he or she relates to others. There are very specific guidelines for what is and is not acceptable, disciplinary measures being taken as a last resort.

● ● ● *Reflection* ● ● ●

Spirituality is not about being 'nice'. It is not about meekly putting up with destructive behaviour. It involves challenge and being prepared to draw the line. An enormous amount of misery is created by putting up with destructive behaviour. Not handing out blame needs to be balanced with discernment and the courage to confront words, actions and attitudes that are damaging to others.

● **47**

Genuine compassion is based on the rationale that all human beings have an innate desire to be happy and overcome suffering, just like myself. On the basis of the recognition of this equality and commonality, you develop a sense of affinity and closeness with others. With this as a foundation, you feel compassion regardless of whether you view the other person as a friend or an enemy.

Dalai Lama

● ●

HOWLERS THAT BLOOM

Jane is responsible for Learnfish, the online learning branch of Happy Computers. She has very strong views about Happy Computers:

> If there is one message I would love you to get over to people, it is that we have a no-blame culture; it's the thing that makes the biggest difference between other companies and ours. What that means is that we accept that staff make mistakes and screw up – of course we do – and we accept the cliché that they'll learn by it. But Henry takes it further; he says we celebrate when people make mistakes because we know we are learning from them.

It was, after all, from the *News on Sunday* mistake that Henry learnt what he really wanted.

This way of celebrating mistakes is hard to take in, but mistakes are appreciated for what they are – vital feedback that can lead to radical improvement. Mistakes are part of a culture in which people are taking responsibility and stepping forward into the unknown, experimenting and innovating. They will inevitably make mistakes; if they don't, they are playing too cautiously. Henry recounts the story of how when Microsoft set up their UK research project, they said to the director, 'If every one of your projects succeeds, you have failed.' Henry believes this is absolutely true: 'Being able to think big, have a big picture, take sensible risks and get lots wrong – I've got lots wrong and that is one of my biggest achievements.'

About two years ago, Jane was tidying up her computer files when she inadvertently, and without noticing, wiped out the company's entire accounts file. Later that day, Henry came over and asked whether she had been deleting any files as he could not access the accounts. After checking and realising what Jane had done, Henry laughed: 'Well, that's a good one.' This wasn't quite what Jane had expected:

> I was gobsmacked that that was his response, he just laughed. That's an example of where I made a genuine mistake and it wasn't wilfully or neglectfully doing something – I just made a genuine error and this company goes, 'Hey, you made a mistake, well done.'

There were positive outcomes to this mistake though. Until then, the computer network had followed the open principles of the company – everyone having access to everything. This problem alerted them to the need to build security into the system; the technician established read-only zones such that the whole IT system was strengthened. And a day and a half later, they had retrieved the accounts too.

Michael, a young graduate, joined the company at the basic level as a smoothie. Within weeks, he realised that one of the things he enjoyed most was design. When Happy Computers won an award, Michael took responsibility for designing and producing the banner for the award ceremony. At the last moment, the printing company was changed, but Michael had not realised that each printer uses different specifications so did not adjust the spec. The banner came back from the printers with letters missing; it was as good as useless and £150 had gone down the drain. Michael recalls what happened:

> It was seen as 'It's a banner', simple as that. It's not a case of 'You're to blame and you're incompetent.' It was for an exhibition, and if we didn't have it there it wasn't going to be the end of everything. I like detail, and if I'm doing something I like things to go well, and I'm very much the sort that if something goes wrong it comes back on me, but here it doesn't. Being reassured that it's not my fault makes a big, big difference. Before I would have probably said, 'That's it; I

EVERYDAY PRACTICE

49

don't want anything more to do with printers and desktop publishing', but now its like seeing I'm there for the next time.

The result was positive; Michael gained information fundamental to his understanding of design work and is now playing a key role in preparing the company's course programmes for publication.

This approach towards mistakes means that there are no cover-ups – all the information is out in the open for all to see and use. Without the fear of failure, there is a willingness to take risks and experiment, with the result that there is steady innovation, development and improvement, and with it joy, fun and exhilaration.

This no-blame approach extends to both staff and delegates. If, as rarely happens, a delegate does not appear to succeed on a course, no blame is attached to either the trainer or the delegate, the matter instead being confronted. Happy Computers' commitment is that every delegate will go away from the course fully satisfied, having achieved what the course objectives promise. For two years afterwards, a help desk is available for delegates to phone in if they need help, problems being sorted out within fifteen minutes. Jane recalled how one student kept ringing in long after the course, and it was apparent that they had not mastered the content. The student was invited to come for a free repeat course, but this still did not get the result. Finally, he was given a two-hour one-to-one tuition session and subsequent phone support. At no point was the delegate viewed as being a problem. As Jane put it, everyone has different learning styles and needs – this particular person had difficulties memorising and needed a lot of reinforcement. Finding a way through was a challenge that the company gladly took on, developing its ingenuity as it experimented with new ways to tackle this individual's particular learning style.

The no-blame philosophy that permeates Happy Computers implies that if people do not achieve, we need to change the environment and create one in which they can be who they really are. It is for the organisation and the people within it to give the support needed for this to happen. Happy Computers is laid-back and relaxed, but it is also a formidably disciplined and rigorous organisation in which high professionalism and excellence walk hand in hand with kindness. Although mistakes are celebrated, excellence is not compromised: anything less than success is not accepted. In this environment, feedback can flourish and be given free of judgment.

• • • *Reflection* • • •

Spiritual traditions such as Christianity and Buddhism advise us to be very, very cautious about blaming and judging others. Our perspective as human beings is often too limited to have validity, and our own failings are too many for us to make free with lightly judging others. The most famous teaching on this talks of removing the beam from our own eye before we try to take a speck out of someone else's. Happy Computers gives an extraordinary example of the liberating effect of forgoing the petty pleasures of blame and judgment.

• • • • • • • • • • • • • • • • • • •

EMOTIONAL LITERACY

Happiness does not come from some sugar-sweet coating of smiles, nor is it born of comfiness and complacency; it is hard won and is the fruit of working practices rooted in emotional literacy. In an emotionally literate organisation, feelings are taken into account. People are aware of their own and others' emotions and work with them productively. The people at Happy Computers are just ordinary people; they get angry, depressed, discouraged, disappointed and frustrated just like anyone else. The difference lies in the way in which these emotions are dealt with.

Some would argue that emotions are, of themselves, neither negative nor positive: it is how the emotion is dealt with that determines this. For

51

example, anger need not always be a negative force, and we do not want to go through life feeling that we are bad whenever we feel angry. I would argue, however, that hatred, dislike, envy, resentment and some forms of anger are generally destructive and based on illusion. For the purpose of simplification, I will define a negative emotion as one which is destructive and life-sapping, and a positive emotion as one which is life-giving. In an emotionally literate workplace, the following are true:

- All emotions are recognised and acknowledged.
- Negative emotions are expressed in a safe, private place with another person there to listen supportively.
- There is an agreed understanding that negative emotions are not to be expressed in the public space.
- Positive emotions of caring for each other, affirming, celebrating, welcoming, sharing and expressing appreciation are actively encouraged.

As a company, Happy Computers may be committed to happiness, but depression is by no means taboo, as Nicky recalls:

> I was feeling a bit depressed towards the end of last year and I don't think many people noticed, but my coordinator certainly did. And she always takes the approach whenever we meet of asking questions like what could we be doing differently, what's going well for you, what isn't going well for you, what do you need, is there anything I can do to help? So it's trying to look at ways around it and at what else can be done to try and do things differently.

A number of things emerged from her coordinator's questions. First, Nicky was overloaded, so her work was shared out with her colleagues. Second, Nicky was not fulfilling all her potential and was feeling uneasy inside because of this. It turned out that although she was a smoothie, she was in fact a natural trainer, so she has now begun to learn how to be a trainer. Third, in Nicky's own words:

> Travelling and visiting other places is very much where my heart lies – I live from one holiday to the next by planning the next one and looking forward to it terribly.

I was angry with my friend
I told my wrath, my wrath did end.
I was angry with my foe:
I told it not, my wrath did grow.

William Blake

● ● ● ● ● ● ● ● ● ● ● ●

Here she was, though, in a permanent job feeling the doors to the world closed. Nicky's coordinator had an idea: 'You could take some unpaid leave if you like; you could buy some holiday, start paying for it now and then take, if you wanted, two months off next year.' As Nicky says:

> It's lovely to know that I have that option. Whereas I was thinking, 'I'm not sure if I want to stay in a permanent job; I might have to leave so that I can go off and do some travelling', now I know that here I don't have to leave; I could take a sabbatical for however long and come back, and it wouldn't count against me. On the contrary, everyone here would be really pleased – it would be seen as a positive thing.

So it's OK to long to travel, it's OK to feel frustrated when you are not doing a job reflecting your real talents, it's OK to be human, but if the longing and frustration lead to feelings of depression, these need to be addressed.

Cathy is a very warm person and many people seek her out:

> I'm having loads of one-to-one meetings with loads of people where they shout and scream, stamp their foot, bang the desk, bang the door. And that is fine. What we say is that it is acceptable to do it privately, but it isn't acceptable to dump whatever you're going through in the middle of the office because that isn't fair on everyone else who is trying to work and has to witness that. Everyone is human, no one is perfect, and everybody has frustrating days. Everybody is allowed to have those days and to speak about them. You can offer solutions, ask why it has happened, what's gone wrong, what could we do differently, what would you do differently?

If you are unhappy, find your coordinator, buddy or friend, find a

Anger blows out the lamp of the mind.

Robert Ingersol

• •

free meeting room, express your feelings and then return to your work, leaving those feelings aside for the time being and instead expressing constructive emotions.

Cathy stresses that:

> It is crucial to express one's emotions – if you've got those feelings, whatever they are, they're real for you, so there is absolutely no point in burying them and someone saying, 'Oh you'll get over it' because all that is going to do is drive you wild. So yes, we absolutely encourage whoever it is to express it, but it has to be done in a contained way.

• • • *Reflection* • • •

This approach is part of the inner discipline that Happy Computers practises, a discipline requiring people to accept that we do have a choice over how we react, that we are able to cultivate our emotions. This is not about repressing these emotions but about understanding and taming them. It involves actively choosing not to harm our colleagues through negativity but instead to support them by being positive.

Each spiritual tradition has much to say about emotions, about the destruction that is wrought by hatred, envy, pride and some forms of anger, and about the heaven that is built through compassion and kindness. Unless a business acknowledges the role of these emotions within the workplace, it is disabling itself when it comes to handling the conflicts and distress that negative emotions generate. It can draw also only haphazardly on the immensely powerful force available and there to be used, that is compassion.

THROWING EVERYTHING UP IN THE AIR

Ensuring that all the details are right for 25,000 delegates entails a great many phone calls and much preparation and follow-up. Taking care of all the administrative functions can become dull. Cathy explains how staff sometimes feel fed up with doing a certain job or want to try something new: 'Probably the most important thing for people is that they are listened to and we change things.'

When Cathy had taken over coordinating the smoothies three years previously, there had been a divide: those who had been there a long time did the most interesting jobs, and the boring bits were left to the newer people. Cathy tried many tactics to wear down the division, but the breakthrough finally came when they posed the question, 'Why do certain people have to do certain jobs?', to which the answer given was 'Well, they don't.' Then they did something quite extraordinary; they threw all the administrative tasks up in the air. Together they made a long list of all the fifty to sixty tasks done by smoothies, put them up on a board and then they went out for lunch. Over lunch, each person ticked the tasks he or she wanted to do. When Cathy and Debbie collated the results, they found that everyone ended up getting what they wanted:

> It was like saying, 'If I could pick my job description this is what it would look like.' We got everyone to get all the things they wanted, and surprisingly everyone wanted different things, so it was really brilliant.

The few unwanted jobs are rotated round so that each individual needs do them only once every six weeks – and no one minds that.

There are, of course, repetitive jobs in the company:

> Things like checking the manuals – someone has each night to check that tomorrow's manuals are correct, no mistakes, because it's front-line stuff. It was a question of wanting to get it right for the delegates and making it work for people here, and I think we worked it out in a very collective way and came up with a solution that people are thrilled with.

This process of throwing all the jobs up in the air is undertaken every six months and works well, dispelling the possibility of stagnation.

EVERYDAY PRACTICE

55

• • • *Reflection* • • •

When everyone chooses what they want to do, their different personalities mean that it all pans out quite simply and naturally, each getting their preference. One body, many different parts making a whole. This particular Happy Computers practice of being willing to throw everything up in the air demonstrates a commitment to people's happiness, a great degree of faith in people's multifaceted talentedness, and a trust in letting go and being open to the new.

Spiritual traditions teach that there is a paradoxical need to hold on to that of true worth which endures as well as to be ready to let go and be open to whatever is being called for if we are to be fully alive. Habit and robotic behaviour, mindlessly doing what has always been done before, are anathema to being spiritually alive to the needs around us.

• •

UNDERSTANDING THE FINANCES

The staff at Happy Computers are all involved in the finances of the company and understand how it runs. However new they are, they quickly become conversant with this area so that they can make decisions within the context of their understanding. This awareness is like salt, seasoning the work, giving it a certain edge. Jane gives her perspective on this:

> Henry would love us all to understand the accounts, and every so often he does a workshop on basic accounting, understanding profit and loss, cost of sale against turnover. He tries to get us all to understand what's involved.

Staff become sensitive to whatever might affect the financial health of the company. There was a tube train strike the week I went in to visit Happy Computers, and Nicky, as a smoothie, had been ringing round delegates to see whether they would be able to get to the courses, cancelling and juggling schedules to meet delegates' and trainers' needs: 'As a small company, the tube strike is going to cost us a lot of money.'

When Nicky used to work for a large American multinational, she had no knowledge of their finances, but at Happy Computers she is alert to each monthly cash flow and the factors affecting it and is concerned to contribute. So she has, for example, devised a new invoice format to improve client payment response time. When dealing with delegates over the phone, she feels empowered to make immediate decisions because she is aware of the financial implications of those decisions. This makes for efficient, fast decision-making, which in turn improves performance and increases customer satisfaction:

> If I am on the phone to a client and I can tell there's something wrong, if we have had to cancel someone off a course because we have two trainers sick for example, I can just say to them, 'OK, I'm going to give you the next course for free.' And that's my decision. Everyone here understands the financial implications of things like cancellations. We all want this company to make a profit, so we're not wanting to give everything away, but we also know how important it is to keep loyal clients. We all have a sound understanding of what things really cost and how much money we need to make, but customer service is really important to us.

As a small expanding company, there have been times when cash flow has been critical. The social audit reports:

> Happy Computers experienced a cash flow crisis in August 1995, after realising a hectic period of growth that had not led to profit. Costs had been allowed to grow faster than sales. All staff were actively involved in finding solutions, particularly cutting cost, and the company returned to profit within one month.

Cathy remembers this time:

> I was fairly new to the company, but I remember everyone pulling together and I remember everyone hoping we got through it because they didn't want to work anywhere else. I remember it being scary, and we often look back and laugh about it.

EVERYDAY PRACTICE

EVERYDAY PRACTICE

The cost-cutting, however, had limits beyond which staff were not prepared to go, as Jane recalls:

> Cost-cutting was a scary phase, but we never cut anything for the delegates – their whole experience here is about everything, not just the good training; it's about the nice lunches, the ice creams, decent coffee; we've never cut back on those, even when it was financially tough. It is part of what we do – it would be like training in a grey room – cheaper but not so interesting. We don't want to do it like that, and it seems to have paid off. We are financially buoyant at the moment, which is really nice after a tough period last year.

The social statement audit also reported that:

> A profit-related pay [PRP] scheme was introduced in 1995 to enable staff to share in any success they created. Initially it was for 10% of profits among all the staff. The staff were given a further choice of whether they wished to exchange £500 of their next wage increase for a further 10% of profit-related pay. Although this discussion happened after a year of losses (expanding to the new training centre), the staff voted unanimously to forfeit the £500 rise and go for the extra PRP. They also decided that profit-related pay should be shared equally among all full-time staff.

There is at times a conflict between people and profit, but for Henry the answer is quite simple: 'We choose people.'

• • • *Reflection* • • •

Taking care of the finances is an absolutely vital part of ensuring the happiness within the organisation. All parts of life are sacred including the financial. How we generate profit, how we steward our resources, affects the lives and well-being of others. Having clear financial targets is not only vital for the viability of the organisation, but also helps to provide focus, energy and zest to the way in which people work.

HAVING A LIFE

Cathy places great emphasis on creating the right work/life balance:

> We encourage anyone who wants to to go part time, anyone who
> wants to to do different hours; we try to do whatever we can to
> make it flexible because we really care about an individual, not just
> on the work level but beyond that. I only work four days a week;
> that's my personal choice and that's what I do, and its about trying
> to create that level of choice not just for people in a high position,
> because that's not fair. Everyone should have equal rights to that,
> and that's what we are about – equality and flexibility . . .

Cathy is the most senior manager in the company and is passionate
about the place but she is also very aware that it is a question of balance.

> I love my job and I love being here, but I want some life outside, and
> when I was offered the chance I decided to take one day off a week.
> My partner drives a black taxi so we tend to spend the time togeth-
> er, and in summer it means we can have long weekends away. I don't
> want my work life to overshadow my family life and vice versa. I
> want to work and do everything, and I don't see why I shouldn't.

Henry spends one morning a week helping in his local primary school,
where he is chair of governors. Shelley, a trainer, a mother of three and
an Orthodox Jew, has very flexible times, working four days a week, taking extra annual leave to cover the school holidays, coming in to work
at 9.30 after the school-run, and taking time off for the Jewish holidays:

> If I have to leave early, everything will be manoeuvred. When one is
> doing a desk job that sort of thing is easier, but I'm a trainer and
> courses run from 10.00 to 5.00, and if I need to leave early that is a
> bit more difficult. But as long as we know well in advance, Suzy will
> rejig schedules, rebook courses, switch trainers, make every effort to
> make that OK.

Jane started work with Happy Computers in 1996 as a trainer,
becoming a techie the following year. Six months later, she left on
maternity leave, but she continued to come in monthly to meet her
manager and maintain crucial contact, bringing her baby along to

EVERYDAY PRACTICE

59

the meetings. Seven months later Jane returned to work three days a week as a smoothie, giving her flexibility to leave early to meet childcare deadlines. Five months later, she returned to full-time work as a smoothie. In 2000, when Jane's childcare arrangements became more flexible she decided to revert to training on four days a week. The company started to provide online training the following month, and Jane joined that team as an online mentor. She has since added training and Learnfish sales to her job description:

> Look at that list of changes! How many companies could not only accommodate my change of circumstances (and career choices) but do so so cheerfully and helpfully. It's one of the main reasons why I work here!

But are there no limits? The parameters are set as the balance between three aspects – individual happiness, financial requirements and excellence of performance. Then it is a matter of smiling and trusting.

Eugene, who takes Fridays off in order to work with a creative therapy group and provide counselling, points out that everyone benefits:

> I feel that my development as a trainer benefits my group therapy work, and therapy work benefits my training. It's a great way to keep work interesting and fresh.

The guilt-laden subterranean tugs that many of us experience as parents, partners, artists, healers and workers are removed here. As Eugene says:

● ●

Every now and then go away, have a little relaxation, for when you come back to your work your judgement will be sure; since to remain constantly at work will cause you to lose power of judgement . . . Go some distance away because the work appears smaller and more of it can be taken in at a glance, and a lack of harmony or proportion is more readily seen.

Leonardo da Vinci

EVERYDAY PRACTICE

I am not made to feel disloyal or guilty about requesting flexibility in my work hours at Happy Computers. It is seen as something that might benefit the company.

This benefit is reflected in concrete, bottom-line terms too: the company estimates that it has saved 2.5% of its turnover from a 99% retention of, obviously happy, staff.

• • • *Reflection* • • •

This flexibility recognises the full complexity of individual staff members and enables them to honour the things in their life that they value – their baby, their vocation, their commitment to a local school, their religion, their love of adventure. Henry is clear that this has enormous benefits for the company as well as enabling staff to stay true to themselves and to the many gifts that they have to offer their families and the wider community.

● ● ● ● ● ● ● ● ● ● ● ● ● ● ● ● ● ● ● ●

DELIGHTS, GENEROSITY
AND BALANCING THE BOOKS

Spirituality is not normally associated with delights and luxuries, and there is sometimes a preconception that it involves asceticism and self-denial. There is indeed plenty of self-denial at Happy Computers, but this occurs on a large scale – it is refusing to make large profits for oneself; it is giving up one's time; it is putting others' needs before one's own ease; it is daily risking uncertainty in order to create something of great worth. In the small things, however, there is a happy enjoyment of some of the good things of life, much spontaneous, some planned. The company abounds with little luxuries that surprise a first-time visitor. At about 4 pm everyone – delegates

61

*There is more in us than we know. If we can be made
to see it, perhaps for the rest of our lives we will be
unwilling to settle for less.*

Happy Computers

• •

and staff – stop for the ice cream of their choice. This is almost a rit-
ual, but one coming at a time of day when all tend to be flagging; it
helps to revive people's appetite for the last hour's work of the day.

Three years ago Happy Computers retrained the book-keeper as a
masseuse. Now she comes in twice a week to give free massages, priority being given to those who spend most time at a computer
screen. Once a month Cathy's neighbour comes in and gives mani-
cures and pedicures for the staff who are happy to pay for them:

> The office calls it disability day because when we have our nails
> done, 'we can't do anything for half an hour afterwards, so the guys
> are often asked to open an envelope or pick up the phone in case we
> damage our nails. I'm not saying everyone does that, it's not every-
> one's idea of fun, but that's one example of something that we do.
> And there is such a buzz goes round the office – "What colour did
> you have?, What did she do to you?" '

For some young people arriving from more parsimonious companies, it is a luxury to be told, 'That's your phone; what you do with it
is entirely up to you.' The luxury of being trusted is yours by right in
this company, whoever you are. Generosity is not an add-on that can
be dispensed with when the going gets rough; it is essential to the
very nature of Happy Computers.

The company recently entered into partnership with the London
Voluntary Service Council to provide low-cost training to small voluntary groups. Given that these form a large part of Happy Computers'
client base, this would in effect be offering directly-competing courses
at half the cost. In view of this, Henry asked: 'Should we cut back on

what we offer them, to cut our costs?' The trainers roundly rejected the idea and insisted that full-quality training be given regardless of the cut-price fee.

The generosity of Happy Computers is to be found in crevices and in numerous nooks and crannies: the free places given to a designated charity, the day off a month that every staff member can take to volunteer for a charity, the ongoing 40% reduction in price for charities, the flowers sent to people when they are sick, the smoked salmon sandwiches. It is there in the yearly cheque given to each member of staff to donate to their chosen charity, in the acre of rain-forest endowed for every fifty courses booked. It is there in the training and development given to all staff (even when they are about to go on a round-the-world trip), in the flexible work hours and support that people receive at an individual level.

But how does Happy Computers balance its books? The fees are not high; the salaries and benefits are above average; cost-cutting does not bite into the generosity; long hours and overwork are not allowed. Three main factors are in play here – high productivity, patient shareholders and staff involvement at a financial level.

Productivity is unusually high, and people regularly achieve amazing results. Cathy is the senior manager and coordinates fourteen staff. This involves weekly meetings, lengthy appraisals and support for each individual; she trains the trainers; she delivers in-house training and has won awards for her work; she delivers external training; she goes to companies to talk about Happy Computers; she is responsible for recruitment, a task over which the company takes great care; she is part of the trouble-shooting team; she takes on any special care needed for staff and disciplinary matters; she is involved in the overall strategy and development of the company; she is a member of the culture club; she heads up human relations, and so on. Cathy's great strength is her eye for detail, each job being tackled calmly and with considerable care. All in a four-day week. But Cathy is not atypical in the company, so how does it achieve this enviable level of productivity?

EVERYDAY PRACTICE

*You will work harder than you have ever worked and
you will have more fun than you have ever had.*

Henry, to a new recruit

● ● ● ● ● ● ● ● ● ● ● ● ● ● ●

- Staff are treated, and treat each other, as magnificent human beings.
- They have great freedom and autonomy so do not waste time checking out whether or not it is acceptable to do something; they make a decision and run with it.
- They know they are really valued so do not need to waste time on appearances, on looking good, on writing impressive reports and on seeking approval.
- They know that mistakes are celebrated so they do not waste time on undue worry, dithering and dilemmas. They take action; if it works well, they go forwards; if it goes wrong, they correct it and go forwards anyway. They are constantly advancing, reviewing, learning, adjusting, evolving, developing.
- Staff members work as a superbly interdependent team of enormous diversity. Differences are welcomed and appreciated, and people complement each other's strengths and weaknesses. They work warmly together, lightly stepping in to support each other imperceptibly, achieving that mysterious and powerful synergy that many speak of but few achieve.
- Staff are highly motivated by the values and the vision of the company and each other; they passionately believe in what they are doing.
- There is little emotional junk clogging up the company's arteries, and there is a high degree of positivity, releasing great amounts of energy.

The results of this way of working are there to be seen in the financial audit: the company has doubled in size, in terms of both turnover and output, roughly every three years.

The next important aspect of balancing the books is that the shareholders are patient. The company's mission will not on its own satisfy the shareholders: they do one day want a return, but they are prepared to take a long-term view of success. For several years, there was in fact no dividend paid out. But an ability to carry the shareholders along in sharing a commitment to the long-term mission of the company is significant. The company has six external shareholders, friends of Henry's who helped to fund the expansion in 1994. They have supported the principle that the companies that thrive in the long term are those which work to the benefit of all the stakeholders – including staff, community and earth – rather than focusing on short-term profit. The number of shareholders increased from eight to thirty in 2001 as many staff and associates also bought shares.

Finally, there is the staff's active involvement in the finances of the company, all employees daily caring for Happy Computers' financial health. This injects a good deal of energy, commitment and strength into reaching financial targets. This brings us back again to the theme of generosity, one of its most salient forms being the way in which staff are willing to bring the whole of themselves to work while they are there, and the generosity with which the company accepts all of what they bring.

EVERYDAY PRACTICE

• • • *Reflection* • • •

There are many forms of spirituality, including an ascetic model in which depriving the senses is seen as a path to God. But that is not the sort of spirituality that we are looking at in this book. Many spiritual traditions honour the role of the senses and the importance of delighting in and appreciating the whole of creation. There is a place for celebration and 'extravagant' giving without counting the cost, as in the Bible story of the fine, perfumed ointment being poured out. There were pragmatists two thousand years ago who criticised the waste. Yet there is a place for frugality and fasting as there is for enjoying and celebrating. Balancing the two is a fine skill.

HAPPY COMPUTERS GENERATES HAPPINESS BY:

- Having a commitment to ongoing human growth and development
- Having a goal and vision over and above profit, a goal that inspires people
- Entrusting people with responsibility for managing their work and with freedom to decide how they reach the business outcomes
- Making awareness, creativity, innovation and fun a priority
- Building a no-blame culture and working with trust
- Extending generosity to individuals, society and the earth
- Being committed to a full state of being 'alive'
- Being connected to the community at both micro and macro level
- Facing up to the dark side, confronting it and expressing it safely
- Being emotionally literate
- Building in flexibility and a work/life balance
- Caring for each other's happiness and taking time to enjoy and celebrate

PUTTING THIS INTO PRACTICE IN YOUR WORKPLACE:

WORKING WITH HAPPINESS

Happy Computers has a tough side of high standards, uncompromising targets and professionalism, but it is also a company full of happiness, fun and imaginative delight. This happiness is based not on some shallow consumer froth but on a number of strands woven together to form an environment in which people are happy and soul qualities such as trust and generosity flourish. The following activities look at creating an environment of happiness appropriate to your company.

AN ACTIVITY TO DO AS A TEAM

The purpose of this activity is to identify what makes people in your workplace happy and to begin to take responsibility for creating that.

Happy times

1 Divide into pairs. Individually, take a quiet few moments to cast your mind back to a time when you were really happy at work.

2 Then each spend three minutes telling your partner what that was like, what you were doing, what was happening, what you felt, what made it special.

3 As a whole group gather in the main elements characterising that time. (People generally remember times when there was trust, working together, laughter, clear focus and a sense of achievement.)

4 Individually, choose the element that you value most and share with your partner why it is important to you.

67

5 Look at your current work situation and see where that element is already in evidence and where it could be increased. What is your role in this? What are you going to do to make it happen?

6 Make a commitment to do it, and share this with your partner.

7 Depending on the openness within the group, either go round the whole group listening to what each person is committed to doing, writing it on a board, or, if that level of trust is not yet there, ask each person to write anonymously the element they are going to work on on a card and place it in a bowl in the middle of the room. Someone then reads out the cards: 'This is what we will be working on as a team.'

AN ACTIVITY TO DO AS A LONE INDIVIDUAL WITH 'NO POWER'

The purpose of this activity is to help you identify where there is already happiness in your work and to generate more. It is based on a Hasidic Jewish discipline to note a hundred blessings a day over a period of time.

A hundred blessings

1 Throughout the day, notice a hundred blessings within your life: your child's smile, your car starting smoothly, the shape of the clouds, the space in the car park, the colour of someone's hair, the warmth of the office, your secretary's patience, the taste of cool water, a colleague's particular way of doing something. Make a mental note of these.

2 At the end of the day, take a few minutes to run through in your head as many blessings as you can.

3 Choose three of your blessings. Next day, give them in some form – a delicious piece of fruit, a smile, some patience – to a colleague who is looking low.

4 Do this daily over a period of a month and see what difference it makes.

CHAPTER 4

PEACH PERSONNEL:

A PASSION FOR PEOPLE

THE PERSONNEL RECRUITMENT company Peach Personnel was set up in Hounslow in 1989 by Denise Russell. Since then it has grown consistently year by year, increasing its turnover and profitability. Originally employing two members of staff, there are now twenty-eight. The company has three branches and a turnover of £6.5 million. It works rather like a transformer: people come in without work and often feeling low and, in time, as they go through the Peach process, they emerge confident and hopefully with a job too. Staff often start out at Peach as junior temps or secretaries and, in time, with Peach care, grow into leaders taking on considerable responsibility, be it heading up an accounts department, managing a large team, providing company training or organising the business plan. Peach has an overriding passion – its concern for people, be they applicants looking for work, members of Peach's staff or clients with a vacancy. Peach wants to help, and in the process it makes money, doing so very ably.

Denise Russell set up Peach because she loved recruitment work and was good at it but did not like working in the average agency. She felt she had found her niche in recruitment but was hampered by the demands imposed from above. 'It all seemed the wrong way round'. Her previous bosses had put profit and figures first, but Denise was convinced that they had got it back to front, so she set out on her own to do it her own way – a gentle way:

> Recruitment is very simple. You put people on the right path, you listen to their needs. It's got to be right. You use your intuition. You retain your values. You put people first and the rest will take care of itself.

Art washes from the soul the dust of everyday life.

Pablo Picasso

● ●

Denise set up a unique agency where people lie at the heart of everything they do. Knowing what makes people tick, recognising their personalities, finding their strengths, helping them work through their weaknesses, supporting people as they take on challenges, taking pleasure in others' successes, being committed to people finding their right place, enjoying one another – these are the core elements of Peach.

Peach is an astonishing company. I have chosen just twelve of the many aspects of life there that relate to the spiritual qualities embodied by the company in daily practice. These directly affect the company's success and make it a people-centred recruitment agency.

1 **Sacred space** – Peach creates a very special space in which to work; it recognises that the environment has a high impact on people's well-being and effectiveness. Aesthetic loveliness is integral to the company. *Peach practices an appreciation of beauty.*

2 **Riding the recession** – Peach faces a recession with care, ingenuity and a commitment to people. When financial pressures are forcing others out of the market, Peach faces the recession head on and seeks to respond to and overcome the particular human challenges that hard times present. *It practises compassion and service.*

3 **Respect** – Applicants are given the highest respect. Whether someone is an unskilled clerk or a major client, each is treated in the same way, with great care. *It practises deep equality and respect for others,* the sort that comes naturally because it is in one's bones.

4 **A first-class reception** – The reception at Peach is unlike most

others. The receptionist greets people as unique human beings there to be helped. *It practises welcome.*

5 **David and Goliath** – Although Peach is a small company, it is not afraid to compete with multibillion-pound competitors. It takes pride in what it is doing. *It practises courage and self-respect.*

6 **When the going gets tough** – Peach is prepared to confront and then lay behind it betrayals, losses and disappointments. It does not wait for issues to go away but openly confronts them and uses the tough times to strenthen itself. *It practises letting go of the past, forgiveness and a willingness to move on.*

7 **A hard place to work** – Peach has a distinctive culture that has no room for gossip, bitchiness or blame. It requires a willingness constantly to grow beyond the petty. It requires the very best every day. *It practises belief in the unlimited potential of people.*

8 **Rewards** – Peach seeks out the good points, actively recognises them and says so. *It practises thankfulness, gratitude and appreciation.*

9 **The lifter and shifter** – Peach pays great attention to detail. Who knows what is more important – the little kindness or the grand strategy? *It practises faithfulness in small things.*

10 **Minimising stress** – Peach works in a particularly stressful area of work where there is constant change. The constancy of its values and its focus on people reduce stress and increase fun. *It practises constancy and balance.*

11 **The unseen leader** – The leader is seen though the reflection of what she leaves behind and through the eyes and stories of other people in the company. *It practises leadership humility.*

12 **The bottom line** – Peach works like a family bank: all contribute what they can and take out when they need to, supporting each other to stay in credit. *It practises mutuality.*

EVERYDAY PRACTICE

SACRED SPACE

Arriving at Peach was like stumbling on an oasis. I had driven through the one-way systems of Hounslow and found myself by yet another barren public car park, littered with debris from fast-food shops. Surely Peach was not here? But a passer-by confirmed that this was indeed the right road and indicated Peach's offices as though they were a well-known feature. She had pointed at a building that seemed quite out of place amidst the small, drab premises that had dominated my view. I looked again and saw a handsome, two-storey, Regency-style building painted in soft oatmeal and reached through a courtyard. It did not seem a likely building for a high street recruitment agency for temps and I had driven past it. I turned my car round and drove between the pillars; a small burnished plaque with the Peach logo indicated that this was indeed the place.

I had thought Peach was a recruitment agency for office workers and temporary staff, but when I drove in I assumed that I had probably been mistaken – this was only the first of my several prejudices to be challenged. The courtyard was elegantly paved and well cared for, with fine wooden benches, a fountain playing over rocks and unusual plants climbing up the trellises. Large glass doors opened into a beautiful airy reception area, reminiscent of a first-class hotel. The fragrance of tall, white lilies was matched by the warmth of the elegant receptionist who rose to meet me and, looking me straight in the eye, said, 'I'm June. How can I help you?' That question, asked throughout the world millions of times a day, had an emphasis that I would come to understand. When June sees someone walk through the door her first impulse is from the heart – 'How can I *help* this person?' When an applicant arrives, there are a number of formalities to be undertaken, but June's overriding task is, as she sees it, to help and to make a positive difference for that person. The environment is an unreasonable celebration of the good things of life: flowing water, graceful flowers, light, soft colour, warmth, simplicity and loveliness.

This is a special place for temps, and office workers looking for work – they are going to be treated as very important people.

Two years ago, these offices were a grubby, derelict building owned by the Gas Board, its courtyard a dumping ground for old vehicles and defunct equipment. Peach took it over, gutted it and created the loveliness that is enjoyed by staff, applicants and clients alike. When you walk in, you know immediately that this is a special place.

• • • *Reflection* • • •

There are many companies that are narcissistic, preoccupied with appearances and lacking any substance. But the beauty of Peach is not that. It is not about looking good but about caring for people and wanting to give them a lovely place to come to. The environment reflects Peach's commitment to people and acknowledges that, as human beings, all of our senses matter, including our sense of colour, of smell, of space and light. The mediaeval cathedral builders understood the human need for intangible beauty to open us up to there being something more to life than meets the eye. The Benedictines know how welcome and hospitality are signs of the reverence with which they seek to greet each human being, especially the strangers, seeing the essence of that person.

For Benedictines the 'essence' is the Christ within each person; for Buddhists it is seeing the Buddha nature within each; for a Sikh it is the divine spark that exists within a human being. At Peach, no such fine term is used: it is simply described as 'treating others as you want to be treated'. Whatever we wish to call this way of encountering another human being, it is about going beyond the functional and the 'what's in it for me?' mentality, and seeing another person in a way that calls forth a response within oneself of 'How can I help you; how can I serve you?' In faith terms this is recognised as the core spiritual response of compassion; in secular terms it is caring that goes beyond the mundane and that reaches into the area of suffering, joy and service. Peach is first and foremost a company of service. When members of staff were asked to choose an epitaph for their gravestones, many decided on 'She treated others as she wanted to be treated.'

RIDING THE RECESSION

Peach started off just as the recession of the early 1990s was beginning. Denise Russell set up in a dark two-roomed office next to the public car park where I had stopped, with only one temporary placement to fill. From this the company has grown steadily, now possessing spacious offices and an ever-increasing turnover. Staff attribute their success to good fortune and to doing the right thing. Amanda, a partner in the company, talks about the process of recruitment and how applicants were interviewed:

> In the recession we had people coming in whose husbands had lost their jobs, and literally people were shattered, and you'd interview people and they'd be in tears because they found it hard to accept the devastating experience of what had happened to them. Then, as happened on many occasions, you place somebody like that and you find them work; I felt that was a huge responsibility. When I was dealing with temps, I felt I was responsible for that person's mortgage, rent, whatever bills they had, and if on a Friday night, I didn't have work for someone to start the next week, I took it very personally and seriously because I knew they needed to earn money, and I thought it was my job to go out and get work for them and particularly at that time.

Many agencies were then failing, but Peach prospered, and Amanda attributes this to the fact that they were very focused on taking care of the candidates. She smiles at the thought of how people from those days still come back to see her, bringing news and photos of weddings and grandchildren:

> One of the temps I placed took photos at my wedding as a wedding present. I think people want to come back here; they temp for us, then move on do something else, and they want to come back partly because they know staff have been here years so there's that constancy of contact and they know we'll treat them right; they know what our standards are and that we'll be honest and straight with them, and if we say we can get them work, we will get them work.

This help has sometimes been straightforward:

In those early days I remember giving jackets and things to people who didn't have one. In recession times, people couldn't afford to go out and buy, so they'd come in and as they were about to go out we'd lend them a jacket, and they'd go off for their interview.

Now, many years later, another recession appeared to be arriving. I ask Amanda how they are being affected, with nearby companies cutting their workforces and a general reining-in beginning. Mandy recalls that they have gone through this before; they are a strong team and will find the best way through it together. It is just another challenge.

• • • *Reflection* • • •

Recessions will continue to occur. Many traditional companies believe that the inevitable response is to cut costs and cut staff, but Peach sees it differently; first and foremost, this is yet another particular challenge requiring compassion, ingenuity and that steadfast 'I-won't-be-beaten' commitment to service. The energy that some companies put into internal competitiveness is in Peach directed outwards to the challenges.

In spiritual traditions great emphasis is placed on the qualities used when facing difficulties. How one faces them is crucial. One does not lay the cost at someone else's door; one practises patience and perseverance; one draws on the good-humoured faith that one will get through; one remains committed to compassion especially when the going gets tough. It is easy to be nice when everything is going well, anyone can do that. The test of the soul-friendly company is how it deals with the tough times.

RESPECT

EVERYDAY PRACTICE

Peach has two sets of customers – the clients who provide the jobs and the applicants who want them. Peach feels very strongly about its applicants. As June says, 'They come in feeling demoralised and they go out feeling ten feet tall. It's lovely.'

When people come in they have no job and are in need. Philip Russell, another partner, is very aware that:

> Temps are quite vulnerable and are coming to us for support and guidance. What we never forget is that we have all been employees and we know how it feels.

As far as possible, the Peach consultant stands alongside the applicants, helping them to overcome the hurdles facing them. This requires understanding and often calls for great sensitivity and tact, the work revolving around the issue of relationships. Amanda explains:

> We need to make a judgement on whether we think we can place that person in work, and only a certain amount of that is in our control. Part of it is your relationship with the client. You can encourage them to take somebody that you think they otherwise wouldn't take. But we really have to make a decision based on our knowledge of our client base and markets. If it's somebody who hasn't got any skills or experience, then what we do for them is we sponsor them, take them under our wing.

This involves showing them how to use the phone and the fax, the Internet, e-mail and all the basic things that people in work take for granted:

> If you've never worked in an office you don't know about that sort of etiquette, or maybe even how to use a photocopier. So skills aren't

● ● ● ● ● ● ● ● ● ● ● ● ●

To be human means to be in a constant process of becoming.

Fred Blum

really that much of an issue because we can always help people get skills. We've got Qwiz which is a free software package that trains people in packages.

I press Sue Wynne, the principal PA, to tell me more about sponsoring:

> When someone comes in and they've got the enthusiasm, they want to work but they don't have the skills and they don't have the confidence, then we look after them. It's about sitting down with them, monitoring them, supporting them. For example, if they have just done a two- or three-hour session on Qwiz, we will write them a note or send them a little gift, something recognising what they have achieved and encouraging them on to the next step. We work at developing them as a whole person, as well as their skills. We get them a booking and then go through with them how that went and where they want to go next and what training they will need for it. It is about seeing them turn around.

This all seems to me to take time and money but Sue responds:

> It's common sense. It's the way we would like to be looked after. And it's good for us; if they are out there working, then that is good for us.

There is no sentimentality or self-congratulation about this approach of caring for people: they enjoy helping people and it happens to coincide with being good for business.

Philip knows that there have been, over the years, hundreds of stories of people who have come in with very limited skills or experience and who have been helped onto the ladder by Peach, but he refuses to claim the high ground for this. It is what he gets pleasure from, and it is great for business. If it were not good for business, that would be another matter. The heart and the head have a fine marriage in this company, as do generosity and profit; they sit comfortably and honestly together, each serving the other.

Helping people to acquire the necessary skills to break into the job market is, for Peach, the easy part. As Amanda explains:

> Then there is the issue of whether we really can help somebody if their attitude is completely wrong. They can be skilled up to the

EVERYDAY PRACTICE

eyeballs, but if their attitude was wrong we can't help them. And we pretty much tell them so.

And what if someone comes in covered in tattoos or daubed in outrageous make-up, dripping with jewellery or with some personal problem? Surely not every company will welcome them. Another agency might fob that person off with some platitude and never contact them again, but Peach is committed to being open and honest. If it is appropriate, they will, tactfully, try to help the applicant see how a company might perceive them and how the applicant might bend a little and, for example, take another look at their appearance. This is done with respect for the person and commitment to the result. When Peach cannot help, for example if someone is after a specialist IT role, not one of Peach's areas, or if an attitude is immovable, the company says so and gives the person details of where they can go to get help. People do not go away empty handed, nor are they given empty promises.

Unskilled people are welcomed with the same respect shown to powerful clients. I question this; surely they will not treat a junior, inexperienced temp with the same care as a big multinational client? But Amanda is emphatic that this is so and that it makes sense:

> Generally, I think we've always believed here that if you do things right, look after people, treat people how you'd want to be treated, an age-old sort of adage, then the money will come, that will happen as a by-product. . . . Why should we treat you differently from an international company? You're a client. . . . It doesn't matter if one of us has seen eight applicants already today; you see the eighth one with as much enthusiasm as you showed the one at 9 o'clock this morning.

Making sure that people are valued is ingrained in the culture and it comes from the people who work there. They believe passionately that if you treat people well your rewards will come.

Caring for each individual is a matter not only of principle, but also of common sense. How, after all, is one to know the significance of any one person, or how their lives might change:

> Who knows what Joe Bloggs who comes in off the street is going to

be doing in a year's time? You can never predict what will happen. Somebody could walk in here today, and we may think we can't help you, you're not up to the sort of quality that we deal with. Well, that could be the daughter of a personnel officer somewhere, and because we've treated that person with respect, that gets around. You just never ever know.

Big companies also have their own way of being unpredictable:

We've got very large companies, but although they're very important to our business, we don't necessarily want to build our whole future around them because it's too unstable. A large company can potentially go broke overnight. They'll make a decision that they don't want to use an independent, they want to use a global recruiter or whatever. So I think it's about not being complacent: you never know what will happen, and you need to treat everyone as you want to be treated.

Both of these unlikely scenarios have in fact happened repeatedly to Peach: a young, inexperienced hopeful did turn out to be related to one of their key clients, and a major company did indeed overnight opt for a global recruiter.

EVERYDAY PRACTICE

• • • *Reflection* • • •

Spiritual traditions stress that power based on worldly status, position, wealth and appearance are not all they are cracked up to be; they can easily be shattered. These traditions emphasise our common shared humanity and our essential equality. We all have the right, responsibility and possibility of achieving real greatness that is not dependent on status. The marginalised often have great and unexpected importance.

A FIRST-CLASS RECEPTION

When I had arrived in reception to be welcomed by June, another person greeted me and beamed warmly. I assumed her to be another member of staff – she looked at home there – but it turned out that she was a new applicant who was doing a typing test. The beaming smile had no doubt come from the fact that she was enveloped in the care that Peach gives you once you walk through the door. Regardless of status, you are treated as an important person. June has strong views about this:

> It's vital; it's the first point of call; you've got to make people welcome and make them feel important, and I stress that without them I wouldn't have a job either. If you haven't got a job and you have to go looking for work, it's a horrible position to be in. So when you go somewhere, you need your confidence building up, not put down, because success in most areas of life is all attitude of mind, in the head, isn't it?

If people are a little dejected when they arrive, June undertakes to encourage them. She is aware that some people feel that they are either too young or too old, or they may have been hit by redundancy and have had their confidence knocked back. As receptionist she sees her job as being concerned with helping individuals to believe in themselves and to start constructing the relationship that Peach wants to have with its applicants:

> These people need building up, and they need to feel totally comfortable and at ease in the first place so that they will be able to open up and talk to you and the consultant. I try to lay the foundations, help get people totally relaxed. . . . Because, as I say, most of us have been in that situation before and it's a horrible time, isn't it? I mean, I'd hate not to have a job. So I appreciate that very much.

While applicants are waiting for the consultant, June encourages them to tell the consultant exactly what it is they are looking for rather than saying what they think they ought to say or making do with something they are not happy with:

*The greatest human quest is to know what one must
do in order to become a human being.*

Immanuel Kant

● ●

I want to help them be able to be totally honest so they know it's OK to say what they want. And of course it's very much a three-way thing [Peach, the client and the applicant], and I always point that out to people. We need them as much as they need us and the client. So it's putting them on an equal footing, once again showing people their worth.

June can recount many examples of people who have come in feeling anxious yet have emerged with confidence and work, and this is what she loves:

A young man came in with no actual qualifications. He came and he was so nervous, you know, when people can't stop their knees knocking, bless his heart. He sort of put his head around the door, with an 'Am I in the right place?' sort of attitude. 'I don't suppose you can help me . . .' 'But – yes, come on in; of course we can help you or, if we can't, we'll find someone who can.' And yes, we got him work at a company testing bits of games and things. He's been there ever since.

June administers the aptitude tests but does it in a way that is reassuring:

It's not a question of a pass or a fail. It's again a getting-to-know-them exercise, and that's what I keep reiterating – that that's the whole purpose of their visit. It's just getting to know them so that we can build up the whole picture, their strengths and weaknesses, their skills, their likes, dislikes. So we're not wasting their time sending them on interviews which are totally unsuitable, wasting their time, our time and the client's time, which is also totally demoralising for them. So I point out that it doesn't matter if they can type or not, it's just to show us, to help us match them.

On the day that applicants register, June sends them a letter thanking them and reminding them of the opportunity to come in for free training in order to develop their computer skills while waiting for a position:

> We do care. Of course it's a business, and all businesses have to make a profit, but underlining that is the fact that this is also a people business and they appreciate that. Our product isn't office furniture; our product is people. And we want them to understand that we'll treat them as people.

June takes a keen interest in people's progress. Before their interview, applicants may feel nervous, so they come in to Peach beforehand, where June welcomes them, gently boosting their confidence, before a consultant takes them through interview preparation. June wishes them well, quietly encourages them on and lets them know it matters. Later she checks how things have gone:

> It's not just a case of you're registered, that's my job done, that's it. . . . I want to know how they're getting on and what happened at the last interview.

As I sit in the reception, the phone is ringing, a staff member is requesting some papers, an applicant is doing a test and another is walking through the door. June juggles it gracefully, swiftly and with ease, enjoying the pace and the demands; it stretches her pleasantly and she excels at it. The more difficult the situation, the more she can test her skills out. Of Peach, she says:

> They believe in giving people the chance to grow to their full potential; they give you every opportunity to grow within the company so

● ●

Life's fulfilment finds constant contradictions in its path;
but those are necessary for the sake of its advance.
The stream is saved from the sluggishness of its current
by the perpetual opposition of the soil through which it
must cut its way. It is the soil which forms its banks.
The Spirit of fight belongs to the genius of life.

Anon

that the employees grow together with Peach, and of course the happier you are in your work the more you are going to achieve, and it works for everyone and Peach know this.

• • • *Reflection* • • •

Spiritual traditions emphasise the importance of welcome, especially that extended to a new person or a stranger. This sets the very first imprint on the relationship that is about to begin. Will that imprint be one of mistrust, indifference, hostility, and robotic processing or will it be one of welcome and all that entails – caring, well-being, connection, trust and mutuality? The tone of the relationship is curiously amplified at that moment of arrival. What sort of place is this? What sort of relationship am I about to enter into?

The Peach welcome is unusual in that it consciously sets out to be a transforming experience, positively changing people's perceptions of themselves.

DAVID AND GOLIATH

An enormous piece of business with a multibillion-pound firm came up for tender. The big multinational agencies, with branches on every high street throughout Europe and America, were there bidding, ready to make their presentations. Top executives were flown in from America, both by the potential client and by the agencies bidding for the contract. A great deal of money was at stake. There was also Peach, a small, unknown, independent company with only two branches, represented by Amanda and some of the team. They were already a supplier to this company in Hounslow, but they were tiny compared with the competition. They had managed to get through the first two rounds of the bidding process and were there with the big boys in this

Stand through life firm as a rock in the sea, undisturbed and unmoved by its ever-rising waves.

Hazrat Inayat Khan

● ● ● ● ● ● ● ● ● ● ● ● ● ● ● ●

final round. Against a backdrop of a fairy castle, Amanda began:

> We would like to tell the story and take you back to when we first started doing visits to your organisation.

Amanda went on to tell how they had met a particular woman from the company back in 1990 and how she had given them their first opportunity. They made a temporary placement, who was, many years down the line, still there as a permanent and very highly regarded member of staff. Amanda went on to describe how they had gone on to make their first permanent placement and how Peach had become preferred supplier. The story continued:

> I talked them through the fact that, in all that time, very much based on this relationship that we had, only three people had managed their account internally – and from their side only three people had handled the recruitment. So over a ten-year span, three people from each organisation had had those three jobs. I pointed out that the key to everything we achieved with them had been the relationship through our internal people and their internal people, and the mutual commitment we had to working through it.

This constancy is particularly important when it comes to the challenging area of giving and obtaining temporary bookings:

> They ring me because they've got a problem and they need a temp, and it's fraught with issues, and things go wrong and it's how you deal with things when they go wrong that sets you apart. Anyone can do it if you've got the perfect person with the perfect job. But life isn't like that and it's about compromise, it's about knowing instinctively what makes somebody right. They might lack a skill in an area but because their personality is such, they are right for that particular organisation. So we talked very much about that and about the shared values.

Peach won the contract because their presentation came from the heart, from their passionate commitment to relationships and to their particular skill of finding the right person for the right job within the unique culture of each company:

> It was very simple: it was just 'this is who we are, this is what we have done for you; we understand your culture, we understand your people, we've taken years to learn it.'

Peach works in a very fluid market, one vulnerable to economic trends, but through its emphasis on relationships Peach builds continuity within the potentially rootless world of temping. Candidates come back year after year, and people who come to work at Peach come, with a few exceptions, to stay. In the past eighteen months only two people have left, an almost unheard of feat in the recruitment world, where high staff turnover is endemic. In the fast shifting world of temping Peach creates a place where there are unchanging values and longstanding staff who positively enjoy the turbulence and constant challenges.

• • • Reflection • • •

We sometimes limit ourselves by our lack of respect for ourselves. We assume that we cannot compete, that we are not big enough, strong enough, important enough, these assumptions being useful in keeping us safe in a small, known area. Stories from spiritual traditions repeatedly tell of ordinary people who find themselves called to do extraordinary things well outside their comfort zone. A precondition to their going forward in that situation is that they respect themselves and acknowledge that they have something worth offering, even if they are only a 'small player'. Peach is a small agency with gigantic clients. They know their own worth and are prepared to offer what they have, even if that is at times scary.

*Life is difficult. This is a great truth, one of the greatest
truths. It is a great truth because once we truly see this
truth, we transcend it. Once we truly know that life is
difficult – once we truly understand and accept it – then
life is no longer difficult. Because once it is accepted,
the fact that life is difficult no longer matters.*

M. Scott Peck

WHEN THE GOING GETS TOUGH

Peach has weathered two very tough episodes in its history, one when
an account was lost and one when two relationships went very badly
wrong. Peach approached these in a clear-eyed, philosophical fashion, a poised balance between passion and equanimity. Amanda
explains how she sees it:

> I know there are going to be bad times but they are few and far
> between, and I think when there are bad times, they are there for a
> reason, they're meant to be, and although I might not know why now,
> I will know why in six months' time. I'll be able to look back and
> think, 'That's why that happened.' I'm not religious, but I believe that
> it is how you live your life that is important. I believe that if you live
> your life and you work hard and you're decent to people, and you're
> loving and you're there for your friends and you're kind, you will get
> that back. But you don't do it for that reason, you do it willingly.

When things do go wrong, which they do in business, Amanda trusts
that there is some greater plan:

> There's no point in looking back and being negative, putting a lot of
> negative energy into something that's gone wrong. You have to find
> the energy to move forward. It's this belief that I just know it will
> come right.

The first difficult occasion occurred when through no fault of its own,
Peach lost an account representing 25% of their business to a large
national agency. It seemed a devastating blow at the time, but they

faced it as a whole team, using their creativity and calm determination to find new clients. They in fact went on to better things, grew stronger and more profitable through the process and are now no longer dependent on any one large client. When Amanda looks back at that blow, she sees it as a challenge that was necessary to Peach's growth.

The second occasion involved an act of betrayal that for a short time badly polluted the company's culture. In retrospect, however, it provided an opportunity for the company to go back to its roots and remember what really mattered most. The culture then reasserted itself with new clarity and grounding.

It was now mid-morning and I had been interviewing Amanda for several hours. When I asked for a specific example of how people care for each other at Peach, she recounted how they had dealt with a major issue that had erupted only the previous afternoon:

> We had a major business issue yesterday. A particular company that one of our consultants, Katie, developed from scratch has, basically, decided to go somewhere else, to a national agency. And last night people were on the phone all round the company, from our other branches to here in Hounslow, checking that people were OK, checking how Katie was. This morning people have come in, arms round her.

Before I arrived, Amanda had explained the impact to everyone:

> People were cheering for Katie, very supportive. They genuinely do care when people have got any problems, whether at home or here at work. They care in the way in which they speak to each other, the way they deliver things to each other; they've got a genuine concern for their colleagues.

Amanda explained how when the going gets tough, there is:

> almost a siege mentality; its like 'we'll group together and we'll work through this – it's meant for a reason – this will make us stronger and better', and that comes from them as much from anybody, almost like 'It's us against the world . . .'

The current situation was highly complex and a large number of Peach temps were being affected:

EVERYDAY PRACTICE

> I came in this morning and everyone was rallying round. Very quickly we went from a huge disappointment yesterday to today thinking 'Right OK. What are we going to do about it? Where are we going to replace that business?'

As I listened I realised that within less than twenty hours of hearing of the blow, the company was moving forward as one body. I commented on how they seemed to have been able to shift their energy quickly; how did they do it?

> For me, personally, last night was devastating and I felt totally stunned, but that changed very quickly. I think it's a belief that it's for a reason. There's nothing we could've done that would alter this decision. We're not sure why the decision has been made, but there's nothing we can reproach ourselves on. We've done everything possible . . . so let's look to the future and think, in six months' time that account will be of no importance; let's start looking forward. What's the point in looking back? You can't change it, and you can't get bitter about it because that's not healthy'. Individually people here are very much like that; they let go and move forward.

This crisis had not ever been mentioned until I had asked for an immediate example of caring. We had been talking as though there were all the time in the world and Amanda had been relaxed and pondering some core aspects of Peach. I had not realised how full and pressured her morning had been before I had arrived. Had I been Amanda, I imagine I would have postponed the interview with this unknown writer, exploring 'soul'. This quality of calm and the ability to make time for people even in the midst of the storm was a quality that I found in all the leaders that I met.

This was a huge blow for the Peach consultant responsible for the account, and she needed, and was getting, support. The account rep-

● ● ● ● ● ● ● ● ● ● ● ● ● ● ● ● ● ● ● ●

The opportunity of life is very precious and it moves very quickly.

Ilyani Ywahoo

resented a mountain of work and had been thought to make a critical contribution to the company's well-being. The response to the loss had been emotional, with clearly expressed distress, anger, hurt, care and love. But now they had let go and become intently focused on the new path that had opened up.

• • • *Reflection* • • •

Most spiritual leaders attempt to teach people about dealing with the tough times, the suffering in life. They teach that setbacks are inevitable but that it is our response to them which is crucial. If we try to deny, avoid or ignore suffering, we are like someone going into a battlefield with closed eyes and a picture of daisies in his mind. The result is disastrous; one is ill-equipped to face or deal with the outcome. If we feel that we should be exempt from suffering, we compound the original situation with indignation and anger, and fruitlessly waste our energy trying to make sense of what cannot be made sense of, trying to push away what cannot be rejected.

Peach has a humble and courageous way of responding to the tough times. Some of the staff have themselves gone through suffering such as a broken childhood family. They accept that there will be betrayals, disappointments and losses, in both their personal and their work lives, but they do not accept that these events should change their values or those things which are most precious to them – relationships, caring for one another, making a difference in people's lives, being successful. They refuse to be distracted for long from this, their main purpose. They confront and deal with the tough times emotionally and passionately but then move forwards convinced that there is meaning, whether or not they can see it.

They live and work as if life were short and valuable, showing the calm urgency that many people only practise when confronted by their own mortality.

A HARD PLACE TO WORK

Amanda knows that Peach is not an ordinary company. Even after many years there she says:

> I still can't believe what it's like here, and I think it takes time for people to believe that it is as it is. We have to almost untrain people when they come. There is Sam; she's twenty-one so she's not an old cynic, she's a young cynic because of her experiences, and she almost can't believe what it's like here.

Sam is very happy at Peach but is adamant that:

> It is a hard place to work. It is hard because it's very different. If you're not the sort of person who can cope with this environment, you might not stay long. It's not at all cliquey. It's very open and honest and you are praised a lot, and if you're someone who doesn't like being praised, who doesn't like people saying, 'Oh well done!' and clapping every time you do something well, then you'll find it really irritating.

There are other aspects that are unfamiliar and that require discipline:

> If you're someone who likes to have a bit of a gossip, likes to slag a few people off in your spare time – because there are companies that are like that, people who generally go out of their way to make things difficult for others – you will not be happy here. Because it doesn't happen. The other person will probably just walk away or not want to know. So it's different. It's not a Peach cult, but we all are very Peachy.

Sam is aware that this is not a good place to be for people who are addicted to passing their time in negativity:

> For some reason there is no backstabbing here. Normally when you go into a company, it doesn't matter what company it is, you'll find that there is always someone slagging someone off . . . You hear it everywhere you go. But here you don't because everything is very open. You're encouraged to be open.

Challenges also arise in that difficulties are confronted head on when

If the only prayer you say in your whole life is 'thank you' that would suffice.

Meister Eckhart

● ●

it would just be easier to let things pass. Sam, who is by her own admission a rampant non-team player, recalls:

> The toughest times I've had here are getting on with everybody. There've been times when I haven't got on with certain members of the team and it has got me down. There was a situation where I wasn't getting on with someone in the team. I spoke to Amanda about it and she said, 'What do you want me to do?'

This was said not dismissively but with a genuine concern to know what Sam needed from her as well as with the knowledge that, ultimately, only Sam could change how she related to that person. Sam recalls:

> I asked for advice and was given advice on what to do in that situation but I wasn't told, and I dealt with the situation myself. I confronted it. I felt quite brave. Because confronting those sort of problems isn't something you always like to do. I suppose when given a problem, it's easier to go over and over it in your head rather than sort that problem out. But I think I was advised and encouraged to confront the problem and get it sorted out before it got worse. Now if there's something I don't like, I'll stand up and say I don't like it. So I don't bottle anything in. And it is better for things to be out in the open.

People at Peach often step way out of their comfort zone, confronting and dealing with issues that are unsatisfactory and clearing them up as they arise.

• • • *Reflection* • • •

Peach has a distinctive culture. It does not follow the ways of the world; it does not conform; it breaks the rules. The recruitment sector is harsh and competitive; Peach is driven by kindness and generosity. Our society puts people down and belittles them, but Peach praises and embarrasses them with appreciation. Most workplaces harbour gossip and blame but Peach requires that you say what you think and then act on it. The sloppy world of idle criticism and accusation is not tolerated. Those who arrive at Peach from other companies find it an alien culture, different, sometimes uncomfortable. They cannot believe that it is possible.

Spiritual traditions speak of a different way and invite us to glimpse a world free of cynicism, scepticism and meanness of spirit. At one level it is easier to stay with what is, with the familiar, with mundane mediocrity, but Peach sets out, without saying it, to create something of inestimable worth – the best. It requires people to believe it is possible and to set aside the familiar and to jump into a culture of openness and goodness. This is not the common way and it makes great demands on people.

• • • • • • • • • • • • • • • • • • • •

REWARDS

Although young, Sam has already worked for two large recruitment agencies and has found it a grim, disillusioning experience, everyone looking after themselves, with casual lies and misrepresentations, tough, unreasonable targets and burnout. She was incredulous when she came to Peach:

I like working here, I like my job, I like the people I work with, everything really. It's just a nice place to work; I feel comfortable. And the biggest thing is I'm rewarded for my achievement. If I do something that's good or if I do something that's special, I'm rewarded for it and it's recognised and I'm paid for it. Rewarded not necessarily in a monetary way. I mean rewarded in the way that people recognise that you've done something good . . . It's just nice to be – I don't know – it's nice to be recognised, I suppose.

Sam recalls big companies she has worked for where she had at times put in an enormous effort and had felt, 'God, what a massive achievement this is and I've really done it well', but it had gone completely unnoticed. As she thinks back to those times of unacknowledged effort, there is a wistfulness and her hands flutter as though representing all her efforts washing away down the drain:

It would just go past and you'd think 'Oh well done, well done.' But you wouldn't get that back. But here you do; it's a nice place to work.

At Peach praise is not given in a patronising manner, the shallow management technique of some companies happy to replace tangible rewards with words, but as a genuine happiness at seeing someone succeed, untinged by envy and competitiveness.

E V E R Y D A Y   P R A C T I C E

• • • *Reflection* • • •

The wisdom of all faiths testifies that the human being is a creature of infinite value and potential. In one tradition it is expressed as our being co-creators with the divine, in another as being stewards of creation, in yet another as being part of the creator. Regardless of whether or not we are religious, each of us who is a parent knows that our children are priceless; that is part of our lived experience.

But the great worth attributed to human beings by spiritual traditions is often discounted when the bottom line takes over to fill the picture. Many people work very hard and receive very little appreciation, their life becoming a thankless task. As a society we are uncomfortable with giving and receiving praise. We find it easier to put ourselves and others down than to celebrate our strengths. This keeps us in the safe and comfortable position of pretending we are worthless, so we can give up trying.

THE LIFTER AND SHIFTER (OR NUMBER 63000)

Driving into the courtyard at Peach I had seen an open, cheerful man clearing up and making it spick and span, rather as if he owned the place. This was Greg, in his own words the lifter and shifter of Peach. He had previously worked for thirty-three years as a prison officer, the last twenty at Wormwood Scrubs. Working there had taken its toll on Greg, and when he had left a couple of years beforehand he had been irritable, bad-tempered, impossible to live with, very over-weight and suffering from high blood pressure. He came to Peach almost by chance, and here he found himself again: 'Here you regain your identity, you're a person.' Sloughing off a dead skin that no longer fitted, Greg also shed his bad humour and some three stone in weight. Shaking his head in happy incredulity, he says: 'This is the best job I've ever had!'

Greg had retired three months earlier and he was low and doing nothing. His wife, Anne, was already working for Peach and had asked whether there was any work he might do there, so the company developed the job for him. Now he is full-time lifter and shifter, doing whatever is needed – the driving, caring for the building, decorating, the odd jobs. He treats the place as if it were his home and garden, and he has full rein to care for it as he wants.

After thirty-three years as a civil servant, Greg had come to feel like a number – when he received his prison pay-cheque it was filled out with his surname and number 63000. Coming to Peach, he came back to who he was. He struggles to find the right words; it is hard to express the change that has come over him. Here he is valued for being who he is, a man who takes a pride in what he does, who enjoys a challenge, who respects people, who does not like sitting around but likes to do the job. Here he is an essential part of the team. He lays this at the door of management: 'It's the way management treat you.' He believes they lead by example:

> They don't shirk anything; there's Amanda, the partner, making tea
> for the whole section. They all muck in together.

Greg gives the example of how, the previous Friday, he had mentioned to Philip that he was planning to put up some large pictures for Amanda in the training room. Greg was concerned that the plaster board might not be strong enough to take the screws. Today, after the long Bank Holiday weekend, Philip has arrived with the right screws in his back pocket. He hadn't forgotten. Similarly, the first Christmas he was there, Greg had been sorting out the tall Christmas tree, and Philip had arrived with the lights; it was Philip who climbed the ladders to put them on, without a word, delicately acknowledging that it might not have been easy for Greg, who was at that stage still much overweight. This care for him in the little details means a great deal to Greg and in turn enables him to take care of the small things.

Peach's work involves paying attention to many details and responding swiftly to unforeseen contingencies. Perhaps a temp has fallen sick and another needs to be chauffeured to the client's doorstep double-quick. Perhaps a staff member has found ants in the kitchen and has no time to sort it. Maybe the temps have arrived to pick up their weekly cheques and there is no refreshment to welcome them. Like the mortar between the bricks, Greg lightly fills in the gaps and does whatever is needed to help the smooth running of the team and the building. Moving his hands like a craftsman shaping the materials to make something work better, he says:

> I've got a free rein; anything that needs doing I'll go and do it. No one's looking over my shoulder. I think about little things to make things work more smoothly . . . I have the freedom to do my job. I love coming in here. There are certain little tasks I do, then I look around and see what needs doing and start doing it. I'm never pestered, never bothered. The customer is paramount, and if there is anything to help the customer be happy, then I'll do it.

Greg communicates a great sense of well-being:

> Everybody's so good to one another, especially to me. They are good to me in every respect. When they ask for something to be done, it is always done with courtesy: 'Greg, could you do me a favour, could you please . . .'.

When I ask Greg whether Peach has a soul, he replies without a moment's hesitation:

> Oh yes definitely. Oh yes, it just keeps beating. It doesn't rest, it doesn't slow down, it keeps at a steady beat. It's got past the crawling stage; it's just walking nicely now. It's not in any hurry, just a regular beat – like a pulse.

It is hard to imagine that this fit, energetic, smiling man in a fresh white T-shirt and jeans was once irritable and unhealthy, an unhappy man with little ahead of him in life. He gropes to find words to explain what has happened: 'This is another galaxy.'

• • • *Reflection* • • •

This story is one of transformation. From being a miserable unhealthy man sitting swallowing lager Greg became a fulfilled person able to give of his best.

At the heart of all spiritual traditions is this transformation, sometimes characterised as going from death to life, or from half-life to full life. The traditions teach that there is an intimate connection between serving and living fully, and that, pragmatically, we would do well to pay attention to the fact that it is when we give that we receive. Our lives work more fruitfully when we are able to serve each other. When this need to serve is blocked people often become demotivated, lifeless, robotic and unhappy, prime candidates for any addiction that will blur the pain. Even those who are weakened by illness, old age or poverty can serve; their gift to others is the opportunity to give to them instead and to learn through their experiences. The role of recipient is not, however, the easiest of roles.

One of the aspects of Greg's story is that we do not need grand jobs in order to serve; we can do it wherever we are in the organisation. Transformation can happen in the mundane: this is in fact the place it is most likely to happen.

*Before enlightenment I chopped wood and carried
water. After enlightenment I chopped
wood and carried water.*

Zen saying

● ●

MINIMISING STRESS

'Work at a recruitment agency can be very difficult and incredibly
wearing,' Amanda explains. Recognising this, Peach takes care to be
proactive in minimising stress. Although some of the inevitable stress
can be fun, any unnecessary or unwelcome pressure is removed.

Philip works upstairs in the accounts and administration section
of Peach. Downstairs holds the hive of activity of interviewing and
placing applicants and meeting client requirements:

> I cannot bear the pressure down there. I don't deal with it very well.
> There you will be with four phone calls holding and then you think,
> I have got it all sorted, and it always changes and you find that didn't
> work, so what do I do now? They are all multitasking all the time.
> They have to stand a lot of pressure. In most recruitment agencies,
> staff typically last eighteen months at it. We want people to stay so we
> relieve the pressure. Where in a normal agency there might be three
> or four staff, we put five or six.

Peach insists that people do not come in early; they are encouraged to
take full lunch breaks, and eating at one's desk is not at all acceptable.
They do not want people staying late and if someone is there after
5.30 pm, Peach wants to know what is wrong: 'Are more staff needed?'

Philip knows how tough the job is for the consultants; he understands the pressures and takes whatever measures he can to relieve
them. He is modest when he simply says, 'It's in our interests.' But
this attitude makes a lot of business sense. The staff accumulate a
great deal of knowledge about the client company cultures and what
will and will not work, about the applicants and their strengths and

97

Life is not the way it's supposed to be. It's the way it is. The way you cope with it is what makes the difference.

Virginia Satir

● ●

weaknesses. This is not transferable knowledge; it grows out of relationships built up over years. In the past eighteen months only two members of staff have left. Most staff have been there for many years, and this low staff turnover is almost unheard of in this sector. Philip is like most staff there when he says, 'I love to come to work.'

People work to their strengths. Those who enjoy juggling and getting the adrenaline flowing work as consultants on the fast-paced ground floor. Those who require a gentler pace and more time for reflection work upstairs. The environment throughout is lovely, and there is a culture of care, fun and sharing so that:

> I don't think of it as work. It's a place where I go to spend a day, and its always good fun.

It is essential to Philip that people at Peach enjoy their work. When one usually cheerful member of staff was not looking altogether happy, Philip commented on it, concerned to know what was wrong. When she replied that she hadn't enjoyed work that week, Philip was taken aback and sat down then and there to look at what the problem was. How could this stress be lifted and shared? Action is always taken before the situation has reached boiling point: this is simply good management, but Peach practises it diligently and swiftly, perfecting it.

But there is more to it than just good business sense. Philip, like the other Peach staff, enjoys people, cares about people and appreciates them. As we talk he looks round the office and spreads his arms out:

> Sometimes I look around me at these people and I think it's all down to them, everything that we do is them.

He has an active appreciation of the staff and what they generate. He recognises that Teresa, who originally came as an administration temp and is now the head of accounts, does the work better than he could do, and he takes pleasure in her achievement. He enjoys thinking of how many members of staff have started out in junior positions and have expanded their roles to fulfil themselves. He enjoys thinking of the many applicants who have come with few skills and prospects yet have found work through the way in which Peach has helped to support and develop them, sometimes over months, until they have equipped them and found them good jobs. Philip's modesty prevents him claiming, or maybe even seeing, that much of this has came from the environment he has helped to create. To him it is just down to good fortune.

People enjoy coming to work, appreciate their colleagues and are in turn appreciated and feel valued. If there is an area of the business someone wishes to take on or new skills they want to learn, they are encouraged to do so. Those who make mistakes are not blamed; management simply looks with them at what went wrong and what to do now. The well-being of both staff and applicants is a top priority. Their families too are valued, and there is plenty of flexibility for working around family needs. People are actively encouraged to take time out in the day to chat and share their lives. Fun and creativity are used at every opportunity, whether it is in training, in making savings in staff meetings, in celebrating a birthday or in presenting or reviewing the business plan.

The business plan is owned by everyone, with an input from each member of staff. There is a clear sense of direction, a shared vision and very practical steps and targets for reaching the goal. The practical underpinning of this with meticulously healthy finances and sound cash flow ensures that there is a sense of material success, security and the means by which to invest in people.

Each of these factors combines in such a way that stress is cut down and replaced by a sense of success and excitement, spreading like ripples on a pond. Philip is relaxed and his attitude permeates the company:

EVERYDAY PRACTICE

I look at my life and I see I'm lucky; I have balance. I take one of my children to school and I pick one of them up. I enjoy being here anyway. I've got a very nice life. I do not run the business to the detriment of my family. This place is just like a family.

Other people at Peach would echo that. What is good for the leader extends to each person at Peach.

• • • *Reflection* • • •

Excessive stress brings anxiety and kills the joy of life. Sit on any commuter train and you will see how little joy is left in people by the end of the day. Central to all spiritual traditions are the experiences of joy and of peace: our lives are not meant to be treadmills of hardship and fear. Stress causes illness, injury, exhaustion, burnout and, at times, death. The cost to business, to individuals, to families and to society is vast. Creating a culture in which antidotes to stress are actively employed is therefore good for both life and productivity. Such antidotes include fun, involvement, balance, a love of people, pleasure in others' achievements, a sense of perspective, shared goals and humility. These antidotes are often embodied in the leader, who infects those around them with the same qualities.

THE UNSEEN LEADER

Walk into Peach and you will see Denise Russell. She no longer physically works there, but it is as if she has left a tiny part of herself in each person there, in the fabric of the building and in the indefinable atmosphere. Peach is her child, and you can see the likeness. The beauty and compassion that are apparent in the environment and in the relationships are the embodiment of what matters to Denise.

When I originally set out to write this book, I thought I would interview the 'leaders' and one other person, but it did not work out like that. Denise had politely declined to be interviewed, saying, 'No I do not work there now; it is better really if you go and see it for yourself and talk to the people who are there doing the work now.' And when I talked to the other people in the company, I did in fact get to 'see' the leader. She was seen in innumerable reflections in those who worked there. She had made herself 'redundant' by quietly and imperceptibly handing over leadership to every other person in the organisation.

• • • *Reflection* • • •

This quality of leadership, the ability to 'hand over', is absolutely critical. It is a legacy that ensures there is no crisis of succession when the leader leaves. It builds sustainability and passes the charisma of the leader on to those who follow, multiplying the leadership exponentially. Many fine organisations have been set up by visionary, charismatic leaders, but those who follow then find themselves in a half-light, not sure where to search for the light left behind by the leader. When they realise that it is in fact inside themselves, there is an enormous release of energy into the organisation.

THE BOTTOM LINE

The bottom line is a natural part of the process at Peach. As Philip puts it:

Peach is a family where all the members know that they have a contribution to make, and that everyone's contribution is of value. Making the analogy of a bank, people will sometimes need to make withdrawals, and at this time it is the duty of their Peach colleagues to support and understand them. However, people are usually in credit and so contributing to the business as a whole. The result is that all employees will make great efforts to ensure the continuing success and existence of the family unit.

PEACH CARES FOR PEOPLE BY:

- Having a commitment to ongoing human growth and development
- Providing a beautiful environment in which to work
- Being passionate and compassionate towards the needs of their clients
- Practising equality, valuing each person regardless of status
- Being welcoming and reassuring, and raising people's self-confidence
- Placing great store on relationships
- Finding out what makes individuals tick
- Confronting and resolving relationship difficulties
- Not tolerating gossip or blaming
- Appreciating and valuing people's achievements
- Taking care over the small things
- Lifting the stress from each other
- Having a leader who shines her light on others and hands leadership over to them
- Working with mutuality: we are all in this together

PUTTING THIS INTO PRACTICE IN YOUR WORKPLACE:

WORKING WITH PEOPLE

People feel very highly valued at Peach. They feel accepted for who they are, appreciated for what they do, supported in times of difficulty, encouraged to grow in confidence and enabled to fulfil their potential. At work, as with candidates, they take time to build up a picture in order to know what makes each other tick. Many of the difficulties at work come from misunderstandings and from unacknowledged and unmet needs. When we know about people, who they are, what they are going through, what they need, we can then understand them, and when we understand them we can accept them and enjoy them.

AN ACTIVITY TO DO AS A TEAM

The purpose of this activity is to appreciate, enjoy and support your colleagues and to make your workplace more people centred.

Building up the picture

1 Sit in a circle as a group. Look at each person in the circle and think of a quality you value in them. Jot it down.

2 Now look at each person and recognise that each will have some difficulty or tough area in their life, whether it is the volume of paper they have to deal with, a child with an ear infection, an ageing parent, a drink problem, the uncertainty of a house move, an overdose of cynicism, failure or rejection. Whatever it is, simply

103

acknowledge that this person is doing the best they can.

3 Take three people and see whether you can work out what each of them needs most at work in order to feel supported. Jot your ideas down.

4 Look at three people and become aware of how they have helped and supported you. Jot this down.

5 Take a few moments to reflect and write down what you most need from your colleagues; what would help you most?

6 Divide into groups of three. Each person then says in turn what they need most at work and explains why.

7 Feed back the 'needs' to the whole group and list them on a board.

8 Ask for one volunteer to suggest a 'need' they would like the whole group to work on and use the problem-solving activity entitled 'The web' from page 146.

9 Debrief the whole activity. What struck people most? What have they learnt?

AN ACTIVITY TO DO AS A LONE INDIVIDUAL WITH 'NO POWER'

This simple activity aims to gather information in order to begin to understand and appreciate the background of your colleagues' lives. This will make it easier for you to empathise with them and realise what makes them tick. Knowing this makes it much easier to reconcile different work styles, to resolve conflicts and to clear up misunderstandings.

What makes them tick

1 Take three sheets of paper.

2 Choose three people at work, one of whom you do not get on with very well. Write each person's name at the top of a separate sheet of paper.

3 Underneath the name note down what you already know about that person.

4 Underneath that write a list of numbers from 1 to 20.

5 Over the next week, unobtrusively and with discretion, find out twenty things about that person, their likes and dislikes, their experience, their strengths, their concerns, where they grew up, what interests them.

6 At the end of the week review what you have learnt. Do you know what makes them tick, what makes them unique? Are you any closer to understanding who this person is? Write down how you see them now, and compare this with what you wrote about them at the beginning of the week.

MICROSOFT UK:

PLANETARY CONNECTEDNESS

The soul of Microsoft is probably a volcano in some ways;
it erupts and when the lava flows down it changes
the landscape for ever.

THIS CHAPTER FOCUSES on human creativity; the ability to bring into being something that was never there before, be it ideas, opportunities, connections, products or new ways of being, relating or seeing. This creativity, which can shape the world, draws on some ancient wisdom about what a human being is, which, obvious though it is, tends to get forgotten in our secular age. Human beings are the source of wealth, their ability extraordinarily unlimited, their minds phenomenally powerful in generating new ways of being and providing for human and planetary needs. When human beings work together with mutual respect and a sense of service, this power of creativity is beyond imagination. It is the stuff of life and exhilarating. Microsoft UK is a very unusual company in that although it is big and powerful, it cherishes human creativity and seeks to create the environment within which it can grow, both for itself and for its customers.

Microsoft is known to all the Western world. It is demonised, despised, chastised and accused of many sins, most of which boil down to two things: first, it is very successful and wealthy, and second, it has taken the lead in the field. It is also respected by many for its software that is now integral to people's work and home lives. It evokes strong feelings, including envy and jealousy, perhaps at times because of its extraordinary success.

Fifteen years ago Microsoft was still in its infancy and was a small player among giants such as IBM. In those days ordinary individuals at work, like myself, were struggling to master one of numerous bewildering, awkward software packages using one expensive computer shared with colleagues. It was a painful business. The software had often been designed by boffins who seemed to think in ways quite alien to any normal person: things often went very wrong too, with whole documents sometimes disappearing. Today we have user-friendly technology that young and old can understand, at a cost that many people in the West can afford. Microsoft has been a key player in the revolution to bring friendly, relatively cheap software to the masses, so that it is now part of everyday life in the developed world. Most of us enjoy the benefits of Microsoft without even being conscious of it; we have become accustomed to it and take it for granted. But when Microsoft first set out, it had little power, and its vision was seen as ludicrous. 'When Bill Gates said a PC on every desk and in every home, they were laughed at, and yet a few years ago in the Western world we got quite close to that.' Now that Microsoft is a powerful company, its prophecy of things as yet untold is seen instead as arrogance.

I shall try here to show the human side of what makes Microsoft a world leader. The people we will meet include architects of the UK company, those who designed its culture and have led it since its inception and those who have joined over the years. I have found it hard to reconcile my experience at Microsoft with the relentless media criticism of the company, although I know from experience that the media thrives on and feeds off negativity. All those whom I met were full, many-faceted individuals who talked freely of their work, their passion and their lives. Pressure of space means I have curbed myself from telling you all about each of these individuals; I have instead taken just one or two aspects of each to illustrate the way in which Microsoft expresses its soul.

1 **Approaching Microsoft UK** – When, as an outsider, I asked to come and look at Microsoft from the point of view of its company

soul, I was readily welcomed and found the character of Microsoft to be manifest from the outset. *Microsoft practises conviviality and welcome.*

2 **Ninety-seven per cent of our wealth is the people** – Finance and people are inextricably linked, and great emphasis is placed on unleashing people's potential – the real wealth. *It practises a belief in people.*

3 **Teams** – Microsoft builds superteams, communities of people who have a shared vision, who know, appreciate, share, trust and support each other. *It practises community.*

4 **Workaholism** – Microsoft is a very enjoyable environment within which to work, and, given the ever-unfolding possibilities inherent in software, one can easily succumb to workaholism. Microsoft is conscious of this and takes steps to counteract it. *It attempts to practise balance.*

5 **The Balkan War** – A little known story of Microsoft was its response to the humanitarian disaster in the Balkans; in response to the concern expressed by staff members, the company volunteered its expertise. *It practises responding to suffering with compassion.*

6 **The newest recruit** – Microsoft does not slot people into functions but instead encourages them to find their passion and develop their own job description. *It practises an appreciation of people's individuality.*

7 **The reluctant temp** – Newly arrived from abroad, an administration worker ignorant of technology was given the space and training to transform her skills and role. She talks of how technology affects those traditionally excluded. *It practises valuing and supporting the marginalised.*

8 **Values in the DNA** – Over a period of two and a half years, Microsoft wrestled with understanding its values and finding ways of fully integrating them into its structures and ongoing processes, practice, appraisals and culture. *It practises living through values and accepts the transformation that this brings.*

9 **Always a start-up** – Microsoft thinks like a small organisation

and acts like a start-up, striving, initiating and seeking to break through. *It practises non-complacency.*

10 **The circus** – Microsoft enjoys adventurous involvement in the wider community. *It practises social responsibility.*

11 **Detachment** – Staff keep sight of the big picture and, amidst all the speed and urgency of work, retain a sense of perspective and calm. *It practises healthy detachment.*

12 **Grit** – Breadth and depth of character is one of the salient aspects of Microsoft staff. The diabetic man running across the Sahara, a distance of six marathons in one week, sums up the grit of some of these people. *It practises perseverance and commitment.*

EVERYDAY PRACTICE

APPROACHING MICROSOFT UK

When I was ringing round multinational companies to see if any would be part of this book, I was a little hesitant. Cold-calling and asking to interview people on soul and spirit at work was an unusual request, and I was unsure how it would be received. But when I rang Microsoft, I was met with, 'Ah! You have come to the right company. You need to talk to Tracey Malone who will set up an interview for you.' The response was open and effective; this was the first person I spoke to after the reception desk, and it led straight where I needed to go. Sure enough, the interviews were arranged, and I went to the headquarters of Microsoft UK to meet the newest recruit and the director of people, profit and loyalty.

Microsoft is housed in three massive, grey buildings on a landscaped industrial estate outside Reading in Berkshire. My first impression was of a number of staff emerging from the main entrance in twos and threes, wearing comfortable summery clothes and heading towards a lily pond where wooden tables were informally placed around the grass and people were meeting and chatting. Once inside,

I waited in the reception lounge, helped myself to pure fruit juice and watched the world go by. Just past reception was a large, light atrium where people were having meetings, clustered around tables or sitting on sofas, a supply of coffee coming from the adjacent canteen. There was an indefinable atmosphere of purpose and conviviality, and there was something missing: status. The insidious signs of status were few; clothing style was relaxed, faces were open, accessories and make-up were minimal. People were engrossed in something that seemed to leave little space for image; something more exciting was happening. This was not a smart place in the traditional sense. It even had a slight air of holiday about it. Overhead a giant screen with clock marked the countdown in days, hours and minutes until the release of XP, the latest Microsoft product.

The outward facts and prejudices, the myth of Microsoft, seemed not to fit with this atmosphere. The media will confirm its wealth of $30 billion and a turnover that is greater than the gross national product of some countries. It has immense power and an immeasurable influence on the twentieth and twenty-first centuries. It has changed the lives of billions of people. But in reality it is quite small, globally employing only 50,000 staff. And inside, the story is quite different from the image. The secret of Microsoft seems to lie right here in its people. The following glimpses of Microsoft, of eight different people and how they help to create the company and its wealth, may help to explain this.

NINETY-SEVEN PER CENT OF OUR WEALTH
IS THE PEOPLE

I was to meet the finance director, but when I had looked him up on the Internet I had noticed that he was also director of human resources. How could any one person carry this double workload? Many companies pay lip service to people but few have a finance director who is also head of personnel. The two jobs go naturally and inevitably together, however, if one knows that the wealth of the company actually flows out of the human beings. Steve Harvey, until recently finance and human resources director, is now director of people, profit and loyalty. He is comfortable with the language of spirituality and sees it in software terms:

> Spirit is what we look for in our people. We talk about similarity of spirit and diversity of strength, and that is what we look for. And quite often you find people that don't fit into Microsoft's culture are the ones who don't have the same spirit, that knowledge in you of what technology can do for people; that's what really helps you get through your day and do what you do, and it's what makes you come back here every day. But if you come to Microsoft and you just want to do a job, then it doesn't work. It's not a place where you can just come and do a 9 to 5 job and walk away. It's more embracing than that, it just grabs hold of you. Because we really do want to change the world of microchip software, that's what we're about. It's that similarity of spirit that we are looking for. If a team doesn't quite gel, what we find is that the spirit's not there; they're not looking for the same things.

Here is a finance director in one of the largest multinationals who sees people as the most important part of the business and spirit as the most important part of the people. And this spirit is not to be neatly defined but has something to do with the passion with which one lives, the sense of purpose one has, the desire to help make a difference in people's lives, reaching forward into a future that contains possibilities we have scarcely dreamt of, not knowing where it will lead but trusting that a way will emerge and that this is a path to be followed wholeheartedly or not at all, and a journey to be made with others who share the vision as without them it is not possible.

Steve also is happy speaking the language of finance:

> I worked out four or five years ago that the finance director can only do so much and that the real money is to be made in the people side. We get now nearly £3 million per employee revenue compared with the average in the UK, which is £150,000. And that sort of magnitude of difference comes from focusing on our people and really making them effective. So the idea is to find someone best at

the job, have a great manager to work with them, then focus on employees being engaged in what they do well every day.

So here are these two worlds meeting, two languages – the language of spirit and the language of money. But I am still a little dubious. For decades we have been told that profit rules; even our schools and hospitals have come to put money first. Surely a company will put profit before people when there is a conflict of interests?

> When there's a real clash between profit and people, what happens here is that the people aspect will always come first; it has to, because that's all we've got. If we haven't got the people, we haven't got anything here.

For Steve technology is there to:

> free up people's time and unleash their talents. Freeing their time is one thing so they can do more productive tasks, and then second it takes over the mundane process stuff and lets them go and do something really special. And we believe in that. I love taking people out of processes and letting software do the job. I love freeing up people to unleash their real talents, do the stuff they really want to do. That's my drive for the whole people vision we have here. We all work round this vision of creating an environment where great people can do their best work. That's what I want them to do every day; I want them to be effective. Come here and do whatever you're best at.

Steve speaks from experience. He has been at the company for twelve years, over which time he has been responsible for the finances of Microsoft UK, one of the most successful subsidiaries in the whole of Microsoft. His ideas have been tested and proved in terms of profit forecasts and investment returns. His words are those of a man who is passionate about his company being successful, making the best software and making good profits, and he has consistently delivered the goods. For him this is inextricably tied up with people, their spirit and their loyalty. It is common sense, and there are very practical implications for how he works and the results he gets.

First, Steve recognises that he has a real strength for understanding people and seeing their strengths:

> I passionately believe I was put here to bring out the best in others, and that's what I do; I spend a lot of my time doing that, working with other people, trying to help them see the real strengths they have and understanding what they could be doing. Looking for the best in them and trying to help that come out. That's what I do.

Second, he leaves plenty of space in his diary for walking around talking to people, being available to listen. When he sees what someone's real talents are he knows that 'if we unleash those talents and then get them to do jobs that match them best, then life moves on ever quicker.'

Third, Steve does whatever it takes to get people to the point where they can do what it is they are good at: 'Bashing down the doors and creating a space for them to come through and show what they'd be great at.'

Fourth, he holds all this in the broadest of perspectives:

> We ask people to try and understand what is people's vocation in life; what is it you were put on this planet for in the first place, what is their major vocation in life?

When he does this, Steve finds that it:

> takes people to a whole higher level of thinking about why they're here, what they're doing, what their role in society is. And it's surprising when you get behind that, when you get to find out what people are really motivated by and where they are really heading.

So now he is in touch with people's fundamental core motivators, and he treats this with great respect. Throughout he takes deep pleasure in seeing people break through to success; it is part of what helps him be who he is. When I ask him what will have been of greatest worth to him personally at Microsoft he says:

> seeing people that I've actually helped bring up through the ranks, if you like, and I worked with them to unleash their talents.

113

This ties in with his longing for:

> A world where people are respected for their strengths and not forced to dwell on their weakness. I'd like to think I can help create that sort of space in the world for people to really flourish, to really release what's really inside them.

Steve's approach has very practical outcomes. First, when disaster hits, morale remains high. The previous eighteen months, for example, had been some of the toughest the company has ever known. An adverse decision in the USA court case saw the Microsoft share price plummet from $120 to $40 within days. The effect on employees was felt very directly. Many people had joined the company with a drop in salary because Microsoft pays less than the market rate but gives stock as well. When the share price dropped, much of their package disappeared. Instead of people whingeing and moaning, however, there was a feeling of 'I'm going to fight for this now.' There was a strong sense of being one body and a determination to turn the situation around to achieve the vision. The vision of the future was bright enough to burn off the despondency of the here and now. They went forward with an energy that did indeed help to turn it around. Contrast this with the downward spiral that can hit giants where, once a dent happens, morale plummets, confidence falls and the cycle of descent becomes inexorable. Microsoft spring back.

Second, Microsoft is able to recruit great people. Over the past few years IT companies have found it hard to recruit, but as Steve puts it, 'We're sitting on a thousand-person goldmine – that's what we have here. Other companies are dying to get their hands on the people we have in this company.' Staff at Microsoft are intelligent, passionate people.

Microsoft is also able to retain its staff. The attrition rate in the industry is 19%, but in the technical community at Microsoft, which is where it is hardest to find staff, the most recently available attrition rate was 3%. People stay because they enjoy the company and want to be there. Similarly, when there are dips in the market, as through

In our African language we say 'a person is a person through other persons'. I would not know how to be a human being at all except I learned this from other human beings. We are made for a delicate network of relationship, of interdependence. We are meant to complement each other. All kinds of things go horribly wrong when we break that fundamental law of our being.

Desmond Tutu

a recession, Microsoft does not lay people off. This increases confidence and morale, which in turn increases performance.

Finally, when times are hard, it is able to go forwards because of the combination of the calibre, teamwork, loyalty and commitment of the staff to get through together as one body.

Over the period I was interviewing at Microsoft, most high-tech companies were being badly shaken with bleak profit warnings and redundancies. The atmosphere at Microsoft seemed far from troubled. Staff were not, however, arrogant or complacent; they were simply absorbed and fully engaged in the work they were doing and the vision they were pursuing, like runners in a race who do not notice the rain.

As I went round and interviewed people, I found repeated evidence that Steve's attitudes are put into practice, that people are greatly prized. I met the administrative temp who was encouraged to find her strength in designing internal websites, the new recruit who chose to develop her own strategy in human resources, the help desk staff who have time to undertake personal development courses and get involved in the community. The leaders in this organisation have created an environment where people treat each other well and are actively valued. The structures, processes, principles and culture combine to give primacy to people and relationships.

• • • *Reflection* • • •

Much pain and suffering has been caused in the areas of education and health from money unashamedly dominating over people. Had teachers and children, nurses and doctors, patients and carers, been valued over financial targets, enormous quantities of mistakes, stress, burnout and consequent waste would not have occurred.

The financial director of another blue-chip company said to me, 'No wonder people are enervated, if their focus is always on money; you cannot worship Mammon and God.' The teaching in spiritual traditions is very clear – primacy must not to be given to money. Spirituality is essentially a very practical affair; it attempts to teach us what works well for us as human beings. This does not mean that money and material considerations are not taken seriously and husbanded, but they are not to dominate one's consciousness and care. If they do, life does not 'work'.

At Microsoft it is obviously very important to everyone to be successful, to reach goals, win markets, make money, but the money is not the thing that dominates – there is a world of difference between being important and dominating. When one looks at what is spent in Microsoft in terms of benefits to the staff and structures for providing customer service, it seems evident that people's well-being and service come first.

• •

TEAMS

Individuals acting on their own are limited; it is through their relationships that they come into being. When the power of individuals is unleashed and harmonised to work with that of others, a tremendous and unpredictable synergy is achieved. One of Steve's gifts is his ability to build teams: 'I'm good at creating superteams, and I am quite happy to make constant changes to teams to actually get the right team for the job in hand.' Even as a child he did this when, as captain of the football team, he built his teams around him, maximising their strengths and helping to focus them on the job in hand.

Steve is very conscious that people have weaknesses as well as strengths and that is part of the reason why a team is so important; members make up for each other's weaker areas. Of himself he says:

> My ego is on the golf course because my number one strength is my competitiveness. I love being competitive, but I use golf as my outlet. I go out on to the golf course and strut my stuff and am a golf-competitive person. If I brought that internally it wouldn't help. But it's knowing that others know what I'm good at and also what I'm not good at. And so I build teams around me to compensate.

Steve recognises that he is not very good at fairness and harmony; he does not really believe in it. He is urgent to get the task done and at times ruffles people's feathers in the process. He also does not look for consensus; he does not want everyone singing from the same hymn book. I notice that his PA, Tracy Malone, is, however, appreciated for her outstanding strength in those very two areas.

The person who speaks most eloquently of how a team works is Ian, who staffs the initial response help desk. His team is first in line when corporate customers are having technical difficulties. The delight Ian takes in his work bubbles out. He likes helping people get their technical difficulties sorted and he finds that the structure, the nature of the teams, means that he can do the type of job that really gives him pleasure. As far as Ian is concerned, 'the whole company is based on team players in teams'. His team works well because:

> We know everyone in the team very well. Microsoft allows us to go out and have long and regular team-building sessions. I think we all know what the ultimate goal is, actually to get customer satisfaction high. We want to cut out all the customer dissatisfaction and we're constantly trying to improve that. And everyone in that team is absolutely dedicated to that and trying to get the calls progressed to a resolution. We all know the job like the back of our hands. The great thing about our role is that if we get someone new in the team, they're not pulled in on the phones within just a couple of days to start supporting customers. We have up to two or three months training. So it's a fantastic environment.

EVERYDAY PRACTICE

117

Each team member is daily on the look out for finding ways to help the team work better, to share information, so that they can create a better customer experience. The main facet, however, that helps the team work effectively is:

> friendliness, it's everyone being so outgoing. We've got the values that we all work towards. And I think everyone is really strong in all of the qualities and all of these values, and it's just an amazing place. I can walk back into the team and if I need something done and I haven't got time to do it, then someone else, if I just go and ask, someone will stick up their hand up and say, 'Yes, I'll help' . . . I think it's knowing that in a time when they may need help, we're going to turn round and say, 'Yes, we'll help as well.' And again it's down to the environment; it's difficult to describe.

Ian is aware how he has changed since he has been at Microsoft:

> I must admit I think a few years ago in a different environment I wouldn't have been so forthcoming in wanting to help people, I would just have probably wanted to get down to the job because I was always so busy. I just felt right, focus on myself, I've got to do this, I've got to get this done by the end of the day. Now I'm still busy, but I think we've got time to actually help others. . . . It's also as well I think people enjoy helping – it's the satisfaction and getting the thanks.

Ian's group works closely with other teams; this helping extends to them too, and Ian enjoys the fact that this is not taken for granted:

> We're always helping the technical account manager. If they've got an issue at all with any calls, they come through to us. We help them out, contact their customers for example, and we always get a thank you. And it's followed up, you know, 'Thanks for your help' – and it's just a great deal. They really do mean it; we actually get the recognition. It's getting pleasure out of seeing a thank you note and whether that's from one of the people that you're working with or whether it's a customer, it's lovely.

Now, the idea of working on a computer help desk being a lovely experience, rather than the sort of job that has most people tearing their hair out, is definitely new to me.

Ian unravels some of the strands of this experience. He describes how each person works for two weeks on the phones responding to calls and then has one week away from the phones. During this week they are proactive, taking on whatever training and development they want to strengthen themselves, and doing whatever teamwork they feel needs attention. Ian explained the different tiers and teams of support he can draw on so that the appropriate level of expertise is brought to bear and the problem is dealt with. He describes the training that is undertaken before anyone takes a phone call. He himself came to Microsoft with few technical skills and little knowledge. There have been extraordinary team-building times, for example battling with walls of fire and disasters at a naval base. Ian touches on the company annual conferences, which are full of surprises – as when the theme was 'Face your Fear' and arachnophobic Ian held a large tarantula. He recalled the tremendous experience of being in a Challenger team raising money for the NSPCC with a team of six colleagues from throughout the company, including a director, facing the challenges as equals.

The best part of it all, as far as Ian is concerned, is never knowing what problem he is going to encounter on the phone that day. Part of his pleasure comes from knowing that the people ringing in with problems are really needing help:

> We can take the pressure off them. So in some ways, hopefully, we're de-stressing them. Because if they didn't have this kind of support, then I can imagine them getting very heavily burdened with these problems and not being able to turn anywhere. That's what causes stress and burnout. That's when you start hating your job if you come in every day thinking 'Oh my God I've got this problem again, what the hell am I going to do?' It's much better coming in thinking 'Well I'll pass it over to Microsoft and they can do the work.' And if we can solve it – perfect.

Fleetingly I get an image of a sort of technical social worker, enjoying solving people's problems. On his own Ian could not do it, as part of a fully harmonised group of teams he can.

Not all the teams at Microsoft are, however, like Ian's. Some, according to one senior manager, seem to be held together more by Velcro, ready to come apart when strain is placed on them, but at least there are instances when the company achieves superb teams and these are consciously prized. There is, at times, a sense of team that is akin to community – that place where people choose to bind themselves to each other in mutual care.

• • • *Reflection* • • •

Teams do not necessarily just happen: a lot of work has been put in to ensure that people can work as a team. Until you know each other it is hard to truly value each other – it takes time and shared experiences in a number of different situations. For Ian's team finding themselves in situations where they were absolutely dependent on each other if they were to succeed, as with the Challenger competition or the wall of fire, simply highlighted what is a fact – that they are interdependent. The reality is that to best achieve their everyday task on the help desk, they are as dependent on each other as when facing a wall of fire. They do it together as a team, sharing, valuing, laughing, supporting, having empathy and making space one for another, knowing that what they do together they could not do alone. The company enables this to happen by recruiting people for their attitude rather than their skills, ensuring that there is plenty of training, giving them time to work and play together in unusual situations, structuring the pattern of weeks so that there is space to reflect and develop, building in flexibility so that give and take is a natural way of working and taking the team as such seriously and valuing it.

All spiritual traditions teach of our interdependence and of the paradox that although we are unique individuals, yet we are one. St Paul wrote vividly of the foolishness of thinking that any one part of the body should think that it is superior, or that any part could be dispensed with. A team working well is an extraordinary manifest-ation of this truth that we are many and we are one. It is a community.

WORKAHOLISM

Part of Steve Harvey's job is to keep the company's staff: there is nothing to stop them walking away as they are highly skilled people who could easily walk into other companies. Steve needs to create an environment in which people want to be and where their needs are met, so Microsoft is an extraordinarily comfortable place to work. There is delicious food, space, light, greenery, a medical centre, a well-being centre, a counselling service, shops, a sports centre and a swimming pool next door, financial advisers and private bankers, dry cleaning, groceries delivered from the supermarket to the company door, personal development training, relaxation areas, meadows to walk and talk in and, of course, all the new products to play with. All this is available to everyone:

> We treat everyone the same here; we don't have any special perks because you're a director compared with someone else. We constantly try to treat everyone the same.

But the ease and comfort of this environment has a drawback:

> It is a place where you really can hide if you want to; you can make this place your life 100% of the time and hide from the rest of the world if that's what you really want to do. It has the ability to destroy a lot of families if they're not careful, because you can hide behind it and live your whole life through it, and that's hard for some people to cope with. Because there are so many opportunities here and so few people, you never get bored, you never run out of things to do. In fact it takes a strong person to say, 'Well hang on, that's it for this week, I need to go and have a life now for a bit.'

Steve is aware that the real nitty-gritty of family life can be hard in comparison:

> Because of the environment we create here, both physically and emotionally, this is a great place to be, and actually life outside is quite stressful in comparison. Going out into the outside world of family and friends can be very hard work. It is a mucky business.

He would like to see families more involved in life at Microsoft:

> I'd like to see us working with youngsters, teenagers, see them grow

EVERYDAY PRACTICE

121

up, help them with technology, help them assess who they are. Give them the opportunities to do what we do with our people here so that the kids have got a better chance of getting the right job that's going to make them excited and motivated. That's where I see us extending out to.

Some of the measures that the company uses to counteract workaholism include recruiting people who show a breadth of character and experience, and who have interests over and above work; encouraging staff to get involved in community concerns; top management setting a good example by usually going home at a sensible hour; undermining any macho I-work-long-hours syndrome through flexitime and family-friendly policies, recognising that it is potentially harmful; and valuing people as whole people whose family and community life matters.

• • • *Reflection* • • •

Addiction is damaging even if it is disguised in the seductive garb of heroic hard work. The fact that one often gets admired for this addiction makes it particularly difficult to master. One of the greatest challenges for Microsoft is to achieve a balance so that the tremendous passion that people have for their work does not consume them, their lives and relationships, destroying their families in the process.

Spiritual traditions teach that all idolatry is a destructive mistake, and letting work take pre-eminence over life itself is a form of addiction and idolatry. It also runs counter to the spiritual traditions that require time to be set aside from work, a time of rest and space, a time that has a rhythm different from the rest of the week. It is a time not of getting things done but of being. In Judaeo-Christian terms this was the Sabbath, which was so fiercely defended. Having a time set aside from work is vital to our humanity and sanity, as well as to the planet itself.

THE BALKAN WAR

Shaun Orpen, director of corporate marketing until 2001, recalls how during the Balkan War, e-mails were circulating. 'What can we do?' So a person from the East Europe/Africa Microsoft desk was freed up to meet and listen to the Red Cross and work out how best the company could help. One of the aspects of the war was that people fled, leaving their possessions and losing all their papers. On the advice of the Red Cross, Microsoft installed technology so that the refugees could be registered and have passports, thus having the papers they needed when the time came for repatriation. The technology had to be tested in the field, and computers that had up until then sat only on desks had to be able to withstand battlefield conditions. At the end of the year, the East Europe/Africa Microsoft division presented their figures. They had failed to reach their budget because of the resources that had been freely put into this behind-the-scenes work, but the other divisions applauded them for having their priorities right.

• • • *Reflection* • • •

One of the constant and the hardest teachings of spiritual traditions is that we need to respond to suffering wherever it is, to let it reach us and trouble us, to be involved and to give what we can to alleviate it. Setting up the technology to produce the paperwork was not a particularly glamorous task, but it was a crucial part of the great patchwork of rebuilding people's lives in which many individuals and groups throughout Europe have been involved during and since the war. Most of us were observers; Microsoft, both as individuals and as a company, chose quietly to get involved and let the bottom line suffer if need be.

THE NEWEST RECRUIT

E C I T C A R P   Y A D Y R E V E

Gill Crowther has been at Microsoft for six months and is a member of the human resources team. Shortly after she arrived she was concerned that she had come to the wrong job:

> I joined for the culture and for the opportunity, and I guess I had underestimated that the job I'd just joined to do was so similar to roles I had already done before. The hard part was coming up with the vision of what it was I thought I should be doing, what was it that I could get passionate about, and then going to my boss and saying so. I can talk about strategic things, but when it comes to talking about me I'm not so good.

Gill had come from working in a pharmaceutical company where it was very easy to have the feel-good factor. She recalled how, within weeks of joining them, 'I could sit in a pub and be Mrs Passionate about "Oh your child's got asthma, let me help", because the ethical side of that really is a plus that you feel good about.' It was harder for her to grasp fully the difference that Microsoft made in people's lives; she knew it in her head but not in her heart.

Gill realised that simply doing a good enough job at Microsoft was not what would work. She needed to find out how she could contribute, how she could make a real difference:

> The enjoyment and the buzz I get is so dependent on me being able to use my own talents, that by completely removing yourself and doing a job that is very different to the way that you would want to operate and feel natural operating, is not just bad in that your performance suffers, it's bad because your emotional health suffers as well.

She worked with an outside coach and with Steve, her boss, to create her role and find out what her challenge was, what would give her the buzz that comes when she's performing really well:

> I did an engineering degree so I have a way of seeing structure. I am now working to see that we have globalised, regionalised and localised measures to make human resources a best-practice place.

The company is growing very rapidly, and we need to be thinking where in our people strategy we should be global and where we need to have some regional guidance in terms of Europe, and where we need to be able to make local changes so that we still feel like a flexible, entrepreneurial great place to be.

Gill had previously worked for a vast automobile company that went global, and she had suffered the intense frustration of sitting in the UK unable to make something happen for three years because of global policy. Using this experience, she is now initiating work on an human resources policy that tries to reflect the complexity of global working and the importance of people within that, combining the constancy of principles with personal freedom. Simple in words but harder to put into practice. The task is how to help HR in a global company speak as one voice while being responsive, flexible and creative within diverse cultures. It is the very antithesis of the deadening homogeneity that persists in some large corporates, in which the desire to keep control stifles freedom and creativity. There is no blueprint to tell companies how to be global companies; it needs to be invented now and is being so through the fresh eyes of a young recruit.

For Gill the vision of Microsoft is of a company where people are the very heart and soul of it.

Finding the right way for everybody to understand what that means is really tough.

This is another area where no history books are there to explain how to do it.

••• *Reflection* •••

When we are missing the mark, failing to use our talents, there is a divine discontent that sets in. We feel uneasy, lacking the buzz that makes for enjoyment. It would have been easy for Gill to go along with the fact that her new job required little effort and was not fully satisfying. It took courage to say, 'I want more please', especially when she was not sure what that 'more' was. She took the time to reflect, to draw on who she was and her experience, and she dared to have a dream. It is not a neat, tidy package carefully rehearsed. It is a dream that is coming up from within her into the light of day.

To express one's dream requires courage. A thousand messages played out over and over again tell us to keep our heads down, especially when we are new: 'If it were possible, someone else, someone more important, would have thought of it. Fit in, conform, do what you were hired for, know your place.' All these messages daily strangle the dream. The founders of the great spiritual traditions, and the movements for change throughout history, have all required that ordinary, often inexperienced, people voice the dream, the thought that it can be different, it can be better. To voice that within many companies would be disastrous, but in a soul-friendly company staff are encouraged to reflect, to voice and to act on their dream and to work from their passion.

• •

THE RELUCTANT TEMP

Tracey Grove came to Microsoft three years ago. She had left South Africa suddenly: 'It was very much a defence reaction against things happening in South Africa; we just moved here as a survival instinct. I had no aspirations.' She registered with a temping agency and they asked her to come to Microsoft:

I said no. A large corporation; it would be very cold; I'd be just a number. That was my impression. But the impression of Microsoft externally is very different from what it is actually like inside. I had the same impression that a lot of people had; I thought that I would just be a cog in the wheel. The agency nagged and, just to get them off my back, I came into Microsoft as PA to the finance director, Steve, and a week or two later I was offered a permanent role and accepted it.

Tracey's life then started to change after that. She had arrived with no technology background at all, having worked only in companies that still did everything on paper. Tracey had no interest in technology and her only experience was a little surfing on the web:

My interest was sparked when, as part of my role as Steve's PA, I had to do a bit of editing on our intranet, our internal website, and this document was probably the most boring in history as it was a legal handbook. Just working with that sparked an interest in me to find a way to make it more interesting, interactive and fun for people to use. There was not much I could do with a legal document like that one, but there was a great deal more I could do with the rest of our intranet, and that's where it all started.

Tracey then, with Steve's support, took on a role in systems and processes because that was what she was really keen to do. Since then she has also taken on the company's web development and has been learning more about Microsoft technology. She plans ultimately to move into a software engineering role. Seeing the new Windows technology at work:

I realised just how this technology can make your business more effective; it's just so unbelievable. And so many companies are doing things in an antiquated way and here things are so advanced. The best thing for me about working here is that I'm at the cutting edge of technology and get to play with all the great tools that come out.

This is the woman who had no interest in technology. Tracey explains in detail how the procurement process is streamlined and how claiming expenses is totally automated, saving a huge amount of time and money:

EVERYDAY PRACTICE

The use of technology allows people to focus on what they are paid to do. It removes their focus from doing those mundane day-to-day administrative tasks and allows them to concentrate on their role, which is to add value to the company, either by bringing in revenue, supporting the customer or perhaps responding to the business's needs as far as finance reporting is concerned. It doesn't matter what area you are in, the technology enables you to work more effectively every day.

Although absorbed by the technology, Tracey sees another side to Microsoft – a soft side that many people do not see because Microsoft does not advertise it:

There's an element here of people wanting to give back to the community. There's a feeling that we have got so much going for us here, we have all these wonderful benefits, we are given so much, and I think that makes people feel they want to give something back because we see that other people aren't all as fortunate as we are.

The company has funded schemes to support Help the Aged with their work with the very frail, and it works on developing software that can make a difference for sick and disabled people. It is easy for cynics to dismiss this, but it is clear that the individuals involved feel passionately about giving something back to the community and making a difference in the lives of those who are disadvantaged. They use the payroll to make automatic payments to a charity of their choice. They bake cakes, climb mountains and cross deserts. They house and provide back-up for a full-time NSPCC worker. There is a commitment to developing software to help people who are disabled, ill or disadvantaged. Individually, staff raise thousands of pounds, and Microsoft as a whole gives millions to charities.

Tracey sees this at a very practical, personal level as technology enables her to keep in touch with her family overseas:

Hotmail is a free internet service and with this my mum, who is extremely technologically challenged, can send me an e-mail through her TV screen with a little keyboard and a remote control, which is probably as near as she would ever want to get to using a

*I remembered the line from the Hindu scripture, the Bhagavad
Gita . . . 'I am become death, the destroyer of worlds.'*

J. Robert Oppenheimer

● ● ● ● ● ● ● ● ● ● ● ● ●

mouse. The new technology is much easier for her to handle, especially since she has osteoporosis and can be bedridden at times.

One of the important things for Tracey is that the software is really changing how marginalised people live their lives:

People who have historically been shut out of the world of technology because they can't see or hear, or communicate as effectively as the man on the street, are having a whole new world opened up for them. Recently, at a company conference, we had a demo where a gentleman came up and presented to us using a Braille keypad with Microsoft software. He was completely blind and no one knew until the end of his presentation. So it really does make a difference to people's lives.

Tracey regards Microsoft as unique among big corporations because it cares and demonstrates this caring attitude both to its employees and in its products:

They really do go overboard about people. They are focused on people, which is wonderful because there are so many opportunities for development, to the point where they've actually mandated that every employee must have a personal development plan and career plan as part of our performance review process. Managers are encouraged to help their people to think about their career. They ask, 'Where do you want to go, be it within or outside Microsoft?' Obviously they hope it will be within, but if it isn't, then fair enough; the attitude is 'How can we help you?' Their whole outlook is so completely different, it's so open, it's 'Go out there and take the opportunity. You want it, you can take it; go for it!'

The company is, however, far from perfect: the amount of information can be overwhelming, especially to a newcomer, and even though bureaucracy has been minimised, it still exists. Tracey has set herself

EVERYDAY PRACTICE

the task of working out internal software solutions to ease the path of new staff, helping them through all the information, and also devising processes that cut out bureaucracy. Overload, bureaucracy, confusion all are disabling and deaden the spirit. Tracey's work may not save lives but it frees people up and enables them to give of their best.

I am a struck by Tracey's metamorphosis. She had been, like myself, a woman with just enough computer skills to get by, yet here she was striding forwards through new territories, harvesting technology skills and applying them with glee. I began to feel my mind-set shifting and my prejudice towards and ignorance of technology slipping. I had complacently assumed that technophiles were missing the point, which is that people need to be with people and that technology can only be peripheral to that and may well distract and detract from it. The false dichotomy of people or technology crumbled as I listened to Tracey, this woman who cares about people, romps through all that technology can offer them and feels great gratitude for the opportunity.

• • • *Reflection* • • •

With every scientific advance comes the choice to use it for good or evil. Spirituality goes beyond ethics and morality; it goes straight to the deepest, simplest human truths of what we are as human beings, creatures who long for happiness, creatures who are sacred. How we use technology is critical; does it dehumanise, or does it free us to be more human? The intention of Microsoft is to provide technology that serves people, making us more efficient and effective. Their intention is also that their technology should enable us to be more fully human, more free of drudgery, more able to alleviate the suffering of those who are marginalised, the people who are old, disabled and sick. Of course it also sets out to provide fun, lots of it, and to make lots of money. But technology is not developed in a moral vacuum, nor is it seen as the answer to everything; its limitations are recognised.

VALUES IN THE DNA

Microsoft is very explicit about its values, and all employees take them on board. These values are respect for the customer, entrepreneurial spirit, cooperation, integrity, passion and empowerment. The company wants the values to penetrate every part of the organisation until they are in its very DNA.

Tony Ettlinger has been with Microsoft for ten and a half years and is responsible for values within the UK company, as well as being director of customer and partner loyalty. He points out that this is a company where everything is measured. People are measured on results; it is a very numbers-driven place. People have clear objectives and work to them. How does one measure the intangible? Given that practising values is not so much about *what* you do as about *how* you do it, how is one to measure them? And if they are not measured, how seriously will they be taken?

> Our performance review process is there not only to try and measure how one's done against some fairly measurable objectives, sold X percent, got X percent of market share or whatever. It also dares to assess people on how they do things.

Tony feels that, before values were brought into sharp focus in the company, it was necessary for senior management to demonstrate them through their own behaviour. Values without a leadership that practises them would get nowhere. Moreover, their behaviour needed to spring from the fact that the senior management cared and worried about the legacy they'd leave behind. They spent twelve months as a management team journalling, coaching and working at understanding how to put their values into practice. The whole company then spent eighteen months exploring what these values meant and how they worked on a day-to-day basis. At Microsoft UK there is now plenty of hard evidence that management does care and is intent on leaving a legacy, and that staff do see and value the values as an integral part of work.

Tony makes it clear that the values are not plucked from the sky

EVERYDAY PRACTICE

and are not based on idealism. They are grounded in good business sense and are there to compensate for what could otherwise be difficult behaviour:

> When we think about the way we want people to work here, yes we want them to be very competitive, but we want them to be competitive against our external competition. We don't want them to be competitive against internal staff or against customers or partners, for example. And so co-operation is one of the values, and highly valued because what you find is that the people who tend to share knowledge and not compete internally are actually very effective employees. And everyone likes to work with them.

The value of integrity is basically about doing what you say you will do, sticking to your word. 'This came from the old employee surveys where one of the things people hated was if person X said "I'd do this" and then they didn't get round to it.' In an organisation of Microsoft's complexity, where there are many interdependencies and links in the chain, it is vital that one can rely on people doing what they say they will do, otherwise the failure of one person to keep his or her word can nullify the efforts of countless others. Over and above the pragmatic effect of integrity, there is the discipline that it brings of being honest with oneself, of self-awareness and of commitment. In addition to making business more efficient, it makes individuals stronger and relationships more trusting.

What happened to Tony when he first joined Microsoft illustrates the sort of kindly culture that is fertile ground for values:

> I started in late October, and I had a brilliant secretary and she said, 'Oh yes, it's coming up to Christmas, you know. We always go down the pub.' There were thirty-six of us at that stage. I said, 'Oh yes.' She went on, 'Yes, and for Christmas everybody has to wear something red.' So I'm thinking about this. She said, 'Well, there's a fancy dress shop down the road.' Anyway, I turn up at the pub. The whole department is pretty much there by the time I get there. I'm the only person in fancy dress dressed as Father Christmas. And she thought it was hilarious, as did everybody else. And that's the kind of way it is here. And I carry a lot of things like that which to me are important.

Microsoft is a place that doesn't take itself too seriously, where people can enjoy each other but not at each other's expense, where people can put their head above the parapet but will not be destroyed, and where having a go is turned into a memory of fun rather than of searing embarrassment.

Neither is software taken too seriously:

> There are many things in the world where technology is completely irrelevant. So for me, personally, it comes back to this point. My sister is a doctor, and every day she's working she's done something very measurably good for life. What have I done at the end of the year that's good for life? So you have to say most of us do not work in areas of the world that to my mind fundamentally you can tangibly say, 'I saved that life' or 'I helped to improve the quality of life there.' But what Microsoft does do is return enormously a lot of the wealth. That's one of the reasons why I think it's a good company. But it is just software.

Despite seeing the limitations of software, the overarching usefulness of Tony's work matters to him. For him the important question to ask is 'Did we work in a way that allowed people to do exciting, new, crazy things that overall improved humankind?' He can see many instances where software does contribute:

> You're a doctor, a paramedic, somewhere and you can't know everything. But if you could, just by speaking to something, get immediate access to the best database that humankind had, that would give you an intelligent answer, which is ultimately what you need . . .

He pauses, lost for words by the size of what he is describing, and finishes, 'These things are within reach of that vision.' He then recalls how when he was a child his father had one of the early computers:

> He was in neuropsychological research. And this thing could barely add up in a day what can be done in a moment now. The power in the software drives the research forward because the software keeps demanding more and more power. So now at a research level, the sort of analysis that's going on, using relatively very affordable computing power, is such that could never have been envisaged when my father started.

Shareholding is offered to all employees so that all can participate in the wealth of the company, and this gives many people the financial freedom that again places them in control. Some who have held shares for many years come to work not because they need to but because they want to. Although the dips in the economic climate sometimes render the shares of little value, the intention of the company is still that all employees share well in the prosperity. At least one director to whom I spoke is personally and passionately committed to ensuring that real sharing of the wealth. 'That creates an enormous freedom, an enormous ability to focus on doing what one believes as an individual is right.'

Tony expresses gratitude for the things that Microsoft has enabled him to do in his life not in terms of technology but in a wider sense:

> I did the London Marathon this year; Microsoft has this lovely matching scheme on charity, so I raised myself just over £2,000, which Microsoft immediately doubled to £4,000 for Age Concern. And I feel good about that. I feel great about all the different team activities I've done and the knowledge I've acquired as a person.

The work on values still has a long way to go, and Tony sees plenty that still needs to be done to really embed them. His own work too is ever-changing. He started out running technical support for all UK customers before moving on to support the internal Microsoft infrastructure for Europe, the Middle East and Africa. He now heads the UK's push on improving the way in which Microsoft interacts with its customers and partners:

> The power of employees is the way they approach things and the willingness, the enthusiasm, to gain new skills. The last few years I've been as happy as my first few years at Microsoft because I've been changing all the time. I work in marketing at the moment. I didn't know a thing about marketing when I started. It's fantastic, you know. I don't know what my next job will be in a year's time, but I can't wait to find out. And if it's not there, OK I'll just hope I'm in an organisation that will allow me to keep changing and growing skills.

• • • *Reflection* • • •

The pragmatism that underlies the focus on values does not detract from their powerful ripple effect. Business has always known that trust is, for rational reasons, vital, but this does not take away the inherent goodness of the trust itself. Values are both practical, as in the instance of integrity, and also of unlimited potential. They can deliver the tangible result while at the same time affecting individuals and relationships in ways that immeasurably deepen and strengthen them. Working with colleagues who only ever say what they mean and always deliver what they say when they say has a profound effect on relationships inside and outside work, as well as on efficiency. The repercussions of the values are unlimited in their scope, but this knock-on effect will happen only if they are let loose in a culture that is essentially congruent with them, a soul-friendly culture where barriers are discouraged, where change and transformation are encouraged and where there is a basic kindliness.

One of the characteristics of the spiritual path is the willingness to be open to constant metanoia, transformation, to be willing at times to have nowhere to lay your head. It is not a rootlessness – the roots are there, but they are in the constancy of values. Much of our limitation comes from wanting to hold on to what we have for fear of losing all; and in the process of holding on, we lose the life that is possible if we will only let go.

• • • • • • • • • • • • • • • • • • • •

ALWAYS A START-UP

Karen Bergin is responsible for Microsoft public relations, community affairs and sponsorship. She is passionate about her work and has occasionally thrown all of her personal time out the window to work from dawn till dusk and more in order to help Microsoft develop its softer side and move beyond being a revenue-oriented, product-specific company. She touches on many aspects of her work and what matters to her:

> We think like a small organisation. We're almost 50,000 employees worldwide, but it's absolutely fair to say that we don't think like we're a big fat corporate, or that we've made it so our future's guaranteed. We just don't think that way. And it amazes me sometimes, even though I've been here three and a half years, that we don't think that way, but I'm delighted that we don't because actually it encourages me as an individual to be always thinking 'Golly! Am I doing the right thing; have I really done that the best way I possibly can?' It gets rid of the smugness. And I think, from an internal point of view, it's an organisation where, because we set ourselves such tough targets to be the very best that we can be, we're very overt about wanting our people to be the very best that they can be so that we can produce the very, very best software.

This carries over into Karen's personal life:

> It forces you to look at yourself and think 'Well! . . . Am I being the very best that I can be?' Not just at work, but also am I the best aunt, sister, partner that I can be? And I find that if you're that way inclined naturally, and I am, when you work in a company like Microsoft it forces you to look at yourself even more closely than you've ever done before. It encourages self-criticism, self-awareness and self-exploration. So, therefore, if you can do that, and if you can be honest with yourself and then combine it with the belief, and have the courage to follow your belief in terms of what you can do to help the organisation move forwards or help your team move forwards, or help that individual move forwards, and if you're prepared to put your head up and stick by your beliefs, it's the most phenomenal can-do company I've ever met. We think like a start-up. We really do. It's quite amazing. We think like the race is just about to begin. Every day. There is an unspoken agreement that we all have got to make this thing fly.

• •

If you want to do it, you can do it. If you've got the passion, take charge of your destiny.

Shaun Orpen

● ● ● *Reflection* ● ● ●

Honesty, self-awareness, courage, belief and a commitment to being the best one can be are part of the start-up mentality that Karen describes. Few would seriously attempt to set up a business without having enthusiasm, hope and courage. These are qualities of the spirit, and if we need these qualities to set out, what makes us imagine that we can manage to sustain a business without them? As we go through the rapidly changing, ever-new crises facing business, the world and our planet in the twenty-first century, we need the ability to start as new. What worked last year will not necessarily work now.

Spiritual teaching, in particular Buddhism, points to the transience within the material world and to the fact that the one thing we can be sure of is that all things pass away and change. If an organisation can therefore adopt the stance of being new, it is well equipped to respond to the constantly new emerging situation.

● ●

AGONY AUNT

Time is regarded as a very precious commodity at Microsoft, and the employees are glad to be using cutting-edge software to make the most of their time. However, as the owner of Microsoft's image and reputation, Karen describes how the time she spends on its people can become all-consuming:

> I run a team; I am what I would call a player manager. I do things, I deliver things, I actually roll up my sleeves and deliver objectives, milestones, plans and plenty of other deliverables. I also have a team to take care of, and while I must deliver all these things to the very best of my ability, I also feel that my team have the right for me to be the very best manager that I can possibly be. I have a duty of care to be the best manager, to care about them and think about their

Half an hour's listening is essential except when you are very busy. Then a full hour is needed.

St Francis de Sales

● ● ● ● ● ● ● ● ● ● ● ● ● ●

welfare. So there are two parts to my role. But I also see myself as being a manager in the wider organisation. So if people want to come and talk to me and they're not necessarily in my team, I always try and make the time to listen.

Karen spends a good deal of time listening to people throughout the organisation:

> Quite often people just need to offload, they just need to talk; they need to check what they're thinking, they need reassurance, they need a different view. And I also think it's important as a manager to facilitate that wherever possible. So one of the people who worked for me one day said, 'What does it feel like to be a friend of the people?' And I said, 'What do you mean?' And she said, 'I've sat beside you for the last year, and I would say that, during that time, you add at least an hour and a half on to your day every day because you're making yourself available for people to come and talk to you, and they do. People just come and talk to you. Why do you do it?' And I said that I couldn't ever imagine not doing it, because that cuts off part of who I am as a person, let alone who I am as a manager. It's me the person wanting to help, can I help, can I do something, a quiet word here, a quiet word there.

Karen received the unofficial title of the department's agony aunt, and they made her an open/closed sign:

> So closed was 'I know you need to talk to me, I know it's really important but actually I've got some work to do now; can you hang on for half an hour?' And open is 'I'm just working on normal stuff, if you want to pop by that's fine.'

• • • *Reflection* • • •

We create a wasteland of functionalism if we are prepared to be
with people only when it helps us meet our objectives. Time can
be more precious than money. Making time to simply be there for
others, to be alongside someone going through a tough time, to
be there to listen, this is the basis of compassion. All spiritual
traditions teach that compassion lies at the very centre of what it
is to be a human being. Taking time simply to be there, to listen,
is an essential element of the soul-friendly workplace.

• •

THE CIRCUS

Rory is a technician who provides customer support. When he comes into Microsoft, he comes in not just to work but to live. His work is technically very demanding, but there is more to working than simply the technology:

> Last month the technical community in my building put on a circus for some local schools. So there are 450 five- to six-year-old kids screaming their heads off at a bunch of computer technicians who spent two days learning how to juggle, how to be clowns and magicians, how to do trapezes and things. They sprinkled some professionals in among us to make it look a bit better, but 450 kids thought it was fantastic. A lot of people didn't volunteer to do it, but the people who put something into it came away with a hell of a buzz. It was a bit scary going out there through a wall of sound. But afterwards the sense of accomplishment for what was effectively 45 minutes worth of sheer terror was fantastic.

As someone who for many years has worked in world development work, I am wary of corporate charity. Tokenistic charity and conscience-salving donations are sickly substitutes for real gifts, real change; indeed corporate intrusion into education has created confusion and fury in the USA. But the giving at Microsoft is of a different order and feels authentic because there is genuine mutuality: everyone wins. With the circus, the technical teams, which rely on building up their capacity for superb teamwork, got the opportunity for two days' intensive team learning, with immediate feedback from 450 children; individuals were stretched and learnt new skills that they could use in their lives with their own children; and the community, the schools, in turn benefited from some enjoyable entertainment.

• • • *Reflection* • • •

Spiritual traditions stress the importance of giving, of charity, but how that charity is given is all important. In Judaism there is an emphasis on respecting the dignity of those to whom one gives. Tzedakah, the Jewish word closest to 'charity', has its root in the word for justice. In this tradition, giving comes not just from caring but from a desire for a more just world. The highest form of tzedakah is to work in partnership with someone so that he or she can become self-supporting.

Spirituality may encourage charity not only because it can alleviate suffering, but also because it answers a fundamental human need to give and to grow in the process. Without giving we tend to remain stunted. In the examples of charitable giving at Microsoft, it is clear that people's dignity is respected and that people learn and grow together through their giving. The giver's main reward is perhaps the insight that comes from the paradoxes so often present when spirit is at play.

• • • • • • • • • • • • • • • • • • • •

Only a life lived for others is a life worthwhile.

Albert Einstein

● ● ● ● ● ● ● ● ● ● ● ● ● ● ●

DETACHMENT

Microsoft is a passionate organisation, and passion can lead to burnout if it is not balanced by perspective and the detachment that comes from holding life lightly within the whole picture. Rory describes an incident in which a corporate customer rang in with an urgent problem – arriving at work one Monday morning, he had found that none of the desktop computers at one of their major call centres for customer service was working. The customer was desperate; it was a major breakdown and he was under a lot of pressure:

> Throughout it I responded to his requests for help at the level of urgency that he wanted me to; I was understanding what the impact of this not working was for him, and treating the call with all the urgency that he felt it required.

Rory did not hand over at the end of his shift but carried on in his own time until the problem was sorted:

> But although I empathise with the customers and think, 'Yeah, I know how urgent this is for you', I'm aware that in the greater scheme of things this is not as important as some other things – such as nursing, doctoring. Most things pale into insignificance against things like caring professions.

It is with this balance that Rory avoids any sense of burnout. Although he takes on the urgency of the customer's concern and will give 100% commitment, he still retains a sense of calm and perspective.

What will this look like in fifty years time? How important will it have been? What does it look like from the perspective of the weakest, poorest person? An enormous amount of human life, energy and time is consumed on things that are not that important. Spiritual traditions teach that we need to keep a broad perspective, remember our mortality, remember the weakest member of society and practise a certain degree of detachment: a detachment that paradoxically increases the quality of care. This of course, must not be confused with indifference, which saps life.

• •

GRIT

Paul Norris was head of technical support and responsible for 140 engineers; he now has taken on a new role of forging a team to work on OEM – original equipment manufacture. The team is working with the people who manufacture, assemble and distribute the hardware, and Paul's role is to make sure that they have the software they need when they need it. He knows that the business climate for their partners and customers has been harsh for the past couple of years and is about to get worse. Finding and maintaining markets is a very tough job, but Paul seems to thrive in severe conditions:

> Last year I became the first British diabetic to compete in the Marathon des Sables, known as the 'toughest footrace on earth'. I ran across the Sahara, or part of it – six marathons in a week. So I personally have a very strong achievement drive. But I don't want to win on my own. I truly believe that winning with and through others is a more powerful way of working generally. I go home and sleep well every night. I hope I've helped people bring out their best.

When Paul is looking at recruiting people, he is looking for character:

> That character is about energy and passion and belief and breadth

of life and experience. That's not to do with which courses they've done. I want to hear about people who've climbed mountains, swum rivers or had their art exhibited in a national museum or whatever, because they are people with a patchwork of experience that we can bring and use within the company. They are rounded people. It's about broadening you as a human being.

Anyone who thinks that Microsoft is full of geeks and dull technocrats will be highly surprised. These are rounded people with grit and tenacity; they do not give up: 'The soul of the company is its passion, its energy, its drive, its determination to make a difference.' That difference has something to do with the way people learn and the way people educate, the way we as a society on earth use knowledge and share it, and there are still massive tracts of the planet that don't get access to it. But it's coming.

When I ask Paul about which of the company values matter most to him he opts for his own:

> For me the value is being able to sleep at night. And that means that everything that I do during the day – and it doesn't mean being nice all the time – that's not what it's about. It means about being at peace with what you're doing. And for me that matters a lot. If I had to go home knowing that I'd sold a dodgy car to somebody, I'd go find another job. So if you bring that analogy to Microsoft, that isn't what we're asked to do. We've got great software, and we spend a fortune getting it right.

For Paul the vision is about selling inexpensive software to millions. And he believes in doing that in a very vigorous way: 'Yes this is a successful, aggressive, competitive, fighting, driven company. I wasn't aware that any of that was not fair.'

Combined with that get-out-there-and-win attitude is a breadth of vision and some human values that could change the twenty-first century globally. This is a company in which the leadership inspires vision, courage and the willingness to go the extra mile that often takes you across a barrier and into a whole new country that you did not know existed.

143

MICROSOFT GENERATES CREATIVITY BY:

- Having a commitment to ongoing human growth and development
- Fostering an environment of relaxed conviviality
- Having an enormous, life-enhancing vision to frame its minute endeavours
- Recognising that people are its wealth and investing in them
- Building teams that work like communities, in which there is trust and friendship
- Balancing hard work with fun, leisure and stillness
- Bringing inventiveness into the service of compassion
- Appreciating individuality
- Valuing every person, including those traditionally marginalised
- Using values to provide a bedrock
- Thinking like a start-up
- Looking for breadth, depth and spirit in people

PUTTING THIS INTO PRACTICE IN YOUR WORKPLACE:

WORKING WITH CREATIVITY

Microsoft is alive with creativity and innovation. This is bounded by the strength of values and the desired business outcomes that provide clear parameters. Creativity is the way in which the company gets through hard times and how it constantly moves forwards at speed. Spirituality perceives the human being as being intimately involved with the creative force in the universe: in Judaism and Christianity we are seen as co-creators with the Creator. The activities below focus on this side of our humanity and spirituality, the company expressing its soul through freely flowing creativity.

AN ACTIVITY TO DO AS A TEAM

The purpose of this activity is to heighten awareness of the infinite number of different ways in which we can do even the simplest task and to become aware of how we limit ourselves by thinking in terms of dichotomies – 'I could either do this, or I could do that' – when in reality we can tackle a task with unlimited creativity.

The line

1 Work in a room big enough to provide space to cross the room diagonally.
2 Divide the team in two, half to be observers and half to play.
3 The players cross the room in turn along a diagonal line. They repeat this six times, each time crossing in a different way. This has to be done quickly and without repeating anyone else's method.

145

4   The observers flank the 'line', sounding bells and clangers if a player repeats the line in the same way as anyone else.

Whereas one is likely to start by thinking 'How am I to find six different ways?', it soon becomes apparent that there are an infinite number of ways of crossing a room, be it as an elephant, scratching one ear, touching your nose or dancing a Chopin waltz. If we can move along a simple line in an infinite number of ways, how we run a meeting, make a report or find a new customer can also be tackled in a vast number of, as yet unexplored, ways.

AN ACTIVITY TO DO AS A LONE INDIVIDUAL
WITH 'NO POWER'

The web

This is a fairly old-fashioned activity, but must be a classic as it still seems to be useful. Take any problem that you want to resolve.

1   Write the name of the problem in the centre of a large sheet of paper in a bright colour.
2   Brainstorm (that is, generate as many ideas as possible as quickly as possible without comment) all the *causes* of the problem and write these in a second colour, radiating out from the problem.
3   For each cause, brainstorm all the possible solutions, writing them down in a third colour.
4   Look at the web you have created and identify what you are going to do.

This activity is obviously more powerful if you can find someone to do it with, but it still works if you are on your own. The web format mirrors the way in which one's brain works, with a web of infinite connections. Some of the causes and solutions relate to attitudes and perceptions, requiring not necessarily outward action but an internal shift. These internal shifts are usually the most powerful steps you can take.

CHAPTER 6

IMG:

CONCRETE AND ENLIGHTENMENT

Central to this book is the story of the Industrial Maintenance Group, IMG, a company based in Dorking that employs about a hundred people and has a turnover of £6 million. IMG produces and distributes the materials necessary to maintain public and commercial buildings, materials such as floor sealants, roofing and concrete repair products. It is not a glamorous business, yet it is a highly competitive market.

IMG uses values as its primary tools for inspiring and enabling the workforce to get results. These values are very practical and are quite explictly spiritual values, used on a daily basis by the staff whether they are in the warehouse, in the offices, in the factory or on the road selling, whether they are running a meeting, writing a report, making a phone call or shifting pots of paint. Running parallel to the values are financial targets, which serve to focus people's work. The overriding concern of the managing director, Roger Gundry, is to enlighten and inspire all those with whom the company comes into contact. This is the deeper purpose of the business; it is about awakening people to the fact that there is more to life than you could possibly imagine, so do not put up with anything less.

I first met Roger by chance. I had been listening to a chief executive officer making a presentation about his company, a large construction business based in Dallas, USA. The company ran on unusual servant–leadership principles, all the employees serving one another. The executive had shown us a video that included a tough-

Be the change you want to see in people.

Mahatma Gandhi

● ●

looking foreman on a building site talking of honour, dedication and love, and people working in offices whose faces were alive with commitment and happiness. At the end of the presentation I turned to the stranger sitting next to me and said, 'I wish I could find a company in this country that runs like that.' The stranger quietly responded, 'That's how we run our company.'

I was taken aback by the claim. We had just seen a large, outstandingly successful American company working in bold, experimental ways yet here was an ordinary man calmly saying that this is what he did. 'Come and see', he said. He turns out to be Roger Gundry.

In this chapter I look at twelve facets of this complex company encountered through meeting some of the people who work there and who shared with me why working at IMG is, for them, irresistibly special.

1 **Enduring values** – These values serve as the basic tools with which people can work in relationship with one another. *IMG practises honesty, forgiveness, tolerance, patience, kindness and treating others how we would like to be treated, with humility and awareness.*

2 **Growing people** – People grow and develop within the company. *It practises respect for people's potential.*

3 **Mind the gap** – People at IMG are actively aware of the gap between stimulus and response, and of their freedom to fill that gap however they choose using the values. *It practises taking personal responsibility.*

4 **Multiculturally relevant** – The way in which the company uses values is relevant and valuable to people of whatever faith – Christian, Muslim, Buddhist – as well as those of no faith. *It practises cultural inclusivity.*

5 **Trusting the process of change** – Individuals undertake changes in their work patterns and positions with a view to enhancing the good of the whole company rather than just their individual preference. *It practises trust.*

6 **Paint pots, packaging and pallets** – However mundane a job is, it is carried out wholeheartedly. *It practises wholeheartedness.*

7 **Talking on the assembly line** – When one factory was taken over by IMG, the culture was turned upside down and silence turned to talk. *It practises conviviality and fun.*

8 **Bacon butties and philosophy** – The factory staff stop each morning to meet and think about the way in which they work and reflect on principles. *It practises reflection.*

9 **Paradigm shifts** – People are open to questioning the assumptions on which they live and change their perceptions of life and the world. *It practises inner transformation.*

10 **Families first** – The company understands that people's families come before the company and it encourages this. *It practises family-friendly ways.*

11 **Enjoying telesales** – Vitality and energy fill the telesales room, and this task, which for others might be dull or repetitive, becomes here a very enjoyable job. *It practises drawing on and providing inspiration.*

12 **The dash** – The gap between birth and death that is our life is taken seriously at IMG and the people there make the most of every day. *It practises appreciation that life is short; do not waste it.*

EVERYDAY PRACTICE

ENDURING VALUES

I meet Roger in a hotel foyer near Dorking, early one morning, the vacuum running around us to clear up the debris of the night before. Roger arrives, greets me and takes out of his case a piece of paper with highly coloured lettering:

> Our purpose is to become the best in the business by any measure, built on enduring values, that will enlighten and inspire all those whom we come into contact with.
>
> **The values on which the company is built are:**
> Relationships
> Honesty
> Forgiveness
> Tolerance
> Patience
> Kindness
> Treating others in a way we would like to be treated
>
> with Humility and Awareness

It is not immediately apparent how selling maintenance products ties up with enlightenment, but what this means in practice will soon become clear.

When Roger set out to establish a business seventeen years ago, he was twenty-three. His ideas were not thought through, but he had an intuitive gut feeling:

> When I was dealing with any person in my company, my objective would be that, after they had had a conversation with me, they would feel better than they had before. That's where it started for me, that's all I could really say was my main driving force at that time. I wasn't really fully aware.

What for someone else might have been a manipulative tactic was for

Roger related more to how he felt about people. He explains to me how that beginning evolved into a company in which values are central:

> It started off with just wanting to help people feel better about what they were doing. It's grown from that. I think these things like honesty, forgiveness, tolerance, patience, kindness and treating others in a way that we would like to be treated are all principles that will bring out the best and the good in people and help them enjoy what they do more and not go home upset. Then they can look forward to Monday morning.

Roger strongly believes that, as a leader of an organisation, he needs to look at the whole picture and take responsibility for the social consequences of how things are at work:

> We can help influence and show that there is another way of dealing with those things which have an impact on what is most important to our lives. At the end of the day, the most important thing in all our people's lives is their families, not the business.

GROWING PEOPLE

I realise that although the business is related to producing and supplying maintenance materials, *how* this is achieved is through growing people:

> We have a hundred people in the company, and I would say that what we do is take people who in the main start off as sales people and turn them into business leaders; that has been the focus since we started.

Roger has been growing his company for seventeen years, manufacturing and distributing materials that are for the maintenance industry:

> If you take a maintenance engineer of a factory or a hospital or a hotel, they have a job of maintaining the property, and we have products that help them do their jobs. For example, we manufacture resins, non-slip floor coatings, concrete repairs; we manufacture roof coatings, cleaning products and lubricants. We have a fac-

tory up in Lancashire, a warehouse distribution company in Tamworth, a telesales operation in Nantwich, our head office is in Dorking, and we have about sixty sales people out on the road. We have within the organisation ten companies, five of which are selling companies, all started by people who joined as sales people, and we have trained them up to be leaders of their own businesses.

This emphasis on developing and taking people forwards has been a key focus for the company:

There are people who join us from all sorts of backgrounds. One of the guys started his career as a mechanic, another read theology at Oxford, another began in catering, another was a maintenance engineer, yet another had a chauffeur's business in London. The lady who runs telesales began her career as a ballerina. So I quite like the idea that they have changed direction and that the company has given them the opportunity to grow within the business, and as a consequence that has helped the business grow.

MIND THE GAP

Spirituality in practice at IMG revolves around awareness and becoming conscious of the gap, for it is the gap that is central to IMG's high performance. The gap occurs at two levels. First, there is the gap between how one is doing something well now and how one could be doing it even better. Identify the gap and then work on it:

It starts with the individual and how they have the capacity to know how well they are doing in their job. So they can measure how well, for example, they are doing on a daily basis. They could say, 'Today I am going to see how well I do responding to the phone calls that I get. . . . Do I do it in a friendly manner or am I a bit short? How long does the phone ring before I answer it?' The idea is to heighten awareness so that they can measure themselves in all sorts of areas and can take responsibility for it.

So the staff are invited to reflect on whatever it is they are doing, to become aware of how they are doing it and how they can now do it better and to set goals, monitor and meet them. That is fairly common to much business practice, but it is the second level of gap that is unusual and which IMG tackles in a unique way. This second level is the use of values in filling the gap between stimulus and response. At IMG it is about becoming aware of the fact that between the stimulus one receives and the response one makes there is a gap into which one can choose what one puts.

Many management gurus, philosophers and teachers have spoken of this gap, in which our freedom lies. One of the most famous people to write about it in recent times is Viktor Frankl, who has recounted his experience in a Nazi concentration camp. When undergoing profound loss and human suffering, he realised that he had a choice of how to respond to whatever was done to him; he could decide how he was going to let it affect him. He realised that he had a choice as to how to respond to the man torturing him, and in this he had more freedom than his torturer, who was blindly following orders and brute feelings.

This is the fundamental human freedom, the freedom to choose our response in any situation in which we find ourselves. What is remarkable at IMG is that the staff are encouraged to insert into that gap of choice some very specific values that can transform situations, the values being those outlined in the mission statement: relationships, honesty, forgiveness, tolerance, patience, kindness and treating others how we would like to be treated, with humility and awareness. People can enjoy and revel in that gap, and it can be the most crucial aspect of whatever job they are doing, be it as a salesperson, a member of the administrative staff or a factory hand.

The staff often use these values when considering how to improve a situation, increase productivity or deal with a crisis. Through training, discussion, daily meetings and seeing the mission statement tacked up on their computers and framed on the walls, staff are highly conscious of the values and how to use them actively. Roger recounts how one employee found himself caught up in a misunderstanding:

Just the other day we had someone who left the company because he felt unfairly treated. He lost his cool if you like, and then he left in anger. . . . I think he was probably right. He wasn't treated fairly and we accepted that, but I got in touch with him and talked about forgiveness and about looking at it in a different way, rather than being angry and reactive, thinking about how he could forgive and that the hurt wasn't intended. He had done quite a lot of things that were not good from our point of view, but by adopting the principle of forgiveness he actually rejoined the company.

● ● ● *Reflection* ● ● ●

I think back to situations in which resentments have festered, self-righteousness has boiled and conflict has spread insidiously through organisations, some of them with the highest missions – schools, voluntary charities, non-governmental organisations. Effectiveness, productivity, staff retention and morale have all suffered for want of the practice of forgiveness. We have been shy of even using the word let alone placing it high on our mission statement and using it as a practical tool. Here is an industrial maintenance group doing just that.

● ●

Elaine, a manager, is getting frustrated with a colleague, and potential conflict is building up. She reflects on her encounter with him earlier in the day and considers her level of practising patience. Let's face it, it was not very high. When she meets him later in the day, she consciously sees whether she can raise her level of patience on a score of one to ten.

The company's approach involves people looking at what they are doing, becoming aware of how they are currently doing it, deciding to do it better, choosing how they want to do that and monitoring it for themselves, whether it relates to how they had a meeting, how they respond to a customer's complaint, how they process the invoices or the patience with which they respond to a colleague. They are constantly looking at how they can do it better and using the *values as a key*. They are doing this not because someone is making them or because they will be checked up on but because, in the process, they themselves get to be the best they can that day, and that is what they enjoy. It is a bit like having a workout at the gym and feeling great at the end of it: it might feel tough at the beginning, but you will see the results. There is a lot of fun, warmth and excitement.

This level of awareness, learning, readjustment, experimentation and improvement runs through at each level; no one is exempt. The managing director, the newest member of staff, factory hands and management are all involved. It is not an easy, peaceful life. There is no resting on your laurels here. There is instead continuous development, higher financial targets to be met and higher standards to be achieved:

> Patience is a part of this. One of the things that we have started to do more at work is saying, 'What can I practice today that I have never practised before that will help me be better tomorrow?' So it is actually when you are planning the day that you ask this of yourself.

The majority of employees whom I talk to bring up the question of values themselves and talk enthusiastically about these as being something that makes the job worthwhile. The mission is visible not only on paper but also in the experience of the staff. People are challenged to grow beyond who they are now to who they can become. They reflect on their experience, heighten their awareness and practise very specific values that directly affect their professional practice. The appetite for constant improvement and development is almost tangible.

What motivates them to work in this way? After all, in many work-places it is inconceivable that one will find this degree of commit-ment, awareness and willingness to change. Imagine how it would transform the public services. Part of the motivation is that employ-ees value and respect the managing director. They feel cared for by him. He has a wholehearted commitment to this mission and to this way of working to values, and he himself practises them. Staff trust him enough to give it a go, and find, once they try his way of work-ing, that it is satisfying and fulfilling. They get to stretch; they are supported and are supporting others. They know that they are in an environment where their best will be welcomed and recognised. They find that they work in a place where they are treated as they want to be treated, and they are able to treat others as they them-selves want to be treated. The result is a deep sense of well-being and contentment. The values that they hold at home are echoed at work, so they feel at home there. This is reinforced with training, the com-pany having invested hundreds of thousands of pounds in personal development and leadership training programmes for all staff.

Roger recognises that at times:

> It's a little bit out of their comfort zone. Just a little incy bit, because if you are outside your comfort zone, that's where the learning takes place. We talk a little bit about just pushing the barriers out a bit, so you can think about it. One of the reasons I mentioned patience is that it is a wonderful thing that you can practise. A lot of people do have a tendency, I think, in a work environment to get very stressed and get a sort of feeling of work being on top of them, but if they practise being patient in the moment when they would have been impatient, that can lead to a lot of exciting results.

• • • *Reflection* • • •

Being prepared to be fruitfully uncomfortable is essential, but some people believe that they should not do anything that makes them feel uncomfortable. Discomfort is at times, for example when we are going against our conscience, a valuable indicator that something is wrong. More often, however, it is simply a sign that we are growing, that we are doing something that we have not done before, something that does not easily fit in with how we have been. The discomfort is a measure of our becoming something other than we were. It is a necessary stage to go through, like digging the garden up before replanting it. Many people resist any growth in awareness because they are not willing to go through the discomfort.

• • • • • • • • • • • • • • • • • • • •

The most vital result for Roger lies in the quality of relationships as it is through these relationships that the work is done:

> If you focus on relationships within the business, rather than anything else, that is what is important. It's the difference between focusing on getting a task done at the expense of the relationships, or focusing on the relationships first. It's being aware of relationships first, whilst keeping the task firmly in mind.

The company invites values and virtues to be meshed together both as an end in itself and as the most effective way to reach the financial and commercial goals they set.

MULTICULTURALLY RELEVANT

The first person I catch sight of when I arrive at IMG is Younis, who happens to be on the doorstep. He greets Roger warmly and swiftly checks on a work issue with him before returning to his desk. Younis is responsible for the IT support for the organisation, his desk a sea

EVERYDAY PRACTICE

of papers and busyness. I ask him what it is that is important to him about working at IMG. 'Let me show you,' he responds and dives into the pile of papers looking for something. 'I can't find it,' he says with good-humoured frustration, 'but it's the values.' And he describes the sheet I have already seen:

> Patience, tolerance, forgiveness, treating others in the way I want to be treated, these are all values that to me as a Muslim are really important. So I can come to work and know that what matters to me in my life also matters here. I know the bosses are not trying just to get the most out of me that they can, so that makes me want to give all I can give to them.

Then came the phrase that I was to hear over and over again from people: 'When I get up in the morning I *want* to come to work.' Work is not that Monday-to-Friday chore that people do to earn money so that they can live; it is the very stuff of their living, it is what they want to be doing, and it reflects what matters to them in life.

For very many Muslims their faith is not an add-on; it is something that colours their entire life, and working for a company that has ethical standards and explicitly practises spiritual qualities is of significant importance to them. This is of course also important to many people who regard themselves as atheists, agnostics or nothing at all.

• • • *Reflection* • • •

Finding a way of working that is relevant to those of all faiths and of no faith, but that is free of dogma, seems particularly important in a world in which much division and conflict becomes crystallised in doctrine. Religion is often seen to divide and to be a source of war. Here values taken from Christianity unite and are a source of shared humanity, cutting across religions and relating back to that which is true to all faiths.

TRUSTING THE PROCESS OF CHANGE

The managing director's vision is all very well, but what about the vision of the person with least power in the company? Roger takes me to meet Carrie, the newest recruit at headquarters, who has been there for four months and works in the administration section of the office: 'Georgeanne is looking at spirituality here at IMG. Could you give her a little time to talk with her about your work?' Carrie's initial smile freezes slightly at the word 'spirituality', her eyes glancing round momentarily, perhaps looking for an escape route, but then she relaxes. Like most people, she is not comfortable with the term 'spirituality', but she is happy to talk about her job. Her work currently involves supporting a sales team out in the field, taking care of their customers and sorting out anything that is needed, including raising morale when a salesperson is discouraged, sorting out complaints and processing invoices. Her job is, however, about to change: a backlog of invoices means that her job will soon simply be working on these. It seems to me that Carrie likes the people side of the job; 'Won't this new invoice-focused work be much less enjoyable for you?' I ask. She replies:

> We looked at it as a whole; the invoicing when I arrived was hell.
> And we think this is what will work.

'But it will be less fun for you', I speculate. Carrie's response is confident; without hesitation she replies, 'If there is a problem I know I can take it to management and there will be a solution.' She does not anticipate a problem; she sees herself as part of the solution and knows that her needs, if and when they arise, will be listened to, heard and met.

So how does she feel about the mission statement? After all, it is unusual to be in a company where the values are explicity Christian. Her response is simple:

> This is about how people treat each other and how we respect each
> other. I'm not a Christian, but these are values that I want in life.

This reflects Roger's hope that the values are relevant whether one is

Love and do what you will.

St Augustine

• • • • • • • • • •

Jewish, Buddhist, Christian or nothing at all, and it did indeed seem that they were helpful to people with or without a faith.

Carrie, at twenty, has ownership of her work; she is ready to give up something she enjoys and is willing to take on a role that superficially looks tedious. She trusts that her needs will be listened to and met, one way or another, along with the needs of the business.

• • • *Reflection* • • •

Many people want to treat others as they want to be treated. This teaching lies at the heart of most spiritual paths. While many people are happy to get on and practise this in their lives and work, they reject all dogma, creeds and trappings of religion.

• • • • • • • • • • • • • • • • • •

PAINT POTS, PACKAGING AND PALLETS

'. . . Values that I want in life.' I had grown up thinking that if work were to reflect values, one would work in the public sector or in a profession where service is recognised as central. Here, however, were an IT supervisor and an invoice clerk who enjoyed their work largely because of service and values. But what of those doing the really manual, tedious jobs? Could they be part of this passion for work of great worth? How does 'enlightenment' fit into the factory floor?

Harris is sixteen. He left school having failed his GCSEs and having gone through four tough, unhappy years of being on the margins. He now has a job packing paint and loading it up on pallets for dispatch:

> I know I've been given this chance. When I wake up in the morning, I could just lie there, but I get up and shower and think. 'How can I make people happy at work today?' When I get to work and I'm told there's a big order to get out I think 'Good, we'll work flat out and everything's ready for it.' If I get in and there's not much happening I think 'How I can get it all just right for when the big order does come in?', so I'll sweep the floor, check the pallets, get everything sorted and the floor clean.

I had known that Harris was likely to be special because, when I had arrived and been introduced, several people had said, 'You must talk to Harris.' Later in the day, a manager I was with glanced through the factory window onto the shop floor and saw someone. She asked me to stop and look:

> Harris has just gone up those stairs you can see at the back; he will come down again in a minute carrying some deliveries or pallets. Watch – he always comes down the stairs differently – never the same twice.

Sure enough, he appeared carrying a large load and danced gracefully down.

Harris brings to his job of packer inventiveness, fun and care. His main aim on any day is to take care of his colleagues and see how he can make them happy. I wonder whether this is because he has, even at a young age, gone through more than the average amount of unhappiness and knows how hard life can be. His goal is one day to become an industrial chemist. Without a single qualification, he is holding down a job, is a valued staff member and knows that the company will do its best to give him support in getting the training he needs, step by step, eventually to reach his ambition.

● ● ● *Reflection* ● ● ●

There is no job too mundane to be made sacred, no job too dull to be transformed by the human being's capacity to bring care and creativity to their work.

● ● ● ● ● ● ● ● ● ● ● ● ● ● ● ● ● ● ●

TALKING ON THE ASSEMBLY LINE

Harris works in the paint factory that Roger took over eighteen months earlier. Roger recounts:

> I heard of a factory which was going bankrupt, and I liked the idea of turning things round. Actually, we had a great story there. In the early days we were up at the old factory and John, my finance director, was there with us. We all went up there to have a go at working on the line, just getting involved with the people there, and we were on this production line, and John was working on it. He is an unusual accountant; he laughs a lot and he is not quiet at all, he is quite a great laugh. He was chatting away on the line to this fellow who had been there before and who was filling up paint tins, and this fellow said to John, 'You are not allowed to talk on this line, it's not allowed.' So John said, 'Well you can now.'

IMG's approach is different, probably a culture shock to start with, but the people who were employed under the old regime are still all there:

> And in many ways I would say that that factory may best reflect our purpose at the moment. They came from such an opposite way, and we had an opportunity of bringing them into this new environment and of taking them from the beginning and completely turning it around.

In the USA some slaves were not allowed to talk or sing, those things which distinguish us as human beings being taken from them. Unfortunately, this happens even now in some workplaces.

• • • *Reflection* • • •

*If we are to appreciate each other, we need to know each other.
One of the simplest ways to do this is to talk. Casual talking time
at work is not a drain on the business; it is vital if people are to
get to understand each other and, through that, come to know
how best to support each other.*

• •

BACON BUTTIES AND PHILOSOPHY

Each morning, one of the factory workers checks when everyone's
workloads will allow for a break, tells them when the morning's
meeting will be and puts the bacon on to grill for butties. As a team,
they meet to read through a thought for the day from a management
guru, have a think and a munch, and then experiment with translating the idea into their own language, Blackburnese, relating it to their
specific experience in the factory and the office. One of them then
writes up the team's version in the company thought-for-the-day
book.

• • • *Reflection* • • •

*Wisdom is not esoteric, nor is it the monopoly of a few learned
people. It is often understood and expressed by ordinary people
who take the time to get together, to share and reflect on wisdom,
and to relate it back to their own experience and insights.*

• • • • • • • • • • • • • • • • • • **163**

The unexamined life is not worth living.

Plato

● ● ● ● ● ● ● ● ● ● ● ● ● ●

PARADIGM SHIFTS

Roger runs a maintenance business, and achieving sales and financial targets is central and essential. What he enjoys most, however, is seeing people grow as they break through to a different way of seeing themselves and the world:

> I am reminded of an example of one of our business leaders, who was a garage mechanic, who came back from a course we had sent him on and said, 'I've just realised that I can learn.' Just that one thought or that different way of thinking that the course had given him has led him on to great things. He always thought that he wasn't capable of learning anything new. He had a paradigm, his mind set was that he couldn't learn anything new; now he believes he can. Of course, if you believe you can, you will. I think we are all about changing paradigms, and there is a huge amount of potential within people, if only they would allow it to occur. So what I love the most about my work is helping to change those paradigms.

People are not lettuces; they do not grow in a predictable way. Roger believes, however, that if you provide an environment in which enlightenment and inspiration are your goals, and where very specific transforming values are actively used, then the conditions for shift, change and growth are there. But it is not always an easy journey. Roger points out that:

> The whole process one is going through can be a very difficult and frightening experience. You've got the situation where, I think, over the last four years or so, I have become more spiritually aware and more aware of what we can achieve as an organisation. That has at times created quite a bit of tension within the company, and various people have from time to time suddenly come up against a brick wall and they don't know where to go. They start blaming

people and being reactive, whereas what they can also do, and in fairness a lot of people have actually done it, is think 'What can I learn about this situation? Where can I find a door that will help me get through this brick wall and go into this new zone?'

This has been a big issue for Roger as a leader. At times he has seen people really struggling and he has not enjoyed it:

> Because you don't know if they are actually going to make it through. Particularly when they have been with you a long time; you start questioning, 'What am I doing here? Is it me that's causing this struggle?' Having thought about it, most people do nevertheless get through the wall, they do find that there is a door.

One of the difficulties is getting people to overcome their cynicism and believe in this way of working, where they are valued and values are paramount. This cynicism can be the element that sometimes turns it all into a battle for Roger:

> If you can make the business a place where people can learn, where they can go home and be much more effective at home, then everyone wins. The one thing is that a lot of people find it very hard to believe that this is what we mean. Because they come from backgrounds where it is not this way. One of the things we are fighting most is mediocrity and the belief that this new way cannot be true. And it takes a lot of energy, and it's a very slow process for some people to really believe that this is what you really want for them. I think one of the things I would like, and one of the things I am learning about and wanting to practise today, is to find a better way all the time of communicating that what I believe in is really true. But if someone has come from a broken home and has had ten years' experience of being trodden on in their previous company, it takes a long time for them to believe that it is different here. So that's an interesting overall battle, and I suppose I do see it, at times, as a bit of a battle.

All the staff, from the young warehouse lads to the junior office clerk to the senior managers, are invited to participate in transformational training, where people explore ideas surrounding perception, language, choice, responsibility and win/win cultures. These courses can radically change people; partners are therefore also invited so that they can understand and be part of the change if they want to. This is not the Japanese model of 'everyone must join the culture'; it is simply an invitation to understand what is really happening in this company.

FAMILIES COME FIRST

I recall the story of the human resources director of a large international auto-mobile company arriving at work at 7 am to find the car park half full; at 7 pm it is still half full. The cost to families, to marriages, to children, is immense. For years people are wedded to their jobs for eleven to sixteen hours a day and then wake to find their family grown up and gone and their marriage cracking and broken. The cost to human lives is immense, and the cost to business in terms of stress, breakdown, burnout, illness and absenteeism not inconsiderable. A brave face but being broken inside does not lead to the best work.

Roger is categorical: 'In our people's lives, families come first.' This is not a principle: it is a statement of fact, a recognition that this is what the people working for IMG care about more than anything else. They are very committed to the company but not at the cost of their family. Which is why partners are invited to training courses. Rachel, a telesales assistant at the company, describes how much her last training session has meant to her and is particularly pleased that her boyfriend has been invited to the next one:

> These trainings change you, and I want him to come and see for himself what it's all about. Otherwise how would he understand?

ENJOYING TELESALES

In general, one of the most soul-destroying jobs in our society is telesales. The work can be repetitive, intrusive, fruitless and sometimes pointless, and the staff working on it find it tough, and companies find themselves with high levels of staff turnover and absenteeism, and with low morale and poor productivity. It is therefore with considerable curiosity that I visit IMG's telesales company in Nantwich.

Carmen, one of the telesales assistants, has told me of how she had previously worked for a traditional call centre where there were babbling voices, hype and fatigue. The staff turnover was high and the atmosphere arid. When the going got tough and no sales were coming through, you were on your own, and there was a bitter anxiety hastening your calls. When I walk into the IMG telesales room there is a very distinctive atmosphere of poised concentration, a curious blend of calm relaxation and strong focus, fun and committed activity. There are about eleven assistants and a sense of quiet and purpose interspersed with frequent laughter, a hum of talking and an undercurrent of bubbling, gentle but strong energy. It is a decidedly happy place.

Today the team is aiming to reach the usual day's target sales although phoning will stop early, at 2 pm, for them to spend the afternoon reviewing their recent training on IMG's mission and their part in it. The pressure is on to achieve the daily quota despite losing three hours of phone time; the atmosphere remains relaxed. I stop one assistant, Katherine, and ask to talk with her if she is not too busy. Although committed to reaching her sale targets that day, she readily takes the time I need, well over an hour, to explain to me how they work.

'Our aim is to enlighten and inspire . . .', she begins. This still surprises me; the English part of me leaps to a sceptical mode, and an image of American hype floats to the cynical part of my mind. It has nothing whatsoever to do with this beautiful young woman in front of me who radiates sincerity; it has everything to do with the cynicism about business that still besets me. Fleetingly, I wonder whether they are using spirituality simply as an added value to increase sales, but if the thought were obnoxious to me, it would be even more so to the staff here as they work with complete transparency. I listen to Katherine and things become clearer. She explains the basic selling technique they use, the way the office is run, the culture in which individuals support each other and how energy levels are maintained.

Looking around at the staff, each with their computer, their phone, their desk and papers, Katherine points out that:

> Each woman is a manager, responsible for managing her workload and task.

People make calls when and as they want. Sometimes a customer will ring and simply have a chat that has nothing to do with buying. Sometimes the assistant will take time out to sort out a personal need. At other times they will go over to help, encourage and coach a colleague who has made no sales yet that day. Every now and then through the day the whole team stops while one member leads them through a brain-teaser or fun activity. The day may well have a theme devised by Sandy, the team leader. Although she herself is responsible for the whole operation and all the staff, and spends much of her time helping, coaching, leading and inspiring the team, she nevertheless sets herself a daily quota of sales to be achieved so that she too knows what it is like for the staff, especially when they cannot make a sale.

I have noticed the large open space that runs through the centre of the room. An image of line-dancing comes to mind and is confirmed: when people are tired from being on the phone, they might stop and suggest to everyone to dance and to get their energy back.

The telesales centre is one of the most successful, productive arms of IMG. Its growth and profitability are high and continue to rise. The assistants reach ever-increasing targets and do it in the way that is most effective and satisfying for them as individuals. Staff turnover is minimal: no one has left in eighteen months – people enjoy themselves too much to leave. Absenteeism, low morale and stress are not an issue. Again I hear the phrase 'I come to work because I *want* to come.'

I return to the question of inspiring and enlightening, and Katherine gives me an example:

> If I say to someone, 'Hello, this is Katherine, I'm ringing to see if you want . . .', then it is going to do nothing for anyone.

*Do people find in you the illumination of the inward
Light, do you incarnate the universal spirit? I do not
want to be told that there is a spirit in all life,
I want to see it, experience it.*

Harvey Gillman

● ●

I privately confess to myself that Katherine's tone of voice sounds fine to me, rather reminiscent of how I sound on the phone. 'But', Katherine continues adopting a different tone, 'If I say, "Hello, this is Katherine, I'm ringing . . .", then that does make a difference.' The energy and commitment in her voice have changed palpably, but almost imperceptibly, with a shift in its quality. Her voice now comes from the centre of herself and even in that brief phrase expresses who she, Katherine, is. My mind recalls something I have not noticed before: when I have phoned IMG, even with the briefest of calls, I nearly always feel better for having rung; there is a lift in my energy.

'You see the difference', persists Katherine patiently. The difference is slight but crucial. In the first instance it is the polite, mildly robotic self talking; in the second an alive, individual human being. 'That's what I mean by enlightening and inspiring', says Katherine as if concluding an experiment:

> Some of the people we are ringing are working in dreary warehouses, dull offices. When we ring them we want to lighten their day, inspire them.

Again, I am ashamed to say, the thought of American selling taints my thinking. Katherine's integrity shines out of her, but what if this is just another sales technique? I probe: 'Why are you doing it – is it to increase sales?' Katherine smiles kindly and patiently; my cynicism does not trouble her. She loves her work, knows what it is about and

Something was dead in each of us, And what was dead was Hope.

Oscar Wilde

• • • • • • • • • • • • • • • •

will explain a little bit more to help me understand. 'I get to talk to wonderful people all day.'

Carmen, another assistant, describes how she approaches work:

> Sometimes, you know, this guy might be working in a dark, dingy warehouse and you think 'How can I lighten his day?' We were driving down to HQ for some training and stopped off to visit a customer. We'd only ever talked on the phone but we stopped to see them in their workplace.

Carmen views her job as a privilege and she does it with all the grace and skill with which one would want to run a business; she is a leader, as is each of the women whom I meet there.

Carmen is also committed to particular community work on a voluntary basis. She has needed time for this as well as for her own development and has received nothing but understanding and support from the telesales office. Her hours have been reorganised to fit around her voluntary work, and she now works part-time in order to be able to fulfil these other aspects of her life, which matter deeply to her:

> A lot of people are consumed by work; they have no other option. For me this is part of my life. My life has been enhanced by being able to work part time.

Part-time working does not, however, diminish Carmen's commitment to her workplace. Instead it allows her to be more fully who she is, a complex, vibrant, compassionate woman who brings her qualities both to the telesales team and to the rest of her life.

On one of my visits the whole team sits in a circle with the managing director to share their concerns about recent difficult changes in the other operations within the company: what affects one part of the company reverberates in them. The meeting begins with a brief activity to explore how even the simplest of acts, in this case passing a pen from one to another, can be carried out either mindlessly or mindfully. Then business difficulties and concerns are discussed. At the end of the meeting the energy level has dipped so the whole team stand up, go in a huddle and do a haka, a Maori war chant, that they have written themselves to help clear their energy and renew their focus. A haka has a peculiar force to it, a pure, implacable energy; it will brook no deflection. As they finish their haka they laugh, shake off any residual tiredness from the meeting and return to work with renewed energy. Several of them are aware that if they tried to describe their workplace, no one would believe them. It is so very unlike the usual, dull, repetitive work many suffer. Who would believe it?

THE DASH

The managing director is motivated by the desire to make a difference, as are many people in the company:

> The way I see it is that you need to be aware of what is possible in the world, aware that we have been given the gift of life, and here I am; I happen to be living here in this town and I seem to have been given a talent to build a business, and the journey has only just begun. I suppose it is the vision that one can see. I have a vision of perhaps this hill where there are lots of happy people and faces, and it's as a result of what you have done. That is the driving force really, the legacy that you might leave when you are gone. There is a little poem about the dash. You know, on a grave you see someone has lived from 1895–1970. The dash is your life. For me it is about building a successful business that's profitable but at the same time doesn't destroy the lives of the people in it; I would just like to show that it's possible.

No margin – no mission.

Steven Covey

● ● ● ● ● ● ● ● ● ● ● ● ● ● ●

PROFIT

IMG knows that personal development must not be at the cost of business objectives. Profit and soul go hand in hand as without the profits none of this compelling journey would be possible. As Nigel, one of the leaders in the company, says:

> You can do all this, but for goodness sake make sure you continue to make the money you need to make in order to make that difference in people's lives.

This balance, between on the one hand, the profits made from providing a service and, on the other, the extraordinary personal spiritual development of people, is critical; it is the meeting of earth with heaven.

IMG ACTIVELY USES VALUES BY:

- Having a commitment to ongoing human growth and development
- Being clear on the specific values it draws on and making them visible
- Taking personal responsibility for their choices and actions
- Being multiculturally relevant to the people working there
- Looking at change as an individual with a view to the whole company's needs
- Bringing wholeheartedness to the work
- Encouraging conviviality and fun
- Making space and time for reflection
- Questioning assumptions and self-limiting beliefs
- Caring about families and recognising them as a priority
- Drawing on inspiration
- Recognising that life is short – live it fully
- Holding clear financial targets

PUTTING THIS INTO PRACTICE IN YOUR WORKPLACE:

FINDING THE VALUES FOR THE COMPANY

Values play a very active role in IMG, but in some companies it is not at all clear what the values are, and in others lip-service is paid to them but they do not make much difference. The purpose of the following activity is to identify the core values that inspire individuals and the team or company.

AN ACTIVITY TO DO AS A TEAM

Imagining you are eighty-five

1 Imagine that you are eighty-five years old and have finished your working life. Look back at it and allow yourself to see what *qualities* you brought to your work, what it is that you will have contributed to the world. Imagining yourself still at eighty-five, see what it is that you will be leaving for the next generation, perhaps your grandchildren. What are the three most important qualities or values that you have used? Jot them down, each on a separate card.

2 In pairs, share those qualities. Collect the cards that people are happy to hand in and then ask one or two people to read them out. These are the qualities that this group is bringing now to the world. Allow the qualities to be heard and silently appreciated, and then place the cards somewhere in the middle of the room in which you are working.

3 Ask people to divide into groups of three and reflect on the qualities that they themselves and their colleagues are contributing. They should then draw up a list of core values that they feel represent the most important qualities for the team.

4 Each group then joins up with another group and they work together to reach a consensus on values, drawing up a poster of words and symbols that represent the team values.

5 Each group presents its poster to the whole team.

6 The whole group sits quietly while individuals absorb everything that has been said and heard.

7 Invite people to name three or four people from the whole group to be entrusted with later using the session's work to draw up a statement of values for the team, department or company, with examples of what the values look like in practice.

This activity helps to ensure that the values are not simply listed on paper but reflect the real living values of the people there. The activity need not take long as it is not principally a discussion exercise. The most important part of it is done in a matter of moments as people allow themselves to get in touch with their mortality and to look back on their lives and see the essence of what it is that they contribute. What people say is not as important as what they actually see in their mind's eye.

The next major piece of work in this activity is the shifting from being in touch with one's own qualities and values to moving over and being really open to what it is that makes other people tick. Again, that can happen in a moment. And if it doesn't, then no amount of discussion and techniques will help. This activity requires some basic spiritual tools – silence, listening, encounter, creativity, letting go, empathy and entrusting.

AN ACTIVITY TO DO AS A LONE INDIVIDUAL
WITH 'NO POWER'

A fulfilling week

1 Again project yourself forwards to be eighty-five and see what qualities you will have brought to your work.

2 Then, still with closed eyes, project yourself forwards to the end of next week and imagine yourself looking back at a fulfilling week at work. What five things need to have happened in your mind's eye for that to have been a fulfilling week? What do you see happening? (Keep this in the realm of possibility rather than fantasy.)

3 Jot down these five items.

4 Reflect on the values that underpin these things.

5 Decide what your core values in life are and talk them over with a friend or colleague. Then begin putting them into practice at some point in each day.

6 Be committed to making the five things happen that will ensure you have a fulfilling week.

7 Ideally, keep a journal where you note down the five items and your core values and keep track of how you are reaching them.

CHAPTER 7

NATWEST:

FROM THE BOTTOM OF THE LEAGUE
TO THE TOP

To understand Roger Thomas' story, you will need to know a little bit about banking in the 1990s. This was a time of savage change during which reorganisations and redundancies left staff shell-shocked. High-street branches that had encompassed many functions under one roof, led by bank managers who had been there for decades and were known and respected in the community, were about to change completely. A staff of forty shrunk to twelve; functions were farmed out to specialist business units; managers were toppled. New government legislation and changes in pensions added to the turmoil. NatWest was particularly ill-positioned to cope. Its board had made unwise ventures in investment banking and had made several unsuccessful acquisitions, and the bank was having to cut costs to recoup almost £1 billion.

In 1994, Roger, who had been at the bank for thirty-five years, was made managing director of the London North region of NatWest bank, the region at the bottom of the bank's national league at the time. Over the next five years Roger turned the situation around until, in 1999 when he retired, his region was joint top of the league. Roger's story is remarkable because he went against the tide of his overarching organisation, creating a region that was distinctive from anything else within the bank and, moreover, he made it a very high-performing business. He did this with virtually no support from above, and he enjoyed himself immensely.

The London North region sprawled northwards from the City of

London to Cambridge, east to Southend and west as far as Maidenhead. Of the seventeen London boroughs lying within the region, about nine were in the top twenty poorest boroughs in the UK, and these were struggling. There were many bad debts as a result of overlending in the 1980s; this should never have occurred but it had been done in order to expand the business in the short term. The context in which Roger took over was messy, complex and bewildering:

> I had no idea how to deal with it. I didn't know what to do. I had no idea and no real experience of such a large and complex business, and I think that's something that most senior executives find when they start out on these roles.

It was not only bewildering, but also fraught with anguish, compulsory redundancies, fear, anger, resentment and suspicion. A whole stratum of management, the very senior middle managers, were to be made redundant, and Roger's staffing levels were to go from four and a half thousand to three thousand in the five years that he was there. But in the chaos and distress, Roger had a fairly simple vision:

> That we could actually make London North into something that could perform very well indeed and be equal to the rest of the regions in the UK. Why not? After all, I soon realised that the people were as good as anywhere, so why should they not be able to deliver as well as anyone else?

Although when he arrived it was as if he were in a mist, Roger knew that whatever he did he wanted to do it whole-heartedly and with gusto: 'to prolong the agony of continual change – death by a thousand cuts – beyond two years, would actually make the whole thing much worse.' He also felt a quiet conviction that:

> If I had long enough with it, and could create a team that really trusted each other and pulled in the same direction, we could actually make that business into a successful business. And also I knew . . . I felt something really deep inside me, as though I were following a direction in my life. I felt that all those things that I had done before, for over thirty years, had been there to lead me to this. So I felt good about doing it.

I have chosen twelve aspects of this five-year story that illustrate the ingredients of transformation.

1 **Roger** – This is someone who happily walked the fine tight-rope of serving those for whom he was responsible whilst satisfying his bosses' requirements. *He practises transformation within the constraints of compromise.*

2 **Henchman or midwife?** – Roger faced the pain of change head on and yet remained open and caring. *He practises courage with compassion.*

3 **Mentoring** – Roger did not attempt to do this unaided but drew on another to help him find his path and follow it. *He practises asking for help.*

4 **Shadowing** – Roger shadowed his staff, listening to, standing alongside and feeding back to them what he saw. *He practises challenging people to change and grow.*

5 **A chain of openness** – Roger and senior managers were critiqued in front of peers and subordinates. *They practise courage and vulnerability.*

6 **Awaydays with check-ins** – Each individual regularly shared who they were and spoke from their own personal experience. *They practise openness and authenticity.*

7 **Learning groups** – People worked in triad peer groups to counsel, observe and relate their difficulties to each other. *They practise mutual support.*

8 **Community evenings** – People actively involved themselves in local charities. *They practise giving back to the community.*

9 **Leadership course** – Managers developed their awareness of leadership skills. *They practise sharing leadership.*

10 **The borough support group** – When one area was struggling, they concentrated on mutual support to change the situation. *They practise committed, concerted teamwork.*

11 **Teamwork** – The leader recognised that it was the team not the leader that makes the difference. *They practise interdependence.*

179

12 **Gems** – Roger set up focus groups where he listened and waited to find the five per cent of gems. *He practised being open to the treasures life offers along the way.*

EVERYDAY PRACTICE

ROGER

The key to Roger's work in transforming the region lies in who he is as a man. His story involves scenes that I would have found hard to imagine or bear; bringing in changes that ended careers, with all the terrible sense of loss, betrayal and despair that can accompany redundancy. But, out of that devastation, Roger drew the seeds to generate something quite unique, something very much an expression of who he is as a person.

Roger delights in people, finding out what makes them tick, listening to them, helping them to see how they could do something well, learning from them, developing them, standing alongside them, egging them on, discovering something new about them. He has a hungry curiosity about people. He left school at sixteen and spent his entire working life in NatWest, so by the time he took on this very particular piece of work he knew a great deal about it. He was a man in his prime, with enough experience now to be able to draw on his intuition and take leaps into what might appear to others to be the dark but which Roger knew in his guts to be correct.

Roger has no pretensions. For five years in this London North region he taught swathes of managers how to listen, mentor and counsel each other. He had no qualifications to do this; he simply got on and did it, very simply and straightforwardly. Now, as I talk to him five years later, he tells me he is studying for a certificate in counselling. I wonder at his humility. It is, however, his passion that, for me, stands out, his passionate desire for people to give utterly and fully of themselves to each other, say what they want and 'for God's sake don't hold back.'

HENCHMAN OR MIDWIFE?

This is obviously not just a rose-tinted story, for the old way of banking was dying and out of the mess was the possibility that something new emerge. Roger was to be involved in both the dying and the birthing. His focus was on the unique entity that he wanted to create – a region where people mattered. Paradoxically, that required helping to speed the inevitable death of the previous regime and involved the lives of several thousand people. Roger feels strongly about his style of leadership:

> How are you going to come across to people? Are they going to think they've got somebody here who is going to hack the business to pieces and attempt to squeeze short-term success while all the pain is being felt, or is it going to be somebody who is straight and honest, concerned with the mid and long term, somebody who will show you the way it is but will at the same time be caring, nurturing and concerned with making this the best place to be? So I chose the latter route because it is more my natural style than just to be isolated from it and to be seen as a hatchet man.

He knew that if he was to create something radically different from what was happening elsewhere in the bank, he had to have people around him who would actually make it happen in the right way. He knew he could not do it just by being a leader on his own.

MENTORING

One of Roger's first actions was to find himself a mentor, Sol, to help him at a personal level. This mentoring process was extremely powerful and enabled him to learn a great deal about himself and his leadership style. He then gathered a team around him who were also mentored by Sol, so while Roger was learning and attempting to adapt his style, he was asking his colleagues to do the same. In addition to this Roger encouraged senior people across the business to follow his lead so that mentoring and the development of the next stratum of leaders gathered impetus:

> I selected seven or eight people whom I would personally mentor. I saw them regularly; they didn't have a choice. I selected them and said, 'I want to mentor you; I want to understand you, I want to understand what people are telling me about you and understand that it is good, I want to know you better, I want you to know me better.'

SHADOWING

Next Roger turned his attention to the twelve area managers spread out over this big region and he decided to spend a day with each, shadowing them to find out how they operated in their own environment and giving them feedback about their style. In that first year Roger spent fifty days, a quarter of his time, out coaching these twelve people, helping to make them more aware of themselves as leaders. For the first time ever, these individuals were receiving specific, first-hand feedback that related to what they were doing there and then instead of generalised feedback from a distance.

Roger used this period of shadowing to learn, to make himself visible, to show what it was that he stood for, what it was that he wanted to create in the business – this culture in which people actually cared about people, developed people and held a mid- to long-term view. Needless to say, this was not the overall culture of the bank. The shadowing was:

> A simple way of being a leader. Rather than being sat behind a desk and isolated from the reality of what was happening. I was involved, I was visible, I could talk to people, I could remember people's names and personal details about them. The whole thing lent itself to saying, 'This is the way we are going to be running the business while I'm here.' And because I was doing it myself, I could then say

to my area managers, 'And my expectation of you is that you have a similar sort of role with your people.' It was about being a role model.

In the past there had been coaching by the more enlightened managers but this had been done very casually, by catching bits of conversation as you walked past someone. Roger's way involved saying:

> 'I want to sit with you, and I want to give you feedback after I've observed you operating.' I was trying to create that sort of culture where the people were getting valid feedback on how they came across to people, especially the customers.

As well as giving verbal feedback, Roger would write to staff at home and would work on one or two themes with each individual so that there was a constancy and continuity. Together they would identify something in the person's style that they needed to work on so that they would come across in a different way. In addition, there would be quarterly reviews in which Roger pulled no punches. These were the private property of the individual; the annual review that went on file was a little more formalised.

This whole feedback process could well have been threatening for people, and crucial to its effectiveness was the intention that Roger held. This was to help and support these people in becoming good at what they did. He cared about them. It was not about observing in order to criticise but to be in there with them, helping them to create the best possible result for themselves and the organisation as a whole.

As well as giving feedback Roger himself received plenty of it. The main area one of his senior colleagues asked him to focus on was performance as it was felt that Roger spent a lot of time on supporting people but not so much on targets and performance. And Roger acknowledged this. As we talk and he recalls the episode he does not comment on the fact that performance was improving all the time he was insisting on looking at people rather than targets.

A CHAIN OF OPENNESS

The bank is organised hierarchically with Roger as managing director, and then regional, area and branch managers. One day Roger was visiting a regional manager, and one of his area managers. The senior manager said to Roger:

> 'Would you mind giving me feedback in front of my colleague?' I said, 'Of course'. So I gave feedback there and then, and what we ended up doing for all of the sessions with all of the people was to do the feedback when we were all together so that the subordinate would hear his senior manager having feedback about his style. And there were instances when we took it beyond that as well, when there would be another manager in there who was reporting to the area manager and the area manager was reporting to the regional manager who was reporting to me, so we would have a whole chain of openness.

This took courage and vulnerability. For Roger it was all about creating the ability to be able to say what you wanted:

> Don't hold back. For God's sake don't hold back because it doesn't do anybody any good. If you come out of a meeting and you've held back, we've missed an opportunity to hear you being angry or being pleased or whatever. Just say it, please. Let's try to create a business in which there is transparency and openness, because not saying what you feel does not help.

● ●

We counsel less mystery and more openness towards those who are worthy of confidence. If men (sic) conceal from their nearest connections in life a knowledge of the actual state of their affairs, they may deprive themselves of helpful advice, and kind participation in trouble.

Christian Faith and Practice

AWAYDAYS WITH CHECK-INS

Roger organised regular awaydays for the top team that were facilitated by Sol, who by now knew the business and all the participants very well. They started the sessions with a check-in, going round the room with each person responding in turn to the questions 'How do you feel today as you come into this room?' and 'Is there anything that you want to share with us that you have brought from outside?' These are very specific here-and-now questions:

> That's a nice simple straightforward check-in, but what I have learnt is that if you stay with the same group of people for any length of time, you start off nice and easy like that and then you lift the barrier all the time, so it becomes a tougher check-in and you get to the stage where you could be asking the people to say, 'How do you feel today, what have you brought from outside this room, and what is it that you believe that this group could do better than it currently does, and how could you contribute to that as a person?' So you gradually gradate the check-ins upwards so they become tougher and more open. We challenged people to talk about themselves rather than talking about 'Well, we don't like this, do we?' We asked them to talk about what they as individuals believed in.

Sol was the conscience of the groups, pointing out when they were missing the mark and failing to achieve the degree of openness and authenticity to which they aspired.

LEARNING GROUPS

Roger would have liked to have mentored all the area managers in more depth but they were spread too far afield. He therefore set up learning groups that met every quarter in which he brought four or five of the top team together with Sol and himself. They would start with check-ins and then run counselling triads – one person as observer, one as counsellor and one as client. In each threesome one person would talk on a counselling basis to a colleague about a particular problem he or she had:

And it usually related to how difficult it was to deal with X, Y or Z manager; it was usually people related. So they would spend fifteen to twenty minutes setting out the problem, and then there would be twenty minutes of counselling. Then there would be twenty minutes of feedback. So we were breaking down all the barriers; we became more trusting of each other. The unspoken message was, 'I've been very open with you and you've been very open with somebody else, so I understand more about you and the fact that whilst you may appear to be somebody who handles the whole thing ever so well and your business is doing well, you have your own particular issues when it comes to dealing with X, Y or Z person.' We became more a group of people who understood each other in more depth.

COMMUNITY EVENINGS

Roger wanted the branches to have a sense of community too:

I had this idea that banks just sit in the high street and, especially in the London boroughs, people travel in from, say, the leafy lanes of Hertfordshire to work in a tough inner-City environment, and they get out of there as quickly as they can when the job is done. It's not a place to stay, and that applied in many of the parts of the region that I had, and I wanted us to become more of a community. So what I did was find key people in the business to set up what we called community evenings.

They would bring together, in a central place, between ten and fifteen local voluntary organisations, such as the local hospice, the Samaritans or the NSPCC, inviting all NatWest staff in the area to come straight from work, have a buffet supper and meet the volunteers from the organisations. Then there would be two or three key speakers to talk about their community work:

There was a guy from the Winged Fellowship, which provides holidays for severely disabled and mentally disturbed people to give carers a break. He was a natural when it came to speaking to 150 people. We had NatWest weeks where the Winged holiday weeks were run entirely by NatWest volunteers, and it was brilliant. The idea was to create an environment in which we encouraged people to work in their local community both in their own time and also in the bank's time. I tried to get NatWest actually to become a community organisation because, after all, we're taking our money from the community so why shouldn't we give something back to it?

In the process of giving back, they received a development opportunity, the bank staff working under conditions different from their own organisation and gaining insight from that experience.

LEADERSHIP COURSE

Roger was concerned that many managers did not have much of an opportunity to learn more about leadership:

They'd got to the stage where they had got all the technical courses and only the select few then went on to do other things. We put together a diploma course in management, for which a whole raft of NatWest people went to the University of Hertfordshire, every Wednesday, from 2.30 until about 9.00; so we gave them time off and they put in their own time. What I wanted to do was to give something to people, give them opportunities to think beyond their narrow environment of the branch or the unit they worked in. So it was very much a developmental, a nurturing thing.

THE BOROUGH SUPPORT GROUP

One area of NatWest was not working at its best, and Roger had received many complaints. He decided to go there, meet the people who had made the complaints and work with the new area manager:

Together we created what we called the borough support group, with about five or six key people. We would meet every two or three months, from 5.30 to about 7.30, and what we did was to do the same thing I described earlier on with the learning group. We gave different roles as counsellor, observer, client, and that worked very effectively. I developed an affinity with that borough and the people that I would never have had if I hadn't done that, and it became the best-performing borough in our region. It was wonderful to see it happening. It was 1% to do with me setting up the group and 99% to do with the nature of the guy who took over and the way he and his team interacted. This borough is not an attractive place, with lots of difficult problems to manage in there. It became a jewel; it did exceptionally well.

TEAMWORK

Most of the ingredients of this story have threads entailing very close teamworking, and even in his confused early stages, Roger realised that this was an aspect that he would need to spend a great deal of time learning about and understanding.

The larger team of colleagues in the early stages consisted of twenty people, and the learning group approach was a way of ensuring that all the team had the benefit of working with Roger's personal mentor. When the number in the team fell to ten, Roger was then able to extend the benefits of one-to-one sessions with Sol to all of the team. Roger is convinced that this is the way for teams to develop and grow together.

> What is the point of isolating the leader in a highly developed and almost élite learning situation with a personal mentor when the team who have to ensure they deliver the business improvement and change programmes are allowed to remain locked in their own personal time warps and have to take their chances in growth terms?

Roger took a courageous stance in committing resources to provide coaching feedback for individual team members while they were themselves actually working with their own colleagues, and he feels strongly that this was the crucial factor that differentiated the region from anything that had previously been done within NatWest. In the past key people had relied substantially on residential courses, and although these did have a place in people's growth, Roger remains convinced that feedback, if both appropriate and given at the time, was an innovation that enabled individuals to learn more about their leadership styles than they could in the relatively sterile and safe environment of a staff college.

Roger is certain that the business could not have progressed without the goodwill of his team members:

> There was a mix of responses; some were prepared to embrace new ideas and work with their own teams, producing innovative ways which went beyond my thoughts, while others were reserved and needed convincing.

Roger's view is that teamwork must be at the forefront of any leader's efforts because, regardless of the individual style of different leaders, be it charismatic, autocratic or delegating, the actual delivery of business targets and objectives will be realised only by the people who have to second-guess where their boss is taking them.

Integral to the development of teamwork was high-quality listening. I asked Roger how he taught all these managers to listen:

> By being me I suppose. I didn't set out to teach; I just wanted, in a sense, to try to inspire people to do things differently, so I didn't go into a long teaching session. I just talked briefly about the fact that we don't actually listen as effectively as we could, we could do it much better, and we can understand people far better than we currently do. We are so busy rushing around. I said, 'Let's try it out.' Then I would set them a task in pairs and get their peer groups to give feedback. And I would give feedback at the end. So I was quite direct; but it wasn't hugely academic, it was more practical. It was more to do with real life, like 'When you said X . . . then', because I think that's the only way that people will effectively learn.

GEMS

Roger is an inquisitive man with an insatiable curiosity that he directs largely towards people. He listens with the ear of a collector of fine valuables:

I do believe that listening to other people can add value to your own life in some way or another. There are very, very few occasions in life when you waste your time completely in listening. Ninety-five per cent of it may be wasted, but there are usually 5% worth of gems in there, and I always wanted to keep people talking because you talk and you keep talking and all of a sudden a wonderful idea or solution will emerge. If you don't talk, you won't find these gems.

With a view to this, Roger set up a focus group of volunteers from across the region who met every three months from 5 pm to 7.30 pm:

I wanted to listen to people who weren't influenced by their bosses. I wanted them to say things to me as they really were, and I wanted to develop a situation in which they trusted me and I trusted them, and I got some wonderful gems from some of them.

Here is an example. One of the people there ran a branch, and she said, 'The trouble with these area managers is that they are under so much pressure that mine comes into my branch, he spends three hours in a room with me talking about my performance and then says, "Look, I'm sorry I've got to go because I've got another meeting ten miles away and I need to get there so just say sorry to your staff, I've got to go and I'm off." So he would sweep in, have his cup of coffee in the morning, do the three hours and then sweep out, and the staff would say, "Who is that guy?" '

Roger is emphatic that this is not the way to run a business:

The business should be about touching all those people when you go in there so they understand what you are about, so your compelling purpose is known to them, rather than actually coming in and doing a desk-oriented performance review. That was such a gem for me to hear because then I go back in to all the area managers and say, 'This is what I heard. Are you guys like this? So what are you going to do about it? This is the impression you are giving people.' So from somebody who has just made a stray remark like that, you can pick up so much that is very simple, just apply it by pushing it back to those who are doing it to the rest of the people. You find these gems.

The words of truth are always paradoxical.

Paul Glendinning

● ● ● ● ● ● ● ● ● ● ● ● ● ● ● ●

THE BACKDROP TO THE STORY

Redundancies

It is perhaps a paradox about Roger that he was, on the one hand, tough and unflinching in ensuring that the complex change and restructuring programme was driven through, which of course involved many redundancies, and, on the other hand, dedicated to people, to nurturing and developing those who remained:

> I knew there were going to be losses, oh yes I knew that. My approach was responsible for that. In some ways, as a leader, you have to be quite tough-minded around some of that stuff as well. You can't only be about the softer behavioural approach, you have to be tough-minded in delivering what the organisation wants and needs. That's a key thing, because if I had actually just done that job and been overly sympathetic and allowed those people to stay there and let the cost base remain high, then I would not have been allowed to do the things that I wanted to do for those who were going to remain. So I had to be very tough-minded, very single-minded around doing that and to not worry about what people thought of what I was trying to do. You have to have that toughness in you otherwise you don't survive.

On your own

An individual can often be motivated to work in soul-friendly ways but then find themselves in an organisation that is unsympathetic. What is encouraging about Roger's story is that he had no support from on high for what he was doing. On the contrary, at national level the bank was insistently cutting costs wherever it could, and there was huge pressure from people at the top for this to continue.

Roger went ahead anyway in organising the mentoring process despite the extra cost since he felt so strongly about working to create this level of openness and nurture:

> I initially kept it very much to myself because I was utterly, absolutely, totally convinced that I could not achieve this on my own. I was also totally committed to creating a business that would differentiate itself from the past and if necessary from the rest of the organisation around it.

He succeeded. When the region eventually came joint top of the league, it was making a profit of about £60 million with a cost base of £150 million.

Soul

I asked Roger whether the North London region had a soul:

> It had a soul where for the first time people listened. People could talk and be listened to . . . You could say things, not all the time, but a good proportion of the time, and you would be heard. . . . So I think that was the soul of it. We all cared about everybody who worked for us. We were London North region. It didn't apply to everybody because I'm not that isolated from it that I didn't realise that there were some people in there who really didn't care a fig about London North region, but the majority of people really knew that this was different from anything they had experienced before and that there were leaders here to whom you could speak your mind without being dashed down.

The legacy

When Roger looks back at those five years of work he sees a transformation that went beyond simply going from the bottom to the top of the league:

> I think I added value to people's lives, I actually gave them a way of doing things which was very different from what they had ever seen before, and I hope this has been sustained because they will have seen a different way, not a top-down way, but a way of working with people.

EVERYDAY PRACTICE

PUTTING THIS INTO PRACTICE IN YOUR WORKPLACE:

LISTENING IN THE COMPANY

Listening is one of the most powerful gifts we can offer, a skill that can on its own transform organisations. Although many words flow and much listening appears to take place, in reality true listening is rare. The biggest block to it is our internal voice, usually our ego. As you imagine you are listening to your colleague, you are often just listening to your inner voice burbling a riposte or comment. Listening often happens in the quiet space between the words, in the silence between the speaking. The activities below focus on how the company expresses its soul through its listening.

AN ACTIVITY TO DO AS A TEAM

Creative listening

Use this approach when a team is dealing with an issue or problem that is likely to encompass a range of different perspectives. People sit in a circle or around a table so that they can all see each other and no one is at the 'head'.

1 One person briefly presents the issue that the group is going to consider.
2 People speak, but they only speak out of silence. Between each contribution there is a silence of a few moments or even minutes while people absorb what has just been said and remain open.

193

3 The process can be helped by the use of a 'conch' – people can speak only if they are holding this. When they have finished speaking they place the conch back in the centre of the circle or pass it to whoever indicates they want it.

This very simple device of using silence, and a conch as a reminder of when to speak, rapidly raises awareness. The speaker becomes aware of the time and space he is using. It encourages those who ramble on to be mindful. It stops people interrupting each other. The reticent person who does not want to fight his or her way into a discussion can find room to speak. The silence is also the time during which reflection and creativity can occur. Instead of people simply pushing ideas to and fro at a superficial level, spontaneous images are given space to arise from within.

Creative listening is no substitute for a sometimes necessary vigorous, heated and swift exchange of ideas, but it complements it and is of particular value after an angry discussion in which the participants have not been listening to each other.

AN ACTIVITY TO DO AS A LONE INDIVIDUAL WITH 'NO POWER'

Active listening

Next time you are with a colleague who has a difficulty or an issue to discuss, just listen. Resist the temptation to advise, to probe, to provide solutions, to humour, to moralise, to join in, to preach, to blame or to refer back to your own experience. Just be empty and listen. Listen for the feeling behind the words, and let your colleague see that you are indeed listening. Resist the temptation to let your mind wander forwards looking for solutions or backwards to try to find parallels in your own life. The ego loves to do that and finds it very difficult to simply be still, be present and listen.

The quality of active listening will give your colleague strength and power. It is not surprising that in macho cultures where colleagues are seen as competitors, very little listening occurs. Thousands of hours are wasted every month in companies where people are going through the motions of listening but are in fact not listening at all. This is one of the biggest areas of waste within an organisation.

CHAPTER 8

SCOTT BADER:

MESHING VISION AND REALITY

THIS MANUFACTURING CHEMICAL COMPANY is surely one of the most unusual and idealistic companies in the UK. It is known throughout the world for its extraordinary vision, and there have perhaps been more papers, speeches, articles and theses written about it than there are people employed by it. It manufactures and supplies speciality resins, polymers and composites, and actively promotes a new and better society. The original company was set up by Ernest Bader in 1921; in 1951, having established it as a highly successful and profitable business, he and the other founder shareholders gave the company away to the workers by setting up a Commonwealth into which all the shares were entrusted.

The company's head office is in a beautiful corner of Wollaston, a village outside Northampton. It is flanked by the old village church on one side and a row of thatched houses on the other. The office itself consists of three parts. As you drive in through the discreet pillars, on which are etched the initials 'SB', you find yourself in an avenue of trees. Ahead and on the right, concealed by greenery and invisible to the eye, is a large, modern, quite ugly, functional factory. Ahead is a great gracious lawn and garden leading to an old Georgian country house that contains the offices. In between lies the Commonwealth building, which houses the canteen and hosts the company meetings and community activities. The Commonwealth brings together the new and the old, the functionalism and the ideals, the present constraints and the past vision. The stories of this company are about the battle to bring the ideal into reality.

All the stories in this book essentially concern this very tussle between ideal and reality, between vision and business demands. In this crack that occurs when the constraints are pressing down upon the vision, something happens: either new qualities are released – the resources emerge that one did not know one had, or pain and longing occur as the ideal once more fails to birth its child. Scott Bader embodies this tussle more vividly than any company I have seen. Its light is more brilliant, and perhaps also its shadow more dark, than that of any other company described in this book as it wrestles in an incredible venture both to run a profitable business and to produce a living Commonwealth.

Scott Bader is aware of itself as a historical phenomenon with a role to play that goes beyond that of a normal business. As Godric Bader, son of the founder and life president, writes:

> Our entire world has entered a turbulent period of fundamental transformation similar to the time we moved out of the middle ages. We who are living through it are only beginning to grasp the extent and meaning of the tectonic shift with whole continents of thought and massive economic re-structuring acting on us locally and globally.

Understanding this historical shift is crucial to understanding the company. Scott Bader seeking to move consciously through that turbulence in a way that provides an example of what business may in the future become. Godric quotes the great thinker Willis Harman, who cogently argued that business is now 'the most powerful institution on our planet'. Holding that power, however, requires that companies also accept that they have responsibility. Godric argues that this tremendous shift is a time of transformation and that 'The role of business in making this a *positive* transformation is absolutely crucial.'

But before we look more closely at the lived vision, let us turn to some facts about the Scott Bader Group. The group employs more than 650 people worldwide and has operations, with manufacturing facilities, in the UK, France, South Africa, the Middle East and

Croatia. There are distribution outlets in all of these countries as well as in Sweden, North America and Eastern Europe, serving over ninety countries. It produces Crystic polyester resins and has developed revolutionary composites and applications that are used in boats, trains, cars, buildings, pipes and many other items. The company's turnover is about £100 million, and it distributes a significant proportion of its profits to charities that support the economic and social development of children and young people in the UK and around the world. The head office in Wollaston is the home of the Commonwealth that safeguards the principles of the company.

Most homes will contain some product produced by a customer of Scott Bader – be it the coating on a cereal packet, a finely crafted ornament or the imprint on a T-shirt. A more illustrious example of its products is the gondola of the world record-breaking Breitling Orbiter round-the-world balloon. In the UK, the products supplied to customers are produced in a large, smelly, noisy factory where resins are processed and, if necessary, pigments incorporated, before the products are packaged for distribution in either tankers or drums.

I have chosen ten aspects of this complex, rich company, that touch on some facets of its soul.

1   **Being oneself** – When the head of finance looks back at his twenty or so years in the company, what he appreciates most is that he has always been able to be himself. *Scott Bader practises authenticity.*

2   **Debate and decision** – Walk into the factory and you will find the fitters discussing issues that matter; go to a general meeting and you will hear any member of staff able to have his or her views heard. Whether a factory operative or a director on the board, all the staff are equal members of the Commonwealth. *It practises democracy and equality.*

3   **Finding parts of yourself that you did not know existed** – When Sue came to Scott Bader after having had her children, she was

working as a clerk in the credit control department. Within fifteen years she held the constitutionally most powerful position in the company as chair of the Commonwealth board. *It practises giving people the freedom to realise their full potential.*

4 **You are not alone in this place** – Ian provides training within the company and, as he teaches people how to drive forklift trucks and produce resins, he also heightens their awareness of their interdependence. *It practises conscious interdependence.*

5 **Small is beautiful** – The company is a relatively small fish in a sea where only the big fish now swim. Its size, coupled with its culture, make it well placed to deliver high-quality, tailor-made products. *It practises quality.*

6 **Ernest and Godric** – The company carries the vision of Ernest Bader, his son, Godric, now articulating the twenty-first century vision at many international groundbreaking events and conferences looking at global transformation. *It practises vision.*

7 **Kindness** – When a fire destroyed someone's house, the staff helped to gather what was needed to make a new home. When one staff member had an epileptic fit, he was taken care of. *It practises kindness in little and large ways.*

8 **Don't hold it up as a trophy** – Although Scott Bader has much to be proud of, it does not take refuge in its past but puts its words into action today. *It practises what it preaches.*

9 **Landing in heaven** – When Keith arrived at Scott Bader some thirty years ago, at the age of twenty-seven, he thought 'I have landed in heaven.' *It practises creating glimpses of heaven.*

10 **Giving it all away** – When Keith received the travel award for long service, he gave all £7,000 worth of it away to disadvantaged children. When the company became well established as a highly profitable enterprise, its owner, Ernest Bader, gave it away to the workers. *It practises altruism.*

EVERYDAY PRACTICE

BEING ONESELF

For Andrew Gunn, the head of finance, the defining characteristic of the company is that 'It really does allow people to bring the whole of themselves into their working life.' People are seen not simply in terms of the particular skills that they bring to their specific day-to-day job. There are many roles within the company – sitting on the Commonwealth board, the pension fund trust, the company board, the community council, charitable projects and so on – that require wider abilities. All are encouraged to take part in the wider activities of the company, its management and its social responsibilities, so whether you are a fitter or an accountant, you are equal when it comes to contributing to these wider functions. After all, there are 'All sorts of attributes and insights and aspirations that people have.'

Andrew describes the struggle between the successful business on the one hand and the principles on the other:

> We're clearly seeking to be involved in an economic activity which is successful. I mean we're not talking about maximising profits, we're talking about being successful so that we can continue to grow and be sustainable and continue to be able to offer employment to the numbers of people that we do. So that's clearly necessary. But we also have these principles that have almost been bequeathed to us with the shares in 1951.

The company encourages people to think about the issues that concern the company – the production, the economics, the impact on the local and wider community and on the earth. Those who come to the company are all different, and although some may be attracted because of the company's particular ideals, the majority come first and foremost to earn a living. Only a minority, of whom Andrew is one, are there primarily because of the philosophy. Out-and-out visionaries are thin on the ground; in fact Andrew would argue that Godric is the only person with the wider vision, the person who is devoted primarily to inspiring everybody:

I think for the rest it is a question of understanding the vision and accepting it and working towards it, and changing the way that you work and behave as a result of it. And it's a very quaint approach, but it's a question of seeking and gradually improving; we're not there but we're on the path.

When I ask him to imagine himself as an old man thinking back to his many years at Scott Bader, looking to see what was of greatest worth, Andrew's mind turns to the quality of relationships there. It is:

the enjoyment and satisfaction of working with a large number of people whom I enjoy working with. Because I think, taking the twenty years as a whole, I've felt that I'm being myself, that I'm not required to put on any particular façade in order to meet any particular requirements of the company. Clearly, there are job-related requirements, but I can be myself, I feel relaxed in being myself, and I think that others probably feel that as well. People are not being forced into roles that they feel uncomfortable with.

Here Andrew is talking not just about job roles but about how people feel free to behave both inside and outside the company:

Generally, because of the relative absence of fear in the company, people can be much more relaxed about themselves and about their relationships with others.

Sure enough, I find that people are real individuals: the grumpy engineer who is fed up with a recent change, the angry fitter who wants greater adherence to the principles and no outsourcing, the manager who says clearly that this is no Utopia and that divisions exist, the operatives having their tea. The ordinariness and the warts are there, and people express them freely, but there is something else besides.

DEBATE AND DECISION

Making a profit is a fairly simple thing around which to build a consensus, but building a company that is to be a model of social and economic justice is much harder, and the views on how this is to be done generate strong feelings and hot debate:

> There are some ways of making a profit that are not acceptable and others that are. And I think clearly we would argue that making a profit by selling goods to make nuclear warhead shells is not an acceptable way of making money. Nor is compulsory redundancy an acceptable way of making profits.

Some of the important decisions, for example on reorganisation, voluntary redundancies, the closure of a plant and the distribution of the bonus, are discussed by members. The chair of the Commonwealth board, Sue Carter, who was currently managing these debates, was elected by the workforce. She feels strongly about the question of democracy, however imperfect it may be:

> I like the idea that it doesn't matter whether I'm in the room with the company chairman or a factory operative, it makes no difference to me; we can discuss the issue on an equal basis.

During her one-year term of office she had to deal with several difficult debates, including an extraordinary general meeting with a resolution of no confidence in the company board:

> Everyone brought out their feelings very rationally, and management were asked serious questions, and it was a very open exchange of views in a very calm way.

Financial constraints had forced management to consider contracting out the canteen facilities. Given the vision of the company, this aroused deeply held views on staying true to the principles. Maintaining the marriage between the principles and the economics is sometimes hard work, involving debate as a whole body in order to resolve the tensions.

Sue recently oversaw a workforce discussion on allocating the bonus. They voted to give a donation to charity but not a bonus to themselves. It was a tough decision that called into question the constitution, which stipulates that a bonus cannot be paid to members unless an equal amount is also paid to charity: 'It's to force us always to think of those less fortunate than ourselves.'

One of the most historic decisions that Sue oversaw as chair was that to extend membership around the world:

> The impact of this is enormous. It means that the decisions that are made affecting the whole company, including the factory here at Wollaston, will now be made with the participation of members in South Africa, France, Dubai. The control of the Commonwealth by the people who are physically here in Wollaston is now potentially extended to anyone who works for Scott Bader anywhere in the world if they choose to take membership. A manager from France could, possibly, have as much say as a manager at head office who, in turn, has as much as, say, the clerk processing the invoices.

Debate is endemic, and because the vision is so very prominent at Scott Bader, it sometimes seems to turn round and hit people in the face. Where other ordinary companies might display silence or indifference, here there are arguments and at times fierce bitterness. Some people care very deeply about the legacy of Ernest and of Scott Bader, and honouring it requires countless decisions; there are often no simple answers.

Apart from talk there is action. Andrew speaks with firm emphasis when he says, 'I feel strongly that the practical act is worth hundreds of hours of preaching.' Later he adds:

> It is to do with doing and saying. The doing and the saying have got to be consistent. And what I don't like is people presenting themselves as knowing the way and the vision who cannot demonstrate practical experience of doing it. I don't think it's worth a row of beans really.

FINDING PARTS OF YOURSELF THAT
YOU DID NOT KNOW EXISTED

Had Sue known all that would have been required of her as chair, she wonders whether she would have taken it on. Her time at Scott Bader has:

> released things in me that I didn't know were there – capabilities that I don't know would've been released anywhere else. When I first came I was just a temp in credit control. People refer to the job of chairman as powerful. I didn't see it as power at all; I saw it as a thing I had to learn, how to get things done, and I wasn't comfortable with it.

Sue struggles to express what is for her remarkable and worthwhile about working for Scott Bader. It is something to do with:

> Just that little bit extra. With me it's made me realise I can do things that I didn't think I could do.

Going beyond what is easy, doing more than one knows one can, giving a bit more than one has: these are the qualities that Sue values in the company and wants to help develop in others. People have come to the company as unskilled labourers and taken on great responsibilities in the company, be these in terms of management or of running the Commonwealth, the community council or the charitable work of the company. Godric sees this internal stretching that makes for fundamental behavioural change as part of the essential work of the company:

> More demands are made on people here than in industry in general; the Commonwealth demands more maturity, it calls for personal change besides change of organisation and it requires the ability to give up false power, status and values to realise true relationships.

YOU'RE NOT ALONE IN THIS PLACE

Ian came to Scott Bader as a factory operative. He had spent all his working life in the army and then had left in order to provide stability at school for his young son. He remembers distinctly his first days at the company:

> I remember going down to the canteen to have a cup of tea with the guys on my shift, sitting across a table from them and talking to them. I remember them turning their heads, and I'm thinking, 'They're saying "You'll have to speak up." ' That's because in the past obviously some people have not taken as great care as they possibly could with things like their hearing. Now, I've had a history where it's been forced upon you to take good care of yourself. And I said to myself and to everybody since, new people as they come in, I tell them 'In ten years' time I don't want you to have to be sitting there turning your head to hear what somebody new is saying. So use your common sense and utilise all the training and equipment.'

Ian now shares responsibility for training and development with many others, providing health and safety training and much of the practical instruction, for example on driving forklift trucks and handling equipment. In any training session, however, he has a particular agenda, which is to help people realise that they are not alone. He focuses on breaking through that impervious layer of consciousness that can cut us off from recognising our impact on others:

> You as an individual have got to take responsibility for your actions or your omissions as to how they affect other people. You're not just working as an individual; you're working as part of a group, a family, call it what you will. We're all responsible for each other. At home you wouldn't just go and make a cup of tea for you, walk in to the living room with a cup of tea and cake when your wife's sat there or there's company. You don't think, 'They'll do it themselves'; you don't adopt that philosophy at home, so why at work? If you're going to work in a manufacturing environment which at the best is not posh or very clean, you've got to take responsibility for ensuring that that work environment is kept in the best possible condition for the next person who's going to come along after you.

EVERYDAY PRACTICE

205

This is Ian's vocation – heightening people's awareness of how our ongoing daily choices and actions affect others, be it the neighbours in the village, colleagues, the company, the world:

> Whatever you do or don't do will have an impact on somebody else. You must ensure you take sufficient action to ensure that whoever comes along next and has to work in the space you've just vacated, or use the equipment you've just left, is able to do so without doing anything else to enable them to do it.

As I listen to Ian I realise that he is talking not simply about cleanliness of the factory floor, but also about the generations who come after us, wanting the space that he is now living in to be left in a good condition for those who will come after him. He knows within himself his connectedness to those who have gone before him and those who will follow, and honours his part in that unbroken human chain. He encourages his colleagues to sense that same reality whatever else they may be doing.

SMALL IS BEAUTIFUL

Scott Bader is small compared with most of the giants in chemicals, having been untouched by acquisitions and mergers because of its constitution. Its size is its strength as it is able to respond to niche markets, build close relationships and give a very personal service to its clients, ensuring that exactly the right resin is produced to meet the particular needs of a customer, however unusual or innovative those may be.

ERNEST AND GODRIC

Ernest arrived from Switzerland in 1912 with virtually nothing but determination and willpower. He built from nothing an international company of world standing. Even those who loved him note that he was at times fiercely and unreasonably demanding and autocratic.

His son, Godric, is an equally remarkable man, but his personality is very different. He is a gentle man, devoid of harshness but not of passion. Like his father he is abrim with idealism and has a longing for human beings to become what they might be, as well as a sadness that this has not yet happened. He is a tireless ambassador for the vision and, at seventy-eight years of age, continues to talk at international conferences on the pioneering model of Scott Bader, listening carefully to new thinking and seeking to integrate his unfolding insights into the company's practice. Philosophy, psychology, science and theology all sit happily with this man. His office is full of life, crammed with ideas and documents that he shares generously with me. There is a towel on the radiator drying after his morning swim in the company pool. The walls are papered with inspirational quotes, posters and invocations, and lined with books of many disciplines.

Godric has spent his life translating the highest of aspirations into the concrete practicalities of running factories and a multinational business. He knows about the compromises, the dilemmas, the disappointments and the daily renewed commitment that are involved in helping people's consciousness grow. Godric is clear that this has been and is a spiritual journey, that it is somehow tied in with the future of the world of business, and that these times have an urgency to them.

KINDNESS

The vision is worth nothing if there is not kindness. Andrew recalls how when a fellow worker had a catastrophic fire at home, she found that individuals throughout the company, whether or not she knew them, went to great lengths to bring things in to help her rebuild her home. It was not 'the company' but individuals who stepped in.

People know and care about what is happening in each other's lives – bereavements, illness, problems in the family. They help each other to have fun as well. Annie, now an elderly and retired woman but once chief cook, is visiting the canteen to help someone out with

207

some sewing. When she worked there she was part of the company racing group, and she remembers how the managing director and his wife would come and pick her up in their car and take her to the track.

Andrew sums all this up by quoting an article from the *Financial Times* about faith approaches to work:

> It refers to a Rabbi in the first century. He had been challenged to stand on one leg and explain the contents of the Torah. And he stood on this one leg and said, 'You shall not do to others things that you would not like done to yourself; the rest is commentary.'

This position shapes policy on redundancy and reorganisation and colours the work experience of most of those at Scott Bader.

DON'T HOLD IT UP AS A TROPHY

A vision can be a destructive thing if it becomes ossified, the past dragging people away from the present and the future. For people at Scott Bader the company vision is something alive and constantly evolving. Ian describes it well: 'Commonwealth values – it's your normal daily life values, that's all it is, just incorporated into the business world.' It is not about talking to people and showing them a glass cabinet:

> Don't look at our values and attitudes and behaviours behind that glass cabinet. Come into the community and see them at work. Don't hold it up as a picture or a trophy. See it in action. That's where it should be. Not stuck up on a wall somewhere saying, this is what we all reckon we do. Let's go and see people doing it, let's see the evidence. . . . There is evidence out there; it is working; there is a community spirit. We're here to help each other. And we can incorporate it with all our other companies as well – associated companies abroad. Because that's the way it is going.

As we walk out of the factory through the gate into the old, peaceful, secluded garden that is there for every worker to enjoy, I see a fragment of that evidence.

LANDING IN HEAVEN

When Godric takes me to have lunch in the canteen, he asks me which table I would like to join. At one table are some very senior managers, on another says Godric, 'some interesting people', a smile of merry appreciation spreading across his face. We head towards the second table and I find myself sitting next to Keith, a man apparently in his prime and sporting a baseball cap. In fact, Keith has been retired for several years, but, like many other retirees, he still comes in for lunch.

> I joined the company in 1961; I came out of the army. That's why I thought I landed in heaven, because I'd never worked in civilian work before in my life. I came out of the army at twenty-seven, walked into this place and thought I'd landed in heaven.

Keith had spent the first fourteen years of his life in an orphanage, the next thirteen in the army. When he came to Scott Bader, it was quite literally the first time in his life that he felt cared for. Shortly after joining the company he developed epilepsy:

> Any time I had an epileptic fit, somebody picked me up, stuck me in a chair, and I didn't do another stroke of work for the rest of the day. And somebody carried on in my job; no problem; there was never any complaint. Scott Bader looked after all the hospital, car, services and everything. Anything I needed I got.

He recalls arriving in the company after his difficult and unhappy childhood:

> But this place accepted me for what I was. When people spoke to me they helped me out. I was brand new to it. I mean, when I walked into this place and saw them valves and gates, it frightened the life out of me . . . never seen them valves before in my life. But there were people here to teach you.

Keith recalls with great affection and respect the managers for whom he has worked, their unshakeable ethics, their skill, and their kindness to him. What, he had asked himself, could he give in return?:

What I used to do, because I had nothing else to give, I had no car, I had nothing, I gave my time. I'd work extra hours for nothing. Or I'd walk round the factory and I'd see people. If they needed a hand, I'd give them a hand. When I had nothing to do, I'd go looking for work. And there were a lot of us did that. You just didn't say, 'Oh that's his job; let him get on with it.' If he was struggling, you went and helped.

Keith is passionate about the Commonwealth and about its being fully understood:

I feel that some people don't understand what common ownership is; it is for the company – it's for the good. And it says in the Constitution, 'each according to his needs, each according to his ability.' I'm a plant operator, so I will get paid a sum for that job plus an allowance for working shifts. Now somebody up here, who's a chemist, a highly qualified chemist, will get a lot more than me. You accept that; each according to his ability. . . . You don't go around saying, 'He's getting more than me and I don't think that's fair.'

Keith is impatient with some of the human weaknesses that undermine the Commonwealth – the petty grievances, the envies, the failure to live up to the ideals:

The problem with common ownership is that you're dealing with people. Ernest Bader was a bit of an autocrat but he had a vision. The hard fact of it all was that his vision depended on us to carry it out. And that's people.

Keith has a stutter and sometimes speaks slowly and with difficulty, but as he looks around the room his words are clear and measured: 'I love this place, and I still do even though I'm retired. It's breaking my heart to see what's happening.' He explains what he sees as the difficulty:

Common ownership also means common responsibilities. So you can't just sit back and take all the goodies and not be prepared to put something back. Otherwise, if everybody's taking the goodies out, then after a little while there won't be anything left.

GIVING IT ALL AWAY

Godric encourages Keith to talk about aspects of himself that he would not otherwise mention. Keith is an instinctive giver, his current disappointment springing, I imagine, partly from the fact that, inevitably, not everyone in the company is like that. Some people simply work there to earn a living and do not have his passionate commitment to the ideals nor his thorough altruism. He plays for a local brass band and, wanting to share his talent with others, teaches schoolchildren for free: 'It's not much of a gift but I pass it on and teach youngsters. I take them through their school grades.' Indeed, one of them has just received a GCSE A star grade and is going to audition for the National Youth Brass Band.

When, after twenty-five years with the company, Keith received the long-service award sabbatical, he gave it away:

> I felt that that sort of money could be put to better use. So I asked if it could be put somewhere that could be used for holidays for children. And that's what they did. I didn't need it. And to spend that sort of money on me . . . I've now got no family, and I thought spending all this money on myself is a waste of money.

He shook his head and continued in a very matter of fact way:

> When I gave it away it was £7,000. At that time I could have had the money or I could have retired half a year earlier. Now, to me that's a waste of money. It's a waste of a resource. You just can't do that.

There is no question of Keith claiming any moral high ground; he was just doing what he knew to be best. Perhaps it is because he knew hardship as a child that he derived more pleasure from knowing that children who needed the money would get it than if he had simply used it up on himself. Perhaps he is the sort of person that one day more of humanity will become if we are to survive. This altruism is a strand that runs through the centre of Scott Bader, typified by the way in which after many years of thought and preparation, Ernest Bader gave his company away.

The firebombs that had narrowly missed the company's premises in London's East End and the aircraft shell that hit the family home had served to drive the Baders out of London in the 1940s to the tranquillity of Wollaston. The horror and terrible violence of the Second World War had shaken Ernest to the core. Surely human beings could not go on destroying each other in this way? Godric recalls those post-war years and how Ernest had decided to take his ordinary company and transform it into something unique. He set out to restructure his company, so that human values:

> essentially Christian, but rooted in all world religions, could find their place and be lived out. These aspirations would offer a way forward from economic violence, power struggles and a money-acquisitive society.

Godric, himself a trained chemist, has a profound understanding of what the company is about at an evolutionary level, seeing it within the historical context of economics, society, psychology, theology and ecology. He understands his father in terms of those perspectives:

> Ernest intuited that violence lay at a very deep level in society and humanity had to evolve to survive. The seeds of violence lay within the structures of the capitalist work system, and how we have to earn our living. He understood how easy it was, as an employer, to exploit people; how more capital gave him more means and the power of economic dictation in the way he was running his company, how the system encouraged personal greed and how greed between nations leads to war.

His concern was not, however, simply at the macro level, it was about starting with the individual human being. Ernest was aware that lives are destroyed when people are forced to work as wage slaves. He agreed with Pope Pius XI when the latter said, 'Dead matter goes out of the factory improved, but men go out degraded.' Ernest wanted his company to be a place where human beings could grow into their fullness. As Godric remarks, 'Personal growth is more important than big profits.'

When Ernest gave away his company to the workers, it was after endless work, many discussions and two earlier abortive attempts. The Commonwealth was established in 1951 and all workers were able to become members of it. It was the Commonwealth that held the shares in trust and that now has ultimate responsibility. This original act of altruism has undoubtedly been a crucial factor in the survival of the company. Over the past twenty years large chemical companies have bought up small ones, and medium-sized businesses have not survived the process. In the UK, Scott Bader is alone in being relatively small and immune to take-overs. Not one of the members of the Commonwealth would profit by one penny from a take-over.

Altruism that is not tempered with hard-nosed common sense can be destructive. A business must make a profit – balancing ideals with the figures is vital and people at Scott Bader are very aware of this.

EVERYDAY PRACTICE

SCOTT BADER BRINGS VISION INTO REALITY BY:

- Having a commitment to ongoing human growth and development
- Having a goal and vision over and above profit, a goal that inspires people
- Practising deep equality and democracy in its structures and conversations
- Being involved in global changes for transformation
- Creating glimpses of heaven and saying so
- Extending generosity and altruism to individuals, to society and to the earth
- Being connected to the community at micro and macro level
- Being authentic individuals, able to be themselves
- Balancing the financial demands with the higher good
- Caring for each other's happiness and taking time to enjoy and celebrate
- Raising people's awareness of interdependence
- Paying attention to detail

PUTTING THIS INTO PRACTICE IN YOUR WORKPLACE:

FINDING THE VISION

Scott Bader has a vision that plays a very explicit role in the company and helps to give it its heartwarming personality. A company without vision is often an uncomfortable place to work: when we do not know where we are going, all roads lead there.

One of the characteristics of the soul-friendly organisation is a clear, living vision. Each person in the organisation knows what that vision is like, everyone is committed to creating it, and each can see their part in it and the practical steps that will enable them to reach it. Few things lower morale more than wandering around not knowing where you are going, whether you will ever get there or whether you will get split up and lost.

AN ACTIVITY TO DO AS A TEAM

The shared vision
The following activity enables a group to find its collective vision by using guided fantasy, travelling into the future by imagination to see what the ideal looks like in terms of specifics. The vision that emerges includes what people see, hear, touch and sense, and covers a range of practical, concrete aspects as well as some of the more intangible elements of relationships and culture.

This activity is powerful in drawing out the essence of the ideal future and works with both cynical, hardened sceptics and young, bright-eyed optimists. It is best carried out in an environment that

215

feels safe and where participants trust the person who is leading it. The activity draws on the whole person – their imagination and intuition, group skills, analytical skills, hearts and the willingness to engage and reach out into the future.

The purpose of the activity is to help people to explore as fully as possible their vision of the company, to see and experience the specific elements that make up their ideal and to identify what is already in place and what they can and will create in their own working day. The activity consists of five steps, which we will go through in more detail below:

1 As a group, relax and visit the future using guided meditation.
2 Share what has been seen in the future, the facilitator gathering in the elements.
3 As a group, lightly analyse the elements in terms of what has already been achieved, what can now be created and what is impossible.
4 In pairs, note the part of the future you yourself want to create.
5 Then, as a group, go round and hear each person's commitment.

Step 1

Ask people to make themselves comfortable and relax, with their backs comfortably straight and their feet flat on the floor. Explain that in a moment, if they wish to join in, you are going to take them on an imaginary journey to visit an ideal future for their company or team. Ask them to close their eyes, relax and become quiet and aware of their breathing. Take time yourself to relax and become quiet and still. Then read the guided meditation below, or adapt or invent your own.

Breathe out any anxieties, let go of any thoughts and breathe in a sense of stillness and peace.

Imagine that you are somewhere where you feel at peace . . . Choose the place you want to be . . . What can you see? . . . What can you feel? . . . As you look, imagine that you can see in the distance a path that leads up a hillside towards some trees . . .

Imagine you are walking along this path . . . There are fields on either side of you . . . The sun is shining . . . There is the sound of birds and insects . . . As you get nearer to the trees, you see the track leading into the woods . . . Follow the path . . . The sun is falling through the leaves and branches, making patterns of light and shadows on the ground in front of you . . . You feel your feet on the earth . . .

Walk along a little further until you reach another path that crosses yours . . . Here you see a signpost, and written on it is 'Your company in five years' time' . . . Turn down that path . . . You may have to walk a long way . . . You are now approaching the company . . .

The company you are going to see is in five years from now; it has been working for these past years from its core values and vision; it is an ideal, successful and thriving company. You are now going to visit this workplace, see the people, the women and men here in this place.

You are approaching the company now . . . What can you see? . . . Go right into the company . . . What can you hear? . . . What can you see? . . . What can you smell? . . . Touch a few things . . .

You can see the people working there now . . . What are they doing? . . . Can you see their faces? . . . Their hands? . . . Perhaps someone is speaking . . . What can you hear? . . . What is this like? . . .

What else can you see? . . . Have a good look around . . . What is it like to be in this place? . . . What sort of feeling do you have here? . . . What is the most important thing that you have seen or heard or sensed? . . . Have a last look around now because soon you will be leaving . . .

When you are ready, open your eyes, stretch out and find yourself back here in this room today.

Step 2

Having guided the participants along their journey, ask them now to feed back, without comment, all that they have seen, heard, touched and sensed. Write these under an umbrella drawn on a chart. Keep the group highly focused and in touch with the vision – no chatting, simply harvest in the elements.

Step 3

Ask people to identify those elements which they already have (circling these in one colour) and then those elements which they could, with others, create (circling these in a different colour). Acknowledge that there are elements that cannot be created and let go of those.

217

Step 4

Ask people to divide into pairs and reflect individually, jotting down what element they most value in the ideal company; what part of the vision they *want* to create and what steps they will take to create it. These steps can be very few and very small. Each then in turn listens fully to his or her partner.

Step 5

Close the activity with each person saying what their commitment to the vision is. Someone can scribe this for the group so that every-thing is there in front of their eyes. The group gets a glimpse of how all the individual parts contribute to the whole vision and to that future of which the group is a part.

AN ACTIVITY TO DO AS A LONE INDIVIDUAL WITH 'NO POWER'

Time-lines

This activity encourages people to begin to see a continuity and pat-tern to the life of their company and to see that there are a range of possible futures – and that they are involved in creating that future.

1 Reflect quietly for a few minutes on how you want your company to be in five years' time.

2 Draw three time-lines, all starting now and going forwards into the future. The horizontal line is how you see the probable future for your company if things continue on their current course. The upper line represents your company's preferred future, how you would real-ly like to see it develop, and the bottom line is for the negative possi-ble future, the nightmare scenario. On each line use words, colours and symbols to depict how you see the future unfolding in each case.

3 Take a few moments to reflect on what you have drawn and what strikes you.

4 Note what parts stand out for you and what you see as your part in each of the scenarios.

CHAPTER 9

BAYER UK:

THE WAY OF CHANGE

C HANGE IS THE ONE constant; it is inevitable, the norm. Despite
this, we still seem to be surprised when change comes along.
We react as though it has appeared out of the blue, when in
fact it is simply there all the time. We are often indignant about it, as
if things have no right to change even though this is the very nature
of existence. And often we resist change even when our action is as
unreasonable and futile as trying to stem the waters of a great river
with a tiny twig. Change involves loss, and loss is painful, but when
we resist change we not only suffer the loss, but also exacerbate and
prolong the pain.

As early as 1931 Julian Huxley wrote that the challenge facing society was to move from a theology of 'fixity' to one of change, in other
words, to move from a world view in which we see reality as consist-
ing of objective things, facts and situations into a reality that consists
of constant flux and flow, a world of relationship rather than objects.
This is the shift from Newton's mechanistic universe to that of quantum physics.

The implications of the scientific revolution that occurred in the
early twentieth century have even now scarcely been absorbed by
much of the business world. That paradigm shift was as fundamental as that of the sixteenth and seventeenth centuries when the ideas
of Copernicus changed how we saw the universe, and it is when we
see things differently that we *act* differently. The Copernican shift in
perception opened up the way for the unprecedented leap forward in
science that took place over the next 450 years and was necessary for

219

Everything is in flux.

Heraclitus

● ● ● ● ● ● ● ● ● ● ● ● ● ● ● ●

the development of the Western world's technological advances. Similarly, the quantum physics revolution invites organisations to leap forwards providing a model of reality which recognises that change is not a consequence of mechanical movement but is integral to matter and life itself.

When we function within an old, dead paradigm that flies in the face of scientific truth, we are building insuperable obstacles into our work, denying the way things are. The scientists who continued to attempt to understand the world in pre-Copernican ways were inevitably going to fail. Those who grasped the implication of the new model of Newton and Descartes were able to make progress in ways that had never before been available to scientists.

Business, be it public or private, operates within the real world and is faced with a similar challenge: either to hold onto the old fixed paradigm or to internalise and work with the new understanding that all is in constant flux and that as this is part of the fundamental nature of our universe, it is a core factor in the way we need to structure our organisations. Companies that insist on doing things in the old, mechanistic way are already crumbling and collapsing. Those which still struggle on are placing intense strain on themselves and on the people working within them. They do so at great cost, as is seen in their high levels of stress, absenteeism, sickness, burnout and staff turnover. People are being asked to work in ways that simply do not work and that are not sustainable. Five-year plans, hierarchical structures, compartmentalised boxes, discrete teams and rigid strategic planning all become obstructive when the reality is of interconnected movement and relationship. The underlying reality within which business is working is itself flow, and the structures and decision-making need to reflect this.

The old phrase 'handling change' implies that there is something we can physically get our hands on, but this is largely an illusion. Change is not something that can be managed as if it were a thing; it flows like water and, like water, slips through the fingers. The company that understands and works with change as a natural medium will succeed in a way that eludes others. Bayer UK/Ireland is a remarkable, and perhaps unlikely, example of such a company.

The oldest company described in this book, Bayer was founded in Germany in 1863 as a partnership between two people experimenting at the kitchen sink. Since then it has gone through countless changes, growing into a vast multinational with a turnover of £27 billion and a global workforce of 120,000. It has subsidiaries and associates worldwide and connections with many major suppliers and customers. Each time these companies see a change in fortune, Bayer has to adapt, and each time the market changes, Bayer has to shift. Change is constant and accelerating in this company, yet there is a sense of substance and calm as if it is relatively untroubled by economic forces. Over the years Bayer has evolved, stumbled, fallen, endured and modernised, continuing to be a thriving, productive company with its profits and soul intact. It is like a giant that knows how to move gracefully.

This chapter tells of some individuals who work at Bayer UK and, through their stories, gives a glimpse of how the company works with change, transforming it from a potentially destructive force into a tool for evolution. Eleven key interrelated elements give Bayer its particular ability to thrive on change; they are elements by which the soul of the company expresses itself:

1 **A family giant** – Bayer is enormous, its products are found in almost every home, yet for those who work there it feels like part of a family in which people are responsible to one another. *Bayer practises strong, longstanding relationships and loyalty.*

I think many people assume, wrongly, that a company exists simply to make money. While this is an important result of a company's existence, we have to go deeper and find the real reaons for our being.

David Packard

● ●

2   **Taking time** – There is an absence of frenetic rush; people take time to do what is important: meeting and greeting, talking and sharing, thinking through decisions. Although there are times when all hands on deck work very swiftly, there is overall a measured pace. Management is flexible and does not force people to work at a speed that is uncomfortable and unsustainable. *It practises calm.*

3   **Candour** – There is a high degree of openness. People from the top to the bottom of the organisation speak frankly and share information promptly. The company does not hide behind image or spin. *It practises candour.*

4   **'Here you are plain Hans'** – Whatever their position in the company, whatever their academic qualification, each person is treated with equal respect; there is a recognition of mutuality and each takes responsibility. *It practises mutual respect.*

5   **Taking care of people** – Bayer is finding different, non-paternalistic ways of caring about people in times when it is no longer possible to offer anyone a job for life. *It practises flexible caring for one another.*

6   **The servant-leader** – The leader listens, inspires and serves those around him. *The leader practises humility.*

7   **Autonomy** – Although the company is vast, each unit works as a small, self-directing body while remaining conscious of itself as part of the greater whole. *It practises agility and freedom.*

8   **The scientist's winding path** – The way in which a Bayer scientist works involves patience, perseverance and detachment, a commitment to scientific truth and an awareness of the ethical and human issues. *It practises integrity.*

9 **Compassion** – If and when redundancies are made, both practical needs and human dignity are respected. *It practises compassion.*

10 **Cultures and subcultures** – Bayer has a strong sense of its unique culture and of the subcultures within it and adapts its management to respect these. People have a sense of belonging within the culture. *It practises cultural diversity.*

11 **The long term and the big picture** – Bayer plays a long game; it invests in the long term and does not follow fashion. *It practises perspective.*

EVERYDAY PRACTICE

A FAMILY GIANT

Bayer is an enormous, successful company that has spread over the earth. It has four arms – health care, agrochemicals, chemicals and polymers – its products affecting nearly all our lives. Discreetly present in virtually every home are Bayer products: the aspirin in the bathroom, the kitchen cleaner, the dye of the carpet, the fragrance in the face cream, the plastic coating on the car, the CD, the armchair fabric. Bayer products are found within everyday goods of many different brand names that sit in every supermarket. As well as these, Bayer synthesises highly specialised drugs and chemicals that have designated outlets.

Although Bayer has a low profile in the UK, its name being recognised by only about 2% of people in the street, it is a family name in Europe. It is a powerful company with technologically groundbreaking products and is at times inevitably involved in controversy. On the day of my visit, thirty-nine pharmaceutical companies, of which Bayer is one, are taking the South African government to court over patent protection.

When I ask the managing director, Lennart Aberg, whether the company has a soul, he replies without hesitation, 'Yes; it is a family.' And with a little laugh adds, 'Don't ask me what that means.' Words are inadequate so I go and look for myself.

223

During my visits to various Bayer sites and people, what strikes me is that this giant company is a very personal, human, natural community made up of many parts, each with its own character and with a sense of being part of a greater whole. It weathered a major restructuring in the 1990s, yet many of the people have been at the company for well over ten years; there is a constancy, continuity and a sense of belonging that reminds one of a family. Lennart himself has been within one or other part of Bayer for forty years and has been happy to do that because of the variety that the company's size allows.

While large organisations can be unwieldly, Bayer for the most part uses its size as a means of building in flexibility. When one part of the company is suffering, the rest of the company will carry it. When someone has exhausted all possibilities of personal development in one area, he or she can move into another part of the company. Life's problems and difficulties can to some degree be absorbed by the diversity and breadth of the organisation.

When Steve Painter, head of communications, was being recruited, the director interviewing offered several analogies of how the company worked. One was of a family, the parents being the headquarters in Germany, the brothers and sisters the business units, and the cousins the subsidiaries:

> But he also used another analogy which was meant to tell me that changes come and changes go by, we weather them one way or another, and he said, 'We are like a spider as well – because we've got a large body at the centre but we've also got lots of nice long legs, and if one of those legs gets pulled off the spider doesn't fall over.'

So if, for example, the bottom suddenly drops out of the polymer market and a business unit is under threat, the body as a whole will remain sound. Bayer uses its size to build a culture of interdependence so that it can bend in the wind of change and survive some very harsh gales. This in turn gives confidence to those who work there so that they can face change with a degree of courage rather than fear.

TAKING TIME

My first visit to Bayer is to meet Colin Pedley, head of responsible care. I arrive a little late at reception, and as I check in, a man who has been waiting to one side steps forward and introduces himself as Colin. We walk over to Colin's office in an adjacent building and he swiftly tells me his story, of how he started work for Bayer in a warehouse seventeen years earlier in Bromsgrove and has risen up to now be head of health and safety and responsible care. Colin describes to me what his first impressions of Bayer had been:

> When I first came, within three to four weeks I thought I had made a serious mistake. I looked at the site where I was, which was fairly small, an autonomous place and I thought, 'There is absolutely no management control here, this will close down in less than a year; it can't survive, it's too relaxed, too easy going.' Because, you see, I had always worked in very constrictive industries where you had such a tight line of control, very blinkered management, very fixed in what you did and how you did it and when I came to Bayer I couldn't believe it.

Colin's first impressions were based on his previous experience of working in macho companies where management got what it wanted by wielding sticks and throwing carrots when driven to do so. When he joined Bayer Colin found its working environment confusing because there it was relaxed and management was scarcely to be seen, and there was flexibility. Having previously only seen people working under duress, he was not sure how things could work without this. His fear that the company could not survive was ill-founded. Bayer, experienced in adapting, went through the 1990s like other companies, obliged like them to operate within the strict, callous rules of capitalism, rules that required increased competitiveness, redundancies, outsourcing, cost-cutting and increased productivity. And yet it remains a relaxed, calm place. The working environment that Colin found in Bayer's warehouse in the eighties is still there, as is Colin. Laying his initial qualms aside, Colin stayed: 'I am a relative newcomer, most people say.'

CANDOUR

As part of his role, Colin holds some responsibility for presenting the public face of Bayer. For ten minutes he tells me how one chemical company has been involved in transforming an industrial wasteland into a wildlife area of natural interest, but he makes no attempt to paint a rosy picture of a worthy company doing good deeds. Instead he simply and openly tells me the story of his life at Bayer and what he loves about his work, what it is like to get up at six in the morning and to drive to Newbury with a sense of freedom, knowing that before he returns that night he will have found enjoyment in his day.

I find the same candour, the same lack of self-promotion and image, present in each encounter that I have. Very difficult, controversial issues are brought up quite spontaneously – patents, animal rights, the ethics of research, redundancies, outsourcing and the environment are all touched on naturally with a similar lack of packaged answers. There is a searching to find a way, to understand, to make sense of issues that are not easily resolved and indeed may be unresolvable at this stage of history. I am struck by the substance behind this company and these people. Despite being surrounded by quickly shifting sands, there is a firm, steady centre of good-hearted people struggling to reconcile the irreconcilable, with no attempt to duck the issues or hide behind glib complacency or pat answers.

This lack of internal hype and image-building is vital to living with change. Narcissism, in which image takes over from reality, provides a thin veneer that clouds the truth, the paradoxes and the complexity. It then becomes easy for people to fall into the trap of believing in their image rather than relying on their real substance. Controversial areas become hidden, negative information gets distorted into positive, so that the real situation is not known by the leadership and they do not have the real data with which to work. At Bayer UK/Ireland, however, there is an openness and authenticity. Those I talk to – the managing director; Millie, who tends the plants; Sara, a researcher; Steve, the head of communications; Clare, a fra-

grance evaluator – show a willingness to engage and talk with direct-
ness about some impossibly challenging situations. This book does
not try to explore the ethics of companies; it is about the spirit of the
company, the soul qualities that underlie every other facet of the
company. The soul quality that is apparent at Bayer is candour, and
it takes courage and a willingness to be vulnerable to work with this
degree of openness.

'HERE YOU ARE PLAIN HANS'

Ian Peacock, head of human resources, tells me how Lennart gently
but firmly sets the tone of informality and respect with which people
relate to each other:

> I think, then, that goes down to the staff you have around the indi-
> vidual business director. So the whole culture starts to take on a
> shape from the MD. It's all on first-name terms. Lennart tells a story
> of a chap coming in from Germany, and of course the Germans are
> usually quite formal and . . . they have 'Sie' as the formal address and
> 'du' as the singular and informal. And until you get to know them
> really well, it's Sie. And of course they arrive in England and we're
> all on first-name terms, and they would be on last-name terms, and
> Lennart tells this wonderful story of a guy coming over and saying,
> 'Yes, well I am Herr Professor Doktor So-and-so.' And Lennart said,
> 'Yes, well that's good, but here you're plain Hans.' And it sets the
> marker right from the start.

This is not informality for its own sake; it is part and parcel of
expressing respect and mutuality towards each person working there.
The illustrious chemist with a PhD offers their part just as an administrative assistant offers theirs; all the parts matter. It is the daily contribution that each makes that counts, not title nor status.

In the quantum world, relationships are not just interesting; to many physicists, they are all there is to reality.

Meg Wheatley

● ● ● ● ● ● ● ● ● ● ● ●

TAKING CARE OF PEOPLE

At Bayer, as elsewhere, the days of having a job for life have gone. Ian outlines some of the financial pressures that are leading to outsourcing – in a company in which long service and loyalty are important, this is not straightforward. Ian unravels what care might mean in a multinational in the twenty-first century:

> I think it does put a lot of pressure on the values. We lay a lot of store by caring for our people. I think that we perhaps need to reflect on what do we mean by caring. Caring used to be, I think, very paternalistic, and I think that again the German sort of approach would have been paternalistic. You get a contract and you've got a job for life, we'll put you in the pension scheme, etc., etc. We will still offer pension schemes, but I think what you will see happening is perhaps our giving more ownership and treating people . . . more as 'adults', and we'll be saying to them a little bit more, how would you like to receive your rewards?

So people choose their rewards according to their circumstances. A younger person setting up home might want some cash towards their mortgage rather than all of it going into their pension. Some might prefer a company car, some might want health insurance, others might prefer to have the cash. Still others might want less holiday and more pay. Potentially, in an exploitative company, this flexibility could mask an erosion and fragmentation of the hard-won gains secured for the collective by the Unions. At Bayer UK/Ireland, the intention is to ensure that everyone gets what they most need, when they need it and within the real financial constraints of the company.

The other central aspect of care is training and responsibility. The company sets out to ensure that each person receives the opportunities for training and development that will make them strong as individuals, equipped with the experience and CV that will hold them in good stead. So the forklift driver trains in computer skills and goes on to lead a computer unit within Bayer. A personal assistant develops her web-building skills and heads some computer development for the company; the chemist turns into a trainer, the warehouse lad into a health and safety expert. Creating possibilities for growth and development within the company are a priority.

Talking to individual people at Bayer UK/Ireland, there is a sense of feeling very cared for. It is a question not of particularly high salaries but of the care that the directors take when making decisions that will affect, positively or otherwise, those who work there:

> It seems that, in the past fifteen years, the senior management, in every decision they have made, have considered the workforce as part of that decision-making process rather than profits. That comes partly from our MD, who comes from a culture, Sweden, where they tend to think more about the communities than they do about the bank balance. It seems that in every decision they make they are thinking, 'Well this is what we need to do; how can we do it and benefit the employees at the same time?'

When I ask Lennart whether this is so, he claims no credit. The process of decision-making is complex and profit must be made, but thought is always given to the impact a decision will have on the lives and well-being of people within the company. This care is about good common sense; it is good for business and good for people. It enables the culture of Bayer to remain intact while tremendous and often painful change is underway.

THE SERVANT-LEADER

When I go to meet Lennart, he slips unobtrusively into the room, careful not to intrude on my conversation with Ian Peacock. Lennart is a soft-spoken man whose words, gestures and demeanour speak of

EVERYDAY PRACTICE

a deep humility. He has tremendous authority and knowledge yet is gentle and unassuming, concerned about people, deferential to others and unwilling to take credit. As we talk, he checks with Ian that he has found the right word or phrase to reflect what he is trying to say; he listens carefully, takes time to think and asks for Ian's opinion when answering my questions.

Lennart's immediate vision is to help this company become truly European; his prime aim is to leave a world that is sustainable for the children and grandchildren who come after us. His personal quiet passion is that people's endeavours are not wasted by the decisions of some unknown person higher up in the company:

> Give people the feedom to do their job. How you do it is up to you.
> You have the power.

Lennart speaks concisely and with authoritative conviction. He *knows* that this is right and that his part is to ensure that people do indeed have that freedom.

I ask about the human cost of the 1990s restructuring with globalisation. He believes that the company has become stronger from the process; that it is not about squeezing more from people but of having found ways in which they can *be* more and so have more to give. The process has brought human growth and greater effectiveness. I glimpse the company taking what, for other companies, have felt like ravaging changes and incorporating them calmly into its wholesome evolution.

I ask whether there are any people within the company who are competitive and harsh, protecting their own territory. Laughing gently, Lennart says that they are rare – if they do come, they find that they do not fit in so leave of their own accord:

'Imagine what a board meeting led by him is like,' says Ian when Lennart leaves the room. It is hard to imagine bluster, positioning and posing at such a meeting. He sets a tone of quiet earnest and naturalness in which other people's self-centredness would have little place.

Servant-leaders do not necessarily recognise these qualities within

What is now proved was once only imagined.

William Blake

• •

themselves. Their care is for the greater whole yet they pay minute attention to the individuals needs and concerns, of all the people around them, both at the grass roots and at top management. Servant-leaders work to create an environment in which people can grow and be fulfilled. They do not see any difference between the most powerful or the most lowly – they see them all as people.

Lennart is unspoilt by his great power, using it quietly to serve people by talking with them and running an efficient, effective business that bears his qualities. He leads by example. When I ask him what he will have valued most from those forty years of work, he says, 'It is the people.'

This kind of leadership is vital if a company is to work through change gracefully. Fluidity and restructuring take away the old sense of security that lies in knowing 'this is how it is; this is my place in this organisation and so it always will be.' When that source of safety is removed, people must know that there is something else they can count on. Knowing that the leader is trustworthy and committed to both their interests and their individual development provides an alternative 'safety net', one based on something real rather than the illusion of an unchanging order.

AUTONOMY

Bayer has some thirty-two sites around the UK and Ireland, one being Stoke Court, formerly the home of William Penn's family and now the home of UK pharmaceutical research. It is also the international centre for Bayer's research on chronic obstructive pulmonary disease (COPD) headed by Sara Dodd. Her jeans, T-shirt and cloud of curls dispel any notion I have of a faceless clinical researcher. In the canteen, we talk about her work:

> The disease I work on is mainly associated with smoking, and I look at the damage that happens in the lungs. We are at the very start of the process, with people doing very basic research that will lead in fifteen to twenty years to a drug that will hopefully make a profit for Bayer, but it is a long way from where I am to where the profit starts to emerge. The company has to be prepared to take a long-term view. They do invest a lot in R&D, and I think they are one of the biggest investors in the pharmaceutical industry in terms of their R&D.

As Sara talks I have the impression that she works for a small company:

> There are only about fifty people in my department; a lot of us have been here for quite a long time, and our department has a pretty low turnover. Our boss has been working here for thirty-three years, so we are very much a family team. We have good community team spirit.

Although Sara looks like someone just out of college, she has a doctorate, has been with the company for over eleven years and has a role not only in research, but also in the wider company, having been voted by her colleagues to represent them on the Bayer UK forum, which meets regularly to look at issues of concern:

> I am in quite a privileged position because I can see the larger picture because I know there are other Bayer sites in the UK, but we all have similar problems and we all get together to try and solve them.

Of the department in which she works, she explains:

> We sort of manage ourselves; we're separate from the whole of Bayer in UK and Bayer in Germany. OK, we get targets set from Germany, but how we meet them is up to us and that tends to go down the hierarchy. We have a flattish structure that has been put in place in the last few years. . . . You do get a sense of empowerment because you almost control what you do; you have a lot of input into it, and by putting a lot in you get more out. Very satisfying.

Not all multinationals are places where one is an insignificant cog in a large machine:

> We do almost work as a little company of fifty. Our boss here sets the targets and tells us our goals for the year, but how we go about achieving them is up to us, as individuals and as small teams. If someone has an idea, it doesn't matter where they are in terms of experience or seniority, people tend to listen and they will give new things a try. A girl who works with me has been here about eighteen months. She's become involved in the process of putting forward new targets that will hopefully lead to new drugs. We need everyone's brain power, we respect everybody's views, and we listen to what everybody's got to say as far as possible.

Sara explains how they decide on targets:

> We all get involved; you have to read through the literature and come up with new ideas as a drug target, and then you read round it and make a proposal, how you would tackle it, its viability. The project gets marked against specific things, and then if we think it's viable in terms of profitability and time, we give it a go.

Developing drugs is often a high-risk area. Only a few projects will actually clear all the quality hurdles and ever see the purchasing light of day. There are certain criteria against which viability must be checked, and staff have to be constantly ready to let go of projects:

> If it is becoming clear that the project isn't going to meet the criteria, then the idea is to say stop this now and move onto something that is probably going to be better.

Among the obstacles to be overcome are ethical considerations:

> Our director could see that COPD was a good disease target to aim for. I think he felt some people might have some concerns because it is caused by smoking, and would it almost give people licence to smoke; but I never felt like that, and I don't know if anyone in the department did . . . Even if we look at people who smoke now, they have a good chance that they are going to get COPD, and then you can't just let them suffer because they smoked. Nobody back in the

233

sixties realised how addictive cigarettes were and how difficult it would be for people to stop smoking.

One of the other reasons for choosing this target is that the department has previously carried out research into asthma so has much experience to build on. This helps to ameliorate business concerns about profitability in a very competitive environment, but the company is still able to take on the unknown and work on areas that may not bear fruit:

> We are not in a situation where we're saying, we know this is going to work and we are only going to do things that we know are going to reach fruition.

The department is close-knit, people dependent on each other for support:

> There is good loyalty and we trust each other. People are very kind; when I had this illness in the family a few years ago, everybody was supportive. When another guy in our department was ill and spent a lot of time in hospital, everybody rallied round, visiting him at lunchtime and after work. You can really count on them.

Sometimes work can be difficult and disappointing: it may take weeks to get a tiny result; an achievement can evaporate as new data emerges; dead ends are rife. At such times moral support and other people's belief in you are vital:

> The people in this department are a great bunch. If you are having a hard time, they all tell you it will be OK and 'keep going', and they have a smile for you, and getting the little achievements out is satisfying. Little achievements mostly get recognised.

People are rewarded by being given the freedom to get on with the job, run with the project. But this requires a certain sort of person:

> Not many people are told what to do day to day, and when they recruit people they must bear this in mind. It needs to be somebody who can be self-sufficient and can get on with things without having to be closely supervised.

EVERYDAY PRACTICE

This willingness at all strata of the company to both give and take responsibility, to make decisions at an individual level, to realise that there will be mistakes and that these are acceptable, all these allow for autonomy within the many departments of Bayer UK. This way of working is vital to the ability of the company to respond with agility to change. In Sara's department much of the research is ground-breaking, so patterns of data are constantly reconfiguring, financial implications are constantly needing to be reassessed, the task evolves and the goalposts change. The response to this comes from thousands of daily decisions made by individuals, both junior and senior, who trust each other, and thus there is a degree of flexibility that a mechanistic, controlling organisation simply could not provide. Without this flexibility change would become disruptive, disturbing and stressful; with it, change becomes an enjoyable challenge.

THE SCIENTIST'S WINDING PATH

Sara's work as a scientist involves qualities of character that are particularly relevant to working with change and to working with soul. First, there is the question of patience and perseverance. As Sara points out, this sort of work is no good for someone who likes a quick result:

> I have been working on a project for over eighteen months and it is just coming to the point where we could perhaps go forwards. We have had a lot of problems, and as part of it I was trying to develop a test that was absolutely awful; it was probably the most arduous thing I have ever done here. It would take days to do the experiment and then it wasn't working, and it was almost soul-destroying. It was like, 'It isn't working; please can I stop now?' But from that I started working on other aspects, and now it is coming to its decision point.

Second, is the ability to achieve a balance between passionate commitment and calm detachment. Sara is the champion of her particular project, working tirelessly on it, encouraging her team and being

He who would do good to another, must do it in minute particulars. General good is the plea of the scoundrel, hypocrite and flatterer. For Art and Science cannot exist but in minutely organised particulars.

William Blake

● ●

committed to getting a result, but she also needs to be willing at any point along the road to let go of the work, with detachment:

> I had been working on another project for a couple of months getting nowhere, but along the path I was saying, 'Well this is working and that is working so perhaps the next step is . . .' But then the next step made it clear that we had got it wrong. So I made the decision to stop doing it. That is important too.

Sara recalls how she had worked on a cystic fibrosis project in which she was deeply involved both as a scientist and as an ordinary human being who cared about making a difference to this illness. As she was working on it, she found that:

> There was information coming from the literature that the target that we were on was not appropriate, and I was trying to purify a protein, which is a long process. But I said, 'What if we do this set of experiments to try and prove whether or not it is important, and then if it is not we can stop?' And that's what we did, and I did this set of experiments which showed that our target probably wasn't what was important for this particular project. In this case getting a negative result is good in itself. You have to be able to be detached from the project so that you can see that if it is not going well and you are not getting the results and the answers, then you stop it.

Given all these stillbirths, what keeps them going?

> What motivates me is getting the small achievements. If all that motivated you was getting that drug, you could easily be disappointed when most of what you work on never even gets anywhere near the patient. This year we aiming for twenty-two new targets,

and out of those one might go forward to clinical trials, so I could be working on one of those other twenty-one things. Therefore, I have to be satisfied that I have done a good experiment today and its's worked and I've got another step in my knowledge, and you have to have that sort of mentality to be able to do it.

Sara's work also takes her out of the laboratory, for example, to the international conferences where scientists, carers and sufferers pool their knowledge and stories. Sara knows all too well the urgency and implications of her work for people's lives. She summarises her work for me as a path:

> When I'm setting up new tests I'll sometimes have time pressures and it is a case of 'We need this new test doing but it is up to you how you do it' and you've got to try different things, and you might get straight to your end task, but otherwise you have to walk the winding path and try it one way . . . It doesn't work, OK I'll try this way or that or this . . . and that's how you learn and put things into place really.

Sara speaks as a scientist but what she describes is the way work is for very many of us who are caught up in life and therefore in change. There is no preset, clear path; all we can do is patiently, in good faith, keep trying one thing, checking it out, trying another, checking it out, and persisting until we get it right. It may then in time be changed again. This applies whether we are a manager, an administrative assistant, a warehouseman or a parent. We are all, if you like, much more part of an experiment than we might care to acknowledge. Sara's cheerful embrace of this reality would be a great example to offices where people moan and complain at every shift of the goalposts as if the shift were a personal attack.

COMPASSION

One of the hardest areas to consider when writing this book was that of redundancy and dealing with loss. Taking someone's livelihood from them is as fundamental as taking the land from a farmer; it relates to survival. Changes in economic circumstances, the loss of a customer the other side of the world, factors completely outside the control of the company will cause a sudden fall in income and require restructuring and possible job losses. Most of the companies in this book pride themselves on not enforcing compulsory redundancy, but with some large multinationals this becomes almost impossible to achieve.

Stephen Graves, managing director of Harmer and Reimer UK, a subsidiary of Bayer, speaks with quiet passion on this subject. It is the most difficult part of his job, and he undertakes it with a full awareness of what it means to individuals. He has a personal commitment to each person getting through it with his or her dignity and self-esteem as far as possible intact:

> In business there are a lot of tough decisions you have to make. For me it's very much a case of not ducking away from those tough decisions, especially if people's jobs are involved, but I believe that whatever you do you should try to maintain that person's dignity; so the way you break bad news to people has to be done in a way that you don't undermine that dignity.

Stephen is aware that individuals react in their own way to the news of losing their job:

> All the training you might have as managers . . . there is no one way, you can never have a preconceived view on how any individual will react to that news.

He meets the individuals concerned, gives them information, explaining the reasons behind it and the business decision that has been

. . . .

It is easy – terribly easy – to shake a man's (sic) faith in himself. To take advantage of that to break a man's spirit is devil's work.

George Bernard Shaw

made, and sets out to help them see that this does not reflect badly on them. Stephen is also concerned to reassure them about practicalities:

> The company has always had a good social plan for people affected in that way, so the financial packages offered to people go some way to softening the news, but they are still in a state of shock and you have to be very understanding and sympathetic to that while pressing and repeating that this is not based on a decision that has been made individually. It's important that they are left with the feeling that they are not culpable for that decision, and if you do that and you can convince them of that, at least they know that they have done their best and that it is other people who have taken a decision to do the structure in a certain way; so it doesn't undermine their spirit and their confidence.

To some, of course, no redundancy will be acceptable.

There are many stories of companies in which redundancies have been dealt with in inhumane and unfair ways, and these have left scars. When redundancies are made the whole body of the company reverberates to some degree with them. The reverberation can be one of shock, distaste and mistrust or it can be one where there is shock but also compassion, trust and respect for the leadership, as in the case of Bayer and Harmer and Reimer.

During the writing of this book, I took a walk past a waterfall in a local beauty spot. Perched on the edge of a rock high above the crashing water and boulders was a man shaking with distress and about to jump in a suicide attempt. When I tried to approach him, he sobbed about the job he had lost and of how he had let his wife and children down by losing his job. In his feelings of guilt and hopelessness and despair he will not have been unique. We do not have the figures of how many people destroy themselves through suicide, alcoholism and illness as a result of how redundancies are dealt with. Nor do we know the full extent of the misery that extends to their families. I do not know what has become of this despairing man. A number of us waited with him for an hour or so in the steadily falling rain, approaching him gingerly, talking and listening to him, and desperately hoping he would find some thread to pull him back. He did not kill himself that day.

EVERYDAY PRACTICE

239

EVERYDAY PRACTICE

Redundancy, crushing though it is, need not be this destroying, terrible experience. Stephen in no way underestimates its potential to hurt, but he takes care and time to make sure that he gives people the emotional and practical care and space that they need to come through in one piece, able to go forwards.

Stephen is a business man who is very aware of the economic forces at work in his industry:

> What I have brought to the company is a greater commercial awareness that we have consistently to prove ourselves as a company in order to keep our security and the security of everyone around us. I've brought a harder-nosed edge to the reality of business, which was needed if we are really to compete against the sorts of company I have worked for in the past, companies where there was no soul. In those companies everything was geared to winning; people were very highly rewarded if they were successful, and the people who weren't were got rid of. Here we were the other way – the company was very much concerned for the individual irrespective of results. I have made people aware that we need to help each other if we want to keep our job security – there is no such thing as a benevolent father any more.

Stephen speaks of the radical changes that have happened over the past two decades in his industry, of the erosion of security and stability. He wonders whether companies still have the right to expect the loyalty of people when they can no longer guarantee long-term employment:

> You really have to go the extra mile to make people feel wanted while they're here with you. If you don't have that and they also feel unsettled and insecure, then what is there . . . ?

He imagines a future in which people don't actually work for companies; instead there are individual contracts, and people hire themselves out to individual organisations for short-term payment:

> And then the whole soul or spirit of a company will no longer exist

because you will be employing dozens of contractual people paid by the hour.

Bayer has many invisible bonds with those who work there, and to the subsidiaries within it. There are contracts and benefits, but there is something more than that: an unreasonable and unfashionable insistence that, even in this day of ruthless shareholder value, when capital moves at a whim, a company can still be a family and people can have practical compassion for each other.

The rate of change has set enormous waves of insecurity in people's lives and these lead to hidden stress and distress that undermine people's ability to live and work in peace. When a company takes this on board seriously, faces up to the pain of redundancies and refuses to farm out to anonymous consultancies the work of laying people off, the surgery to the corporate body can be clean and careful, and some of the fear and mistrust is removed.

CULTURES AND SUBCULTURES

There are four pillars to Bayer, each of which is quite different. One reason why Lennart was happy to stay for forty years in one company was the variety he encountered: working with people in agrochemicals was very different from working with those in pharmaceuticals, for example. Part of Bayer's work concerns the mass production of commodities in vast factories, with millions of tons of resin being taken out in tankers; part is supplying raw materials; part is rarefied research that never sees the light of day. Some work relates to selling plant food, some is veterinary work, and some is about developing unique perfumes. Stephen captures this plurality well. He describes his company, Harmer and Reimer UK, a fragrance and flavourings house that is a subsidiary of Bayer:

> Our business is a very creative business – it's not a commodity. We are selling one product to one customer, which is a very particular approach. As a consequence the people whom you employ as your

EVERYDAY PRACTICE

creative people, flavourists or perfumers would never find themselves working in Bayer itself, which is a much more conventional
company. Ours is a much more artistic feel so you attract a very different person.

This has consequences for the style of management and the sensitivity that is needed. Stephen describes to me the process whereby a perfumer takes a blank canvas and creates a unique perfume:

When you are dealing with perfumers who are artists in their own
right, they can be quite emotional as people. You cannot manage
perfumers in the same way that you manage a salesman. The
approach needed doesn't conform to the laid-down guidelines. You
manage that person within a certain framework, but you have to
make certain allowances in dealing with people who, if the creative
juices are not flowing, may get up, leave the building and disappear
over Marlow bridge for three hours.

In a normal set-up this would not be acceptable, but within the fragrance industry it is necessary. The perfumer will come back, his or
her thoughts clear, and be able to produce what is needed, working
until 10 at night if the creativity is flowing.

Bayer is complex with subsidiaries that are themselves part of
multinationals that have their own distinctive cultures:

We have got a culture working within a culture, and how you blend
these two together requires balance. You have the bureaucracy of a
very structured company, and you have that other aspect where you
have to give freedom and flexibility to people in order for them to

● ● ● ● ● ● ● ● ● ● ● ●

*If one advances confidently in the direction of his
dreams, and endeavours to live the life which he has
imagined, he will meet with a success unexpected in
common hours.*

Henry David Thoreau

achieve their objective. As MD I have to balance my duty to reflect the company culture guidelines and stay within the rules but also recognise that you mustn't stifle the creativity. Once you stifle that, you lose the essence of what will make you successful, which is what all the board and the shareholders are interested in – the results of the company.

The money markets are fickle, and countless other factors affect an organisation the size of Bayer, many of these being outside the company's control. What it can control, however, is the way it responds, by paying close attention to its own unique culture. At Bayer UK/Ireland there is a recognition of the value of the culture of the company and that of the subsidiaries. When a company loses sight of its culture, it loses many of its soul qualities – loyalty, community, belonging, service – and without these the company becomes a sterile machine.

THE LONG TERM AND THE BIG PICTURE

Bayer has grown over nearly 140 years, during which it has gone through devastating changes. Its ability to ride these changes has depended largely on its willingness to look at and invest in the long term, to see the big picture. The current fashion and pressure is to break a large company up and realise the shareholder value, but at Bayer the leadership attempted to remain one company, one family, with internal diversity, even if this went against shareholders' short-term gains. This is a battle that changes weekly.

The price of company culture is impossible to gauge, and in the short term many 'savings' can be made by ignoring the culture of care. Conversations can be more abrupt, people's needs and idiosyncrasies can be bypassed, older people can be made redundant, research can be tailored to the market money-makers, marketing ploys can increase sales, contracts can be shaved to a minimum, the daily watering of the abundant real plants at headquarters can be replaced with a quarterly dusting down of plastic ones. But in the process, something indefinable and elusive is lost. The current culture of Bayer has been built up through millions of encounters and decisions, many of which demonstrate care for people as a priority. This culture is an investment made with a view to the long-term needs of people and the environment in the twenty-first century.

BAYER WORKS WITH CHANGE BY:

- Building its foundation on strong, long-standing relationships
- Developing a sense of family, community and interdependence
- Pacing itself, taking time for careful decision-making and time for people
- Developing open, honest communication
- Treating all with equal respect and involving all in responding to change
- Developing each individual so that they are equipped for change
- Having strong leadership that is trusted and in touch with the grass roots
- Fostering autonomy
- Encouraging patience and perseverance, passion and detachment
- Practising compassion when change is painful
- Honouring its culture and subcultures
- Building in flexibility based on trust

PUTTING THIS INTO PRACTICE
IN YOUR WORKPLACE

AN ACTIVITY TO DO AS A TEAM

The purpose of this activity is to gain an awareness of the breadth of change over the past fifteen years, to see how changes in one's own life are part of the larger picture.

Recognising change activity

1 Consider change from the social, technical, environmental and political perspectives. Choose one perspective to focus on and join with others in a small group to explore recent changes that have occurred in this area by comparing life fifteen, ten and five years ago and now.

2 Divide an A1 sheet of paper into four to identify these changes in whatever way you wish – words, diagrams, pictures.

3 Present your findings to the rest of the group and listen to their findings from the other perspectives. A general discussion will provide you with opportunity to explore change further and see how multifaceted it has been.

4 Reflect on changes in your work and how these relate to the global changes you have identified.

5 Identify the positive changes that have occurred in your work over the past fifteen years. Focus on the gains.

6 Reflect individually on how you as a group contribute to that positive change and share your thoughts in groups of three. Feed back to the whole group.

245

7 Acknowledge the individuals who contribute to that positive change.

AN ACTIVITY TO DO AS A LONE INDIVIDUAL
WITH 'NO POWER'

The purpose of the activity is to help you to recognise the amount of change that has happened and is likely to happen in your life and to reflect on how you respond to change, especially that happening currently at work.

Five years ago

1 Think back to five years ago. Take a blank piece of paper and write down what you were doing in your life then.

- Where were you?
- Who were the people in your life then?
- What was your main concern? What were your hopes?
- Where did you then think you would be in five years' time?
- What changes have happened over those five years?
- What is no longer in your life?
- Who and what has come into your life that was not there before?
- Could you have anticipated this? What have been the surprises?

2 Reflect on your answers. Note how you tend to react to change.
3 Consider a change that is happening currently at work. How have you been reacting to it? What three positive qualities do you bring to situations of change?

CHAPTER 10

THE CHIEF CHARACTERISTICS OF SOUL-FRIENDLY COMPANIES

E ACH OF THESE COMPANIES has its own distinctive character and
personality. You will not be able to replicate these, nor would
you want to, as your company has its own character and will
develop in a way unique to its own soul. There are, however, eight
characteristics to be found in all these companies, and these are helpful when looking at your own workplace.

EIGHT CHARACTERISTICS

Leadership

The companies described in this book have a particular style of leadership in which there is a paradox: the leader leads with considerable
authority but also hands the leadership over to others within the
company. The leader enjoys people and instinctively serves them,
deriving great pleasure from helping people grow. This style of leadership has a contagious quality, infecting the people who work there
so that they in turn develop into leaders who become involved with
people and help their colleagues to grow. Instead of seeking success
for themselves, each comes to work committed to others' success, so
each succeeds through helping and being helped. In the process they
feel cared for, supported, appreciated and fulfilled.

The leaders at all levels of the organisation practise a beautiful humility. They do much listening; they are often in the background; they are often away from their desks and are in there alongside people, listening, helping. They are not full of themselves, on the contrary they are convinced that they are quite ordinary people, just doing what comes naturally to them. In reality, however, they are extraordinary, but their humility enables them to work with lack of ego or image, with no need to defend or guard themselves, and so they have a freedom to be fully human. They are servant-leaders.

The least important is the most important
These companies recognise that if the bottom of the ladder is not sound and firmly rooted on the ground, the whole ladder wobbles. They therefore place great value on those who have traditionally seemed to be at the bottom of the ladder – the factory operative, the receptionist, the odd-job man. These people are pivotal to success. If customers arrive in your car park and step into a pile of rubbish, or if they walk through the door and are greeted by a careless, indifferent receptionist, too busy to even see them, then the possibility of magnificence is immediately seriously jeopardised. If the fine-quality service you want to give a customer in terms of a product has been botched by the factory operative, or if the letter you sent has been left crumpled by the postman in the mailroom, you are bound to fail. If your customer's strategy depends on sound software for the next three years, yet your new programmer knows that the fundamental error in front of her will not come to light for at least two years and that speed is all that management wants now, your customer service will fail in the long run.

Those people who appear marginal are central to the success of any operation, and these companies instinctively know that. They appreciate these people and give them the freedom to turn their work into the fine art that it is.

Balance

These companies recognise that no one person or one style is suffi- cient to meet the task. Therefore they tend to welcome a mix of personalities and experience, old and young, women and men, black and white, able-bodied and disabled. The masculine qualities in the company are equally balanced by the feminine qualities. Women are very highly respected and powerful, and the old macho culture of thrust, clumsy competitiveness and the strutting ego is not to be found. There are plenty of strong men in these companies, but they have an inner strength based on authority rather than an outer strength based on fear. As a result of this balance, compassion and canniness go hand in hand.

Financial targets

These companies have clear financial targets with regular milestones and monitoring processes along the way. There is nothing soft and fluffy about their rigorous financial management and commitment to financial success.

A greater purpose

The companies I have described know that there is more to life than meets the eye, that just making shareholder profit is really not enough and that the old-fashioned habit of wanting the greater good is necessary. They practise the virtues of generosity, compassion, doing the right thing and caring about the wider community and the world in which they live and work. Being able to sleep at night is important to them, working with decent people for something that is worthwhile essential.

The intangibles

These companies place value not only on the bottom line. They also place great value on the intangibles such as culture, a sense of community and team spirit. And they *work* on them and invest in them. Courage, risk, trust, patience, integrity, loyalty and happiness all carry

249

great weight. Words such as 'soul' and 'spirit' are not meaningless here; they may not be defined but they have a place. And whether it is recognised or not, there is tremendous personal vulnerability in these companies, individuals being prepared to stand up for what they believe to be right, to experiment with no guarantee of success, to dare to work with vision and step into the unknown, to rest their feet on the intangibles and fly. Language is itself seen as something powerful, the words used in these companies being clear of clutter, pretence or victim talk. Perception that precedes language is understood to be of the highest importance, and attitudes are what they look for when recruiting.

The intangibles are the stuff out of which the products, the processes and the profits grow. These companies recognise this and take great practical care of the intangibles.

The small detail and the larger picture

Attention is paid to physical detail as the sacred is in the everyday, in the small things that show mindfulness: the colour of the rooms, the paintings by a local artist, the imaginative toilets, the inspirational quotes on the walls, the plants, the calendar of multicultural festivals, the fruit juice, the water, the recycling boxes, the lighting. This thoughtfulness over details takes care of people's physical needs and leaves them free to take care of each other, the customers and their work.

But these companies also see the larger picture. They are not alarmed by short-term changes. They do not respond reactively but have a vision of where they are going and work with the long term in mind.

Agape

Although few of them would use this word – the Greek for 'love' – this is what these companies do: they love where they are, they love what they are doing, they love those whom they are with. They have clear financial goals, sound relationships, and the rest follows.

CHAPTER 11

WHAT NEXT?:

A 21-DAY PROGRAMME, TOOLS AND A QUESTIONNAIRE

A 21-DAY PROGRAMME

WE HAVE LOOKED AT SEVEN soul-friendly companies that know how to make money without destroying the soul. But what about your company? What can you do to make sure that your company has soul as well as profits? Are there changes that you can bring about?

There are many paradoxes surrounding spirit, one of which is that change can happen in the twinkling of an eye, and that change takes an entire lifetime. Tiny things that you could do tomorrow could change how you experience your company forever, and it will take a lifetime to master those changes.

The culture of a company is a complex and subtle web that holds the organisation together so it must not be tampered with lightly. It is no good tinkering without recognising the knock-on effect on the entire system, and outsiders should tread with great respect. If the culture of a company is to change, it must occur from the inside; it must evolve from what is already there, the people, their hopes, their abilities, their values and visions. It is an inside job, and it may well require an outsider to act as a catalyst for and midwife to the change.

In this chapter I suggest a twenty-one day programme of activities that will begin to change your experience of work. If you are the managing director or financial director, you hold enormous power and will be able to shape the culture of your company. If you do not have that 'power', you still play a crucial role in your organisation and hold power, but you will not be able to change the culture alone. If you try to do so you are likely to get hurt as you push up against resistant forces. What you can do, however, is to begin to bring soul qualities into your own work and that of those colleagues nearest to you. You will then become an inspiring leader whatever your position in the company. If you look back over the pages of this book, you will see that the leaders are at times the sixteen-year-old factory hand, the odd-job man, the receptionist, the telesales assistant, the multinational managing director. They are simply the people who make a difference in the lives of those around them; without thinking about it, they make space for soul.

You can do the first two weeks of the following programme on your own, but it will be more effective if undertaken with someone else so that you can encourage each other. Start on a Monday.

WEEK 1: GETTING STARTED

Day 1: The here and now; taking stock

The purpose of today's exercise is to find out where you are right now at work. It is rather like a dipstick. You are using it to take a measure of your thoughts and feelings about your workplace.

Choose an empty book to serve as a journal for the next three weeks. No one else will see what you write in here – it is your own private space. You can do whatever you like here, so be uncensored, and you can visit it whenever you like.

> Start the journal by writing down the date. Then write down your thoughts and feelings about your workplace now. What is the main issue facing you, and what are your feelings towards it? Put the journal in a safe place.

You will return to this first entry at the end of the three weeks so that you can determine what changes have happened over that time.

Day 2: Be still

The purpose of today's exercise is to begin to use silence and to tap into the power that lies within silence.

Before you go to work today, take five minutes to sit quietly. Make yourself comfortable with your back straight. Become very still, empty and quiet. Become aware of your breath. Then use this simple meditation of Zen Buddhist master Thich Nhat Hanh:

In Out
Deep Slow
Calm Ease
Smile Release
Present Moment
Wonderful Moment

On the first word of each line breathe in, and on the second gently breathe out. Allow your body and mind to become still and calm, and be aware of your breath and the word in your mind. Repeat the meditation over the five minutes.

At your next meeting at work today, quietly, and without anyone noticing, do this same meditation once. This will take but a few unseen moments as papers are being shuffled and latecomers are arriving, and it will enable you to approach the meeting with a clear and calm mind.

Day 3: Values and visions

The purpose of today's exercise is to find out what really matters to you more than anything else in the world, what your core values are, your highest vision. These will then serve as the prism through which you can pass the daily tasks that face you.

Sit quietly and take a moment to sense the stillness and get in touch with your breath, perhaps using yesterday's meditation. Then imagine the doctor tells you today that you have a serious illness and only twelve months to live. Once you have absorbed that, allow yourself to get in touch with what you want to accomplish in that year. What is it you want to do before you die? Jot these insights down in your journal.

If your first reaction is, 'Well, I'd leave work', you have found out something important – things must change. But now imagine that, because you will need to support those you love, you will stay at work over the twelve months before your death. What will you want to have accomplished at work over that period? Jot your thoughts down in your journal.

Now change the scenario and imagine that you are strong and powerful and in fact have plenty of years of life ahead of you. What is your highest vision? What would you really love to accomplish if you were free to do whatever you wanted? Jot this down in your journal.

Day 4: The hero

The purpose of this activity is to find the qualities of a human being that matter most to you.

Allow to come into your mind a hero, someone you really admire, and write down all the adjectives that describe this person. Carry this person around with you at the back of your mind today at work and at times see your workplace through your hero's eyes and ears.

Day 5: Review and examen of consciousness

The purpose of today's exercise is to review how things are going and learn a powerful technique for raising awareness. This is drawn from the Ignation tradition and has been used for hundreds of years. I have adapted it slightly from its traditional form.

At the top of a page in your journal write 'Examen of Consciousness' and put the dates from day 1 until today. Draw a diagonal line from the top to the bottom of the page. Enjoy a few moments stillness and then note down any of the highs and lows of this past week, placing the lows below the line and highs above. Below the line come the moments of irritation, disappointment, unease and annoyance, the negatives. Above the line are the moments that bring a smile to your face or a sense of satisfaction to your heart. Together these make up a whole. There is no right or wrong to it; it is simply that there are in one's life areas of 'consolation', a sense of well-being, and areas of 'desolation', where something needs to be learnt, understood or released. If you spend ten minutes each day on this reflection you will begin to develop an awareness of where you find peace in your life and where you need to tackle some issues.

When you have completed the exercise turn the page and write down 'What I have learnt', jotting down any insights that you have had over the course of the week.

What do you intend to do differently as a result of that learning?

Over the weekend

Go for a long walk. Recall a time when you were really happy at work and you were working at your very best. What were the elements of the situation? What was really going on?

WEEK 2: BEGINNING TO CREATE YOUR VISION

This week will explore beginning to change your experience of your workplace by bringing into it your values, your vision, listening, thankfulness, inspiration and risk.

Day 1: Visioning

The purpose of today's exercise is to set out on this week with a clear sense of where you are going in terms of your values and vision.

Think of the week ahead. Picture it in your mind's eye as an open space into which you can put what you choose. Then project yourself to the end of the week. What will you have accomplished by then? What is your vision for the week? What are the values that you want to use through the week? Write down in your journal your priorities, your vision in a nutshell and the values you want to see at play this week.

Now turn back to the passage you wrote about the hero and read the adjectives you listed. Each of the qualities that you see in your hero are in fact qualities you have to some extent yourself. Preface each adjective with 'I am . . .', and recognise that these qualities are part of you. This is likely to feel uncomfortable but do it anyway.

Day 2: Listening

The purpose of today's exercise is to begin to develop your listening skills.

> For one minute become aware of all the sounds around you: the sound of a car, a bird, a radiator, a voice, your stomach rumbling or maybe just silence. Simply listen and become aware of these sounds.
>
> Now consider how good a listener you are. Really good listeners simply listen actively with all of themselves; the inner voice that is thinking of a reply is silenced, the thoughts flashing back to one's own life are laid aside. In everyday life there are many opportunities for active listening, but there are also many road blocks (Figure 3). Ring any five road blocks that you have used this week.
>
> At work today really practise listening during one conversation. It may feel uncomfortable at first; it is very threatening for the ego to really listen, but persist and practise.

This skill of listening is the core skill for soul-friendly workplaces. It will on its own transform any work environment.

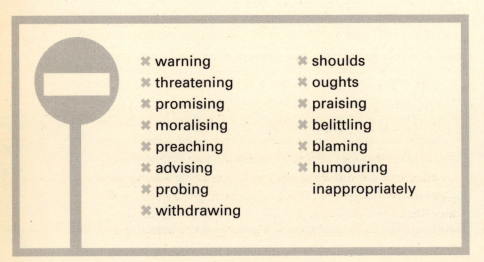

* warning
* threatening
* promising
* moralising
* preaching
* advising
* probing
* withdrawing

* shoulds
* oughts
* praising
* belittling
* blaming
* humouring
inappropriately

Figure 3 Road blocks to achieve listening

Day 3: Thanks

The purpose of today's exercise is to bring more thankfulness into your workplace.

> Think of ten colleagues (fingers are useful here). As each comes to mind, identify a quality you appreciate in them; think of something they have done for you or the company, and in your mind thank them for it.
>
> Now mentally scan your actual workplace. What is there that you can be thankful for? Think of someone at work who has really helped you over the past few weeks and find a way today to thank them for the difference they have made to you.

Day 4: Lifeline

The purpose of today's activity is to find the sources of inspiration in your life.

> Draw a line across a double-page spread your journal. Put the date you were born at the far left and the current year at the far right. This line represents your life. Place on it chronologically the people, the books, the ideas that have affected you and made a difference in your life. When you have completed this, sit quietly and see what strikes you about it. Then, when you are ready, write down:
>
> • What you have learnt from the exercise.
> • Its implications for your work. What do you intend to do in the light of it?

Day 5: Review and risk

The purpose of today's exercise is to continue to practise reflection and review. It also introduces the idea of risk-taking.

> Do this exercise in the morning. As at the end of last week, carry out an examen of consciousness, drawing a diagonal line across the page and reviewing your week so far, both the negative and the positive. Then note down what you have so far learnt from this week. What do you intend to do differently in the light of that learning?
>
> Look back to Monday and the values and vision that you set out with. Have you used the values and reached the vision? You have

one day left now in front of you. How can you use it to reach your vision? Now be prepared to take a risk. Any day on which you play safe and take no risks is a day when you are not stretching your limits and are needlessly restricting yourself. What could help you either move towards your vision or strengthen it? Take a risk in order to do this. (Make sure, however, that it is not a risk that will jeopardise anyone other than yourself.)

Risks are delicious; they are why people climb mountains, swim oceans and create all that is new. A day lived without risk is like a plate of potatoes without salt. Risk involves discernment, demanding that you judge the appropriateness of your action, courage to step into the unknown, and trust to accept that whatever the outcome, you will handle it. Use these qualities of discernment, courage and trust today at work, and take a risk.

Over the weekend

Go for a long walk and ponder your last two weeks at work. What do you appreciate about your workplace? Recall all the positive experiences that your work has given you, the relationships, the insights, the skills, the experience, the income, the benefits and the challenges.

WEEK 3: CHOICE AND COMMITMENT

As human beings, we are not made to be alone. We need each other, and the quality of our relationships affects every aspect of our work. You will need someone to help you with this week's exercises.

Day 1: Have to and choose to

The purpose of this exercise is to get in touch with our freedom, our power to choose. It also begins to raise an awareness of the effect of the language that we use. Have your friend or colleague help you with this exercise at the end of the day, shortly before you go home.

One of you is A and one B. A starts talking, and B listens without interruption. A verbally lists each and every tiny thing he or she has to do in order to get home and to bed, prefacing each action with 'I have to . . .'. So, for example, 'I have to go out of the door. I have to go down to the car park. I have to turn the key in the car lock. I have to . . .'. Go through each step until you turn off the light to go to bed. B simply listens. After two minutes A runs through the same scenario again but prefaces each action with 'I choose to . . .'. Then reverse roles and B talks and A listens.

Notice what it felt like as the speaker. What was the difference in energy when it felt as though each action were compelled rather than the result of choice? What did it feel like as the listener? What was the difference between hearing the tale of compulsion and hearing that of free choice?

Talk over the experience with your partner. What have you learnt from it?

Day 2: Free-writing and issues

This exercise, which the writer Julie Cameron describes as 'morning pages', is a way of unravelling an issue and gaining insight and clarity. It is based on the premise that if we look within ourselves, we will find the answers that we need. Give yourself about forty-five minutes for this exercise.

Sit quietly for a moment and then set out with the intention of gaining some insight into a work issue that you have chosen. Write in your journal the equivalent of three sides of A4 paper on the issue. Write without pausing and without reflection. Simply write whatever comes into your head, your thoughts, feelings, questions. Write fast so that your writing catches up with your thoughts, use abbreviations if you need to. If you get stuck, write about being stuck and then return to the issue. Do not stop and do not censor. This exercise is not about writing fine prose but about uncovering in the course of your writing what you know inside yourself.

The first two and half pages may well feel like drivel; do not be discouraged but continue until all three pages have been covered. The last few lines usually hold what you are looking for.

What have you learnt?

Day 3: Discernment

We are constantly inundated with decisions to be made. The exercise today aims, by drawing on your inner wisdom, to help you to develop your discernment so that you can ensure your choices are based on your values and vision rather than on short-term expediency.

Copy the chart below into your journal. Think of a choice that you are going to make, for example whether to take a new position in the company. Sit quietly and become still. Then hold the choice in your mind. Brainstorm all the pluses and then all the minuses of choosing to take the new position. Then brainstorm all the pluses and minuses of not taking it. Now sit quietly again before reviewing your brainstorms. What strikes you about what you have written? Are you surprised by the 'result'?

If I do take the new position		If I don't take the new position	
The pluses	*The minuses*	*The pluses*	*The minuses*

Day 4: Strategising

The purpose of today's exercise is to begin to think through how to get a result that you want at work. You will need a partner for this exercise.

Decide what it is that you want to make happen at work. One of you is A and one B. A will ask B the questions in Figure 4, listen to the answers and jot down the essence of the replies. B will simply reply to the questions. When you have completed the sheet of strategising questions, swap roles.

How do you make your choices?

Putting aside all modesty, what have you achieved so far in this area?

What particular strengths do you have?
What particular abilities do you have?
What particular talents do you have?

What have you tried that has worked?
What have you tried that didn't work?
What does this teach you?

What circles do you move in? Who are the people you can most easily reach? Is this really where you want to be?

What are the major things holding you back?

What is the next challenge for you?

Who will support you?
Who understands you?
Who will work with you?

Where do you choose to put your energy?
What aspects in this area do you want to work out?

What can you do if you get stuck?

In your personal development, is there one thing that you could do that would make the rest easier to do?

What goals can you set that are manageable, that will help you get a sense of what you are achieving as time goes by?

What are your next steps?

Figure 4 Some questions to help you strategise

Day 5: Review

The purpose of today is to review where you have reached.

> Find a quiet place and take ten minutes to write down your thoughts and feelings about your workplace. Then do an examen of consciousness for yesterday at work.
>
> Go back to the entry that you made in the journal on day 1 and see whether there is any change in how you experience your workplace and your colleagues. Note down any changes that have taken place.
>
> Scan through the exercises that you have completed over the past three weeks.

- Which of them did you find useful?
- What have you learnt?
- What do you intend to do in the light of the learning?

Over the weekend

Take a good long walk and let your workplace come with you. Decide on the best contribution that you can make and the contribution that you *want* to make. Who at work can support you in this?

And now . . .

Over the next few weeks begin to vision, to listen, to reflect, to take time for stillness, to discern, to take risks, to journal, to thank people, to use courage, to trust and to have fun.

TOOLS OF REFLECTION

A twenty-one day programme will not fix your workplace. Practice is needed if change is to be sustained, and spiritual traditions provide some very specific tools to help develop that practice. The overall purpose of these is transformation, the route being through reflection on our experience. By such reflection we understand and integrate our experience into ourselves.

Spiritual traditions have many tools for the task, some of the best known of which are prayer, pilgrimage, walking and almsgiving. I have, however, chosen, eight tools that are particularly relevant for today's secular society. I have used these with groups over the past twenty years and have seen countless people transform themselves and their organisations with them.

- Stillness
- Listening
- Story
- Encounter
- Celebration
- Grieving
- Visioning
- Journalling

Stillness

This is the first and most essential of tools as it takes one to the source. Stillness is the place where our own busyness, preoccupations and prattle stop and the source of our being starts. It is from here that all deep creativity springs. A musician about to play will first seek and reach into stillness and silence; a dancer about to fill the stage with movement will start by getting in touch with complete stillness. If we want our work to carry unquantifiable worth, we must learn to know stillness and use it regularly. The Eastern traditions all emphasise this tool and train it through meditation. In the Western world, it is the basis of Quaker tradition. In secular society we know that when we are stunned, for example at Dunblane or the attacks on the World Trade Centre on 11 September 2001, then we as one people call for silence.

How to apply stillness:
- When you arrive at work take a minute simply to be still and silent.
- Throughout the day take time to look out of the window and empty your mind.
- Before a meeting invite everyone to be still for a minute of peace and quiet.

Listening

Listening is a skill that few have mastered. To really listen to someone we need to lay aside our mind's internal chatter with its urge to hold opinions, give advice, make comparisons, anticipate and interrupt. Ignoring this requires a high degree of discipline. Our ego rebels and wants to listen to itself rather than another. When we listen we may hear things that do not fit into our tidy little world; something that contradicts a dearly held belief, something that makes no sense, something that challenges and overturns our prejudices. This sort of listening requires openness, humility and a degree of courage. All spiritual traditions invite people to listen, to hear in this way.

Apart from listening to others, we also need to listen to the voice within ourselves. When we are quiet and still and listen carefully, we have the possibility of doing this. Some call this their intuition or their conscience; others call it their gut feeling. Spiritual traditions recognise this as a sacred voice and a source of wisdom.

All the managing directors and leaders of the companies we have met in this book are exceptional listeners. They spend part of their day walking around, being available to listen to people. As a result they are able to base their decisions on people's lived experience.

How to apply listening:

- At your next team meeting listen to your colleagues. Pay complete attention to them, looking at them, listening to them and hearing what lies behind their words, what it is they are really trying to say.
- Next time you are in a one-to-one conversation listen carefully; when the other person finishes speaking, remain silent and leave them space to go on speaking when they are ready. Do not fill the gap.

Story

Every spiritual tradition relies on story to communicate what is incomprehensible to the rational mind but is required by the full human mind. Stories help us to make sense of experience. They imbue what appears to be random data with meaning and sequence.

Stories are the carriers of concepts that attract us yet elude us, the intangibles. For well over two and a half thousand years, for example, millions upon millions have told and retold the story of Passover to somehow share the human longing for freedom and justice.

In the companies I visited people communicated what the company was really about through stories. Stories go beyond opinions, beliefs and dogmas, reaching into that part of us that other human faculties cannot touch. Stories communicate those aspects of life that cannot be captured in any other way apart from art. In these companies people touch on the intangibles through telling stories. This is how we learn to make sense of the chaos and awesome enormity of life; they help us to bring together into the present, the past and the future.

How to apply story:
- Go for a walk and tell yourself the story of your life in the company – how you began, where you are now, how you got there, where the future may lie.
- Next time a colleague starts to tell you a story, listen carefully to where his or her story is leading.

Encounter

Encounter is about relationships; it happens when the barriers around us drop away and we are able to become permeable – open to giving of ourselves and receiving from another. Encounter is the basis of meaningful relationships. There is an exchange whereby something of someone else flows into me and vice versa.

When people are very damaged and are suffering unresolved trauma, they may perhaps protect themselves from further hurt by placing a barrier between themselves and others; they may thus be unable to encounter others unless they receive help. We perhaps must not venture to intrude here. If, however, people are basically emotionally healthy, we can enter into an encounter with them. When we do so we run the risk of being changed, of never being the same again. We receive from the other person an insight, a glimpse of life, a story that irrevocably reaches into our mind; then how we see the world is changed. This may be a tiny imperceptible shift, but the encounter has changed our perception forever.

In all these companies I visited there were people who were able and willing to encounter others. This quality of relationship transforms an organisation; empathy, growth, insight, compassion and a tremendous amount of learning spring from this capacity to encounter another.

How to apply encounter:
• When you are next with someone at work, be prepared to be open.

Celebration

I have been told that people in Central America who have been forced off their land, attacked, terrorised and made refugees appoint a committee for celebration as soon as they have set up a refugee camp. They know that, without celebration, they lose hope and that without hope all is lost. In celebration three ingredients come together – the past, the present and the future. People stand firmly in the present, recall the past and now turn to look to the future. All spiritual traditions place great emphasis on our human need for celebration, to eat and drink together, to recall past times and to commit ourselves to the future with others. These traditions also urge people to give thanks and to express joy.

Celebration in our materialistic culture is often but a shadow of its real self, an embarrassing mockery of the real thing. Celebration should be far more than going to a smoky pub for some mass-produced food and some alcohol.

In the companies in this book celebration is there on a daily basis. It is sometimes planned, often spontaneous, but nearly always exuberant and joyful. It overflows and is heart-warming. It may be seen in home-baked cakes for people's birthdays, flowers to congratulate work achievements, cards of thanks, jumping with joy when an award comes in, stopping work just to be happy together when the project is achieved. At least one of the companies throws a party at which the business plan is presented creatively and playfully, people celebrating the plan and their part in it. There is gratitude, thankfulness and a sense of blessing; no one takes it for granted.

How to apply celebration:
- Next time a colleague achieves something, send them a card to congratulate them.
- Next time someone helps you, get them some flowers as a thank-you.
- When you present your business plan, turn it into a party. Look back over the past year, see where you are now and then celebrate where you are going.

Grieving

Being human involves us in suffering and loss. We age, we get ill, we eventually lose those we love, and we die. On the way we fail to get promotions, we lose dreams, we have countless small pains and disappointments. As long as we fail to acknowledge these, they stay inside us and are an unseen burden. A barrier may then grow up between ourselves and those who do not know our grief. Soul-friendly companies know how to grieve, not to wallow but to face up to hurts and express them, listen to them and share them. They know how to cry and to weep, how to comfort and console each other. Having done so, they are then free to get back into the fun and energy of living.

Each of the companies described has a willingness to share appropriately and caringly the difficulties that people experience within their professional and personal lives.

How to apply grieving:
- Make time just to be with people and listen.
- Next time something in life knocks you off centre, have the courage to share what you feel with a colleague. Do not shrug it off as though it were nothing.

267

Visioning

Visioning is a skill that some naturally have and that others need to learn to develop. It is the ability to feel the future as though it were now, to picture the future, to use that vision to create the future that might otherwise never exist. Visioning does not need to be grand. It can occur in the way in which you approach any day, meeting or piece of work; picture what it will be like by the end. A vision might also be enormous: several of the leaders we have encountered have vast vision.

Philip, a senior manager in IMG's warehousing company, goes into the warehouse each morning before anyone arrives. He senses the air, cool before the bustle of the day, and in his mind's eye gently runs through all that is likely to happen that day, what will be shifting in, what out, who will be involved. He walks through the warehouse, scans the shelves and pictures the people involved. At the end of each day the air feels different: it is warm, and there is dust in the air from all the activity. Philip reviews how the day has gone. His visioning is immediate, simply a case of taking the space to project his mind forwards over the whole of the day, picturing it in its many facets and in terms of how these relate to each other. For him relationships underpin the whole enterprise, and seeing how each person will fit into the day is central to his management.

One of the important elements of vision is that the i's are not dotted and the t's not crossed. There is still room for others' vision to flow in and expand and shape one's own.

Spirituality and vision are inseparable. Spirituality points to a way of being, working and living that is fuller than we can imagine and depends on each person to create it out of the nothingness and the dross. Without vision it is impossible; it is like having a tree without a trunk.

How to apply visioning:

- Before your next meeting take a few moments to think about not only what you want from the meeting, but also what is the highest possible outcome. Picture it, see what it looks like, hear what it sounds like; get the feel of it.

Journalling

Journalling is one of the most flexible and multifaceted tools available. Having a journal is like having a safe room where you can any time bring into the light of day those parts of your experience that are otherwise hidden. It is a place to ask questions, voice fears, doubts and frustrations, give thanks, highlight the good, and park and recycle the negative. Not all traditions advocate journals, but it is a cornerstone of the Quaker path.

How to apply journalling:
• Buy an empty notebook and use it to review what you have learnt each day.

SUMMARY

Spiritual tools are very practical. They are meant to make our lives happier and fuller, but they have had terribly bad press for centuries. Despite that, try them for yourself and see how they work. They are powerful tools, so it is wise to use them with care, ideally in a community where the checks and balances of other people will help to moderate them wisely. It is not without reason that, until the past few decades, spiritual tools have largely been overseen and bounded by the clergy, who have spent years studying them. Take time to use there tools well and appropriately; just because you pick up a paint brush does not mean that you will become Leonardo da Vinci overnight.

QUESTIONNAIRE:

HOW SOUL-FRIENDLY IS YOUR WORKPLACE?

This questionnaire will help you to measure how your company is doing in terms of its soul-friendliness. It will help to highlight your strengths and also show where there is room for improvement. Ideally complete the questionnaire as a pair, with one person asking the questions, listening to (without comment) and recording the response of the other person.

When completing the questionnaire, give your first spontaneous response. If the question makes no sense to you, score zero. If you can reply, 'Yes, definitely!' to a question score 5 for it. If the answer lies somewhere in between and lots of qualifying statements spring to your mind, take a moment to ponder then, following your gut reaction, place your company where you think it stands *overall* on the line from 1 to 5.

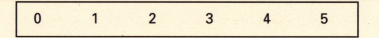

| 0 | 1 | 2 | 3 | 4 | 5 |

1 Do your leaders have a commitment to individuals' personal and professional growth and development?

2 Is there a vision that is exciting and makes people want to get up in the morning to bring it into the world?

3 Do people have the freedom to choose how they want to reach a result?

4 Is there fun and humour?

5 Do people take risks?

6 Is making money balanced by other values and goals?

7 Is there a sense of buzz and excitement?

8 Is the company involved with the local community?

9 Are personal difficulties and hardships shared by colleagues at work?

10   Are people open about their weaknesses and willing to be vulnerable?

11   Is there flexibility of work patterns that honours people's needs outside work, such as their family and community?

12   Do people enjoy one another?

13   Is your receptionist valued, appreciated and included in decision-making?

14   Are differences of personality and culture respected and taken into account?

15   Are people well remunerated for their work?

16   Are people open with each other?

17   Are there opportunities for celebration?

18   Do your leaders really like and enjoy people?

19   Is the best of the past valued by newcomers?

20   Are people able to be themselves?

21   Do people feel fulfilled?

22   Is there a sense of shared values and endeavours?

23   Do your leaders hand over leadership to others within the organisation?

24   Are mundane tasks tackled in creative ways?

25   Are people willing to make mistakes and readily acknowledge them?

26   Is there a lack of envy and resentment around salaries?

27   Is there plenty of energy and vitality?

28   Does the company have a green audit; does it care about the planet?

29   Are people able to air their frustrations and irritations in a safe way?

30   Are people appreciative and thankful of each other?

31   Are long, tough hours unacceptable?

32   Do people delight in delighting each other?

33   Is your cleaner valued and involved in decision-making (and would he or she agree?)

34 Is there a place for those who have a faith to practise it?

35 Are people's physical needs taken care of; are there light, peace and freshness?

36 Are there regular (at least weekly) feedback mechanisms?

37 Is there conviviality and welcome?

38 Do the leaders know what it is really like for the people on the ground doing the job?

39 Is there investment in the long-term development of the company?

40 Are there good and frank discussions about issues such as old age and the meaning of life?

41 Is there mobility within the company?

42 Is there a sense of the company having a higher purpose?

43 Is the language used in the company free of negative victim language?

44 Is there experimentation with new ways of running meetings?

45 Are mistakes accepted as an inevitable part of life; is it a no-blame culture?

46 Does everyone understand the impact on company finances of their everyday actions?

47 If buzz and energy levels dip, are there strategies for renewing them?

48 Does the company have an ethical code of conduct?

49 Are professional difficulties acknowledged, faced up to and dealt with promptly?

50 Is there strong teamwork in which people count on one another for help and support?

51 Is stress kept at a healthy level and excess stress removed; can people sleep at night?

52 Is there empathy for each other, including the customer?

53 Are the operatives on the 'factory floor' valued and appreciated?

54 Is the company multicultural and inclusive of old and young, women and men, black and white, able-bodied and disabled?

55 Is there beauty in the company?

56 Is there plenty of positive authentic feedback?

57 Do people want to come to work?

58 Does management listen?

59 Is there healthy detachment, a sense of perspective that does not take anything too seriously?

60 Is there an absence of hollow brand hype?

61 Are people free and able to develop their work roles according to their strengths?

62 Does the company have a distinctive culture?

63 Is leadership shown throughout the entire company?

64 Are people entrepreneurial, devising new ways and products?

65 Do people trust one another at work?

66 Is financial greed regarded as unacceptable?

67 Is there passion; do people know this matters immensely?

68 Are the suppliers to the company working in humane conditions?

69 Are the tough times faced with courage and adventurousness?

70 Is there zero tolerance of turf wars?

71 Can women enjoy both a family and career progression?

72 Do people treat each other in the way in which they want to be treated?

73 Are there respect, care and compassion for the leaders?

74 Is there an awareness of and care for people's disabilities?

75 Is there a place where people can take time to be quiet and still?

76 Is there real listening between individuals?

77 When people achieve something, is it recognised and appreciated?

78 Do your leaders care about and serve people?

79 Is there a lack of selfish ego?

80 Do people work with integrity; is their word their bond?

81 Do people feel free and excited about life and its possibilities?

82 Do people actively use values to help them resolve situations?

83 Do people recognise that in any situation they have a choice?

84 Are there programmes of training to help people to develop their awareness?

85 Do staff empathise with, and care about, the customers?

86 Is fairness felt to be important in trading with customers and suppliers?

87 Do people feel fully alive?

88 Do you have a sense of your company as a community of which you are proud to be part?

89 Is there a willingness to share the costs equally, for example, the pain of cost-cutting?

90 Is there zero tolerance of bullying, gossip and bitchiness?

91 Can men have both a full family life and career progression?

92 Are words and concepts such as happiness and joy acceptable and used?

93 Are the young really valued and listened to?

94 Are the feminine qualities prized?

95 Do people have their own professional space in which to work?

96 Is it an environment where it is safe to say what you think?

97 Would people still come to work even if they did not need the money?

98 Do your leaders lead with humility?

99 Is change accepted as a vital part of life?

100 Is there substance behind the image and words?

Measuring the results

Soul-friendliness is not a precise, mathematical science so don't worry about exact figures. This questionnaire is intended as a general guide only.

Total	Comment
Above 400	We had better all come and study at your feet.
300–399	You are a very soul-friendly company.
250–299	You are a soul-friendly company with scope for developing new aspects.
150–249	You have plenty to build on, but plenty left to do.
100–149	There is room for improvement here.
50–99	Seek urgent medical attention.
Below 49	Many people will be spending their lives in quiet desperation in your company and the profits will eventually suffer. Get help.

Which items did you rate with a 5 on the questionnaire? These items are where your strength lies. Note them, appreciate them and share them with colleagues.

Check through the items you rated between 0 and 2. These are the areas on which you can focus to expand the soul-friendliness of your company.

If you want to carry out a more detailed analysis of your answers, there is a section on pages 277–8 that splits the questions into groups associated with particular aspects of soul-friendliness. However, there is also a very simple 'litmus test' you can perform, as follows.

THREE STALWART INDICATORS TO TEST
THE ACCURACY OF YOUR IMPRESSIONS

All the companies in this book have infinitesimal absenteeism, little sickness and very low staff turnover; they are well below the national average on all three counts. These three factors are a good indicator of the soul health of your organisation. So, in your company:

• Is the rate of absenteeism below the national average?
• Is the amount of sickness below the national average?
• Is staff turnover below the national average?

If you can answer yes to all three questions your company is likely to be quite soul-friendly.

Soul-destroying workplaces are literally intolerable for people. They have to find some way to get out or they will fall sick, leave or absent themselves through hangovers and other escape mechanisms. Every human being has a soul, and if that soul is being destroyed it will seek some way to protect itself.

ANALYSING YOUR ANSWERS IN DETAIL

Copy your answers into these columns, then add up your total for each row						Total	Soul-friendly facet being measured
Questions 1, 21, 41, 61, 81							Commitment to human growth and development
Questions 2, 22, 42, 62, 82							Shared values and visions
Questions 3, 23, 43, 63, 83							People taking responsibility
Questions 4, 24, 44, 64, 84							Awareness, creativity, innovation and fun
Questions 5, 25, 45, 65, 85							No-blame culture, where there is trust
Questions 6, 26, 46, 66, 86							Healthy attitudes to money
Questions 7, 27, 47, 67, 87							Commitment to full aliveness
Questions 8, 28, 48, 68, 88							Sense of belonging and being connected to the community
Questions 9, 29, 49, 69, 89							Facing up to, confronting, expressing and moving on with difficulties
Questions 10, 30, 50, 70, 90							Strong teams, where people respect and appreciate each other
Questions 11, 31, 51, 71, 91							Work–life balance and flexibility
Questions 12, 32, 52, 72, 92							People enjoying and caring for each other
Questions 13, 33, 53, 73, 93							Deep equality and respect for individuals
Questions 14, 34, 54, 74, 94							Multicultural and personality diversity
Questions 15, 35, 55, 75, 95							Physical well-being

ANALYSING YOUR ANSWERS IN DETAIL

Copy your answers into these columns, then add up your total for each row						Total	Soul-friendly facet being measured
Questions 16, 36, 56, 76, 96							Listening, openness, honesty commitment and feedback
Questions 17, 37, 57, 77, 97							Celebration, conviviality and happiness
Questions 18, 38, 58, 78, 98							Leadership with humility
Questions 19, 39, 59, 79, 99							Sense of perspective and detachment
Questions 20, 40, 60, 80, 100							People being able to be themselves, i.e. authenticity and integrity

CONCLUSION:

WHAT IF?

THE POTENTIAL OF EACH COMPANY

THE COMPANIES WE HAVE MET are superb, but if they stand still and do not develop, they will die. Soul is inherently evolutionary; it never stops still for long. It is constantly evolving, bringing in yet more life. If, as an individual or a company, you think you have arrived and got everything sorted, you have definitely got lost. There is no finished product here, no limit to what soul is or can and will become and any company that thinks it can package up the soul has got it all wrong. Each of these companies in the book has changed and evolved even over the course of my researching and writing the book. What has stayed constant in each, however, is the steady, calm centre, the soul that does not change.

Each of these companies is, in soul terms, still in the embryonic phase; each inevitably has the potential to develop way beyond where it lies today. Operating now within the wasteful rules of capitalism, they all struggle with endless compromises, each trying to square the circle, each succeeding or failing to some degree. A million and more choices every week will determine where and how these companies evolve, but here are some possible paths that lie ahead.

High performance and happiness

What if a computer training company has found a principle that leads to phenomenal high performance and happiness? They currently train people to develop their computer literacy, and they have lessons they can teach other sectors on how to achieve high performance. In the process, they have the potential to spread happiness into the mainstream corporate, public and voluntary sectors. Our health service is sick with the lack of soul-friendliness, and this company could inject happiness and performance.

Employment and skills

What if an employment agency has found the way to make the unemployable employable, to find people their place in the workplace? They have the potential to transform employment agencies and bring a wave of those previously unemployed into the workforce. In alliance with a computer training company, they have the potential to ensure we as a country do not have a shortage of people equipped with IT skills.

Connectedness and planetary awareness

What if a company has discovered the potential of planetary connectedness and how to develop it? This is still in infancy phase, with only a small percentage of the world's population online. Many first need water, food and health before computers. Nevertheless, this technology can enable people to get the information they need, make informed choices and make connections with other people in order to raise awareness. This raised knowledge and level of awareness could potentially change our ability to deal with the current planetary crisis in which the earth can no longer cope with human short-sightedness and our ignorance of our interdependencies.

Sales and manufacturing

What if a company has discovered a way of transforming a manufacturing, telesales, sales force into a body of people who touch the lives of everyone they meet? They have found a way to wake people up to the fact that there is more to life than one could possibly imagine. They have the potential to inspire call centres and the wider corporate world.

> *So all over the world, children work in fields with toxic*
> *pesticides, in dangerous mines and in rubber and steel*
> *factories where small fingers and hands are sliced off*
> *or mangled in heavy machinery. Many of these children*
> *are producing stuff for the export market: canned fish,*
> *tea, rubber for tyres. But their plight has never*
> *captured the world's imagination.*

Naomi Klein

● ●

Awareness in the financial world

What if one man has discovered a way of turning a bank division around regardless of the overall culture of the company? What if, through his indomitable individuality, he teaches the business leaders of financial organisations how to trust their intuition and to use feedback and mentoring in order to transform their organisations, to humanise them and to make them excel?

Economic ownership

What if a company has found a way of sidestepping the worst features of capitalism and removing the power of the faceless shareholder? What if this company's experience offers a vital alternative model as the current economic system stumbles over its internal contradictions and seeks a new third way, a way not based on destructive competition? What if the company can help society to look at the economic root causes of many of our conflicts and hardships?

The environment

What if a giant chemical/pharmaceutical company has already found environmentally sound ways of working in order to be way ahead of environmental legislation and retain a competitive edge? It has the scientists, the experience, the substance to tackle some of the global-

281

sized problems facing the earth – pollution, waste, desertification, carcinogens. It also has the persistence and perseverance to find an answer to some of the diseases that are devastating the Third World. What if this giant taught multinationals how to stay human and take environmental responsibility?

The companies whose stories I have recounted are not alone. When first I set out to find companies, a good number of small businesses fell into my lap quite readily, all as astonishing as those outlined in this book. There was HUB, a company within the Institute of Directors, a body that was looking for and supporting honour in business. It was led by a remarkable woman, Oonagh Harpur, who combines spiritual awareness with financial expertise. There was Glaxo Smith Kline, with its head of Human Resources, Asif Khan, for whom all work is done for the greater good and woven with an Islamic commitment to compassion and responsibility. Next was OPRAF, the franchising company led by Roger Salmon, an organisation that, despite the folly of ideological privatisation, worked with courage, great honesty and leadership within the murky swamp of political short-sightedness, civil service timidity and a general unwillingness to fund a modern railway system. Few would have had their strength to maintain integrity within the quagmire. At Bridgehead, an outstanding small software house, the same people have for thirty years enjoyed solving people's software problems and caring for customers and colleagues with love, balance and integrity. There is Hewlett Packard whose finance director worked four days a week so that he could study for a degree in divinity on the other day. This is a company whose chief executive officer wants it to be a shining soul. When cost-cutting came, it was shared imaginatively throughout the company.

All these companies exist in the harsh world of economics and in the disillusioned world of secularism. The words that they use, how they live, will mean nothing to the totally disillusioned, cynical person who has given up hope. But to anyone who has eyes to see, the soul qualities found in the stories of the people there can inspire you to make it happen where you are. All things are possible to those who dare to dream of heaven and ground it in the humdrum of daily life. Then the sacred is brought to life.

Corporations hold much of the power to determine the future of our earth. People are hungry for a world that has meaning, stability and sanity, and the companies in this book offer a passionate, powerful and people-centred way of working that can transform life, not only at work, but also in the wider world of family, community and the planet. They show what spirituality at work looks like in practice, offer other companies ways forward and point to ways of expressing spirituality that are relevant to today's world.

A FINAL WORD

Ernest Bader, founder of Scott Bader, dedicated his life to making a business that would carry within it the seeds of transformation. He had an overwhelming desire for those who worked there to be free and to be most fully what a human being can become. The company often caused him great pain, frustrating him because people could not see what *he* saw. When, as a very old man, he died, involved with the company right up to the end, his last words were, 'Do they not see that it is love?'

CHOPSTICKS

A women who had worked all her life to bring about good was granted one wish: 'Before I die let me visit both hell and heaven.' Her wish was granted. 'Where would you like to go first?', asked the angel. 'To hell', she replied. She was whisked off to a great banqueting hall, where the tables where loaded with delicious food and drink. Around the tables sat miserable, starving people, as wretched as could be. 'Why are they like this?', the woman asked the angel. 'Look at their arms', the angel replied. She looked and saw that long chopsticks,

283

secured above the elbow, were attached to each person's arms. Unable to bend their elbows, the people aimed the chopsticks at the food, missed every time and sat hungry, frustrated and miserable. 'This is indeed hell! Take me away from here!', she said.

The woman was then whisked off to heaven, where she again found herself in a great banqueting hall with tables piled high. Around the tables sat people laughing, contented and joyful. 'No chopsticks, I suppose', she said. 'Oh yes there are', said the angel. 'Look – just as in hell, they are long and attached above the elbow, but look . . . here people have learnt to feed one another.'

All shall be well and all shall be used and all manner of thing shall be well.

Julian of Norwich

BIBLIOGRAPHY

Autry, James A., *Love and Profit: The Art of Caring Leadership*, Avon Books: New York (1991).

Bach, Richard, *Illusions: The Adventures of a Reluctant Messiah*, William Heinemann: Great Britain (1977).

Barrett, Richard, *Liberating the Corporate Soul: Building a Visionary Organization*, Butterworth Heinemann: Boston, Massachusetts (1998).

Blue, Lionel, *To Heaven with Scribes and Pharisees*, Darton, Longman & Todd: London (1975).

Blum, Fred, *Depth, Psychology and the Healing Ministry*, Arthur James: London (1990).

Bolt, Laurence G., *Zen and the Art of Making a Living: A Practical Guide to Creative Career Design*, Lightning Press: New York (1992).

Brueggemann, Walter, *The Prophetic Imagination*, SCM Press: London (1992).

Burns, Sally and Lamont, Georgeanne, *Values and Visions: A Handbook for Spiritual Development and Global Awareness*, Hodder & Stoughton: London (1995).

Caddy, Eileen, *Opening Doors Within*, The Findhorn Press: Scotland (1987).

Cameron, Julia, *The Artist's Way: A Course in Discovering and Recovering Your Creative Self*, Macmillan Publishers Ltd: London (1994).

Caniford, Jack & Hansen, Mark Victor, *Chicken Soup for the Soul: Stories That Restore Your Faith in Human Nature*, Vermilion: Florida (1999).

de Chardin, Pierre Teilhard, *The Phenomenon of Man*, William Collins Sons & Co.: London (1959).

de Chardin, Pierre Teilhard, *Le Milieu Divin*, Collins: London (1960).

Chopra, Deepak, *The Seven Spiritual Laws of Success: A Practical Guide To The Fulfilment of Your Dreams*, Bantam Press: London (1996).

Covey, Stephen R., *The Seven Habits of Highly Effective People: Powerful Lessons in Personal Changes*, Simon & Schuster: London (1992).

Crwys-Williams, Jennifer (Ed.), *In the Words of Nelson Mandela: A Little Pocketbook*, Michael Joseph: London (1998).

H.H. Dalai Lama, *The Art of Happiness: A Handbook for Living*, Hodder & Stoughton: London (1998).

H.H. Dalai Lama, *Ancient Wisdom, Modern World: Ethics for the New Millennium*, Little, Brown & Company: London (1999).

285

Doyle, Brendan, *Meditations With Julian of Norwich*, Bear & Company: Santa Fe, New Mexico (1983).

Edwards, Gill, *Stepping Into the Magic: A New Approach to Everday Life*, Judy Piatkus: London (1993).

Edwards, Gill, *Pure Bliss: The Art of Living in Soft Time*, Judy Piatkus: London (1999).

Elkins, David N., *Beyond Religion*, Quest Books: Wheaton, Illinois (1998).

Farrow, Jo, *The World in My Heart*, Quaker Home Service: London (1990).

Feng, Gia-Fu and English, Jane, *Tao Te Ching*, Wildwood House Ltd: Aldershot, Hampshire (1972).

Ferrucci, Piero, *What We May Be: The Visions and Techniques of Psychosynthesis*, Turnstone Press: Wellingborough, Northamptonshire, Britain (1982).

Foster, Richard, *Celebration of Discipline*, Hodder & Stoughton: London (1980).

Foster, Richard, *Freedom of Simplicity*, Harper & Row: USA (1981).

Fox, Matthew, *The Reinvention of Work: A New Vision of Livelihood for Our Time*, Aquarian: New York (1994).

Gawain, Shakti, *Creative Visualization: Use the Power of Your Imagination to Create What You Want in Your Life*, New World Library: San Rafael, California (1978).

Guillory, William A., Ph.D., *The Living Workplace: Spirituality in the Workplace, A Guide for Adapting to the Chaotically Changing Workplace*, Innovations International: Salt Lake City, Utah (1997).

Hampson, Tom and Whalen, Loretta, *Tales of the Heart: Affective Approaches to Global Education*, Friendship Press Inc: New York (1991).

Handy, Charles, *The Empty Raincoat: Making Sense of the Future*, Hutchinson: London (1994).

Handy, Charles, *The Hungry Spirit: Beyond Capitalism, A Quest for Purpose in the Modern World*, Hutchinson: London (1997).

Harding, D.E., *On Having No Head: Zen and the Re-Discovery of the Oblivious*, Arkana: London (1986).

Heider, John, *The Tao of Leadership*, Wildwood House: Great Britain (1986).

Hoe, Susanna, *The Man Who Gave His Company Away: A Biography of Ernest Bader, Founder of the Scott Bader Commonwealth*, Scott Bader: Great Britain (1978).

Hughes, Gerard W., *Oh God, Why?: A Journey Through Lent for Bruised Pilgrims*, The Bible Reading Fellowship: Oxford (1993).

Jeffers, Susan, *Feel the Fear and Do It Anyway: How to Turn Your Fear and Indecision into Confidence and Action*, Century Hutchinson: London (1987).

Johnson, Spencer, Dr, *Who Moved My Cheese: An Amazing Way to Deal with Change in Your Work and in Your Life*, Vermillion: London (1999).

Johnston, William, *Being in Love: The Practice of Christian Prayer*, William Collins Sons & Co.: London (1988).

Klein, Naomi, *No Logo*, Flamingo: London (2000).

Kuhn, Thomas S., *The Copernican Revolution*, Vintage Books: New York (1957).

Lampen, John, *Mending Hurts*, Quaker Home Service: London (1987).

Lasch, Christopher, *The Minimal Self: Psychic Survival in Troubled Times*, W.W. Norton & Co.: USA (1984).

Leech, Kenneth, *True God: An Exploration in Spiritual Theology*, Sheldon Press, SPCK: London (1985).

Lewin, Roger and Regine, Birute, *The Soul at Work: Unleashing the Power of Complexity Science for Business Success*, Orion Business Books: London (1999).

Lewis, C.S., *The Screwtape Letters: Letters from a Senior to a Junior Devil*, Geoffrey Bless: London (1942).

Lloyd, Humphrey, *The Quaker Lloyds in the Industrial Revolution*, Hutchinson & Co: London (1975).

London Borough of Kent, *Diving Deep and Surfacing: Exploring the spiritual dimension of education*, London Borough of Kent: London (1998).

London Yearly Meeting of the Religious Society of Friends, *Christian Faith and Practice in the Experience of the Society of Friends*, Headley Brothers: London (1960).

Lundin, Stephen C., Ph.D., Paul, Harry and Christensen, John, *Fish!: A Remarkable Way to Boost Morale and Improve Results*, Hyperion: USA (2000).

Marriott, J.W. (Jnr) and Brown, Kathi Ann, *The Spirit to Serve*, Harper Collins: New York (1997).

Maufroy, Muriel, *Breathing Truth: Quotations from Jalaluddin Rumi*, Sanyar Press: London (1997).

McDonagh, Sean, *The Greening of the Church*, Geoffrey Chapman: London (1990).

de Mello, Anthony, *The Song of the Bird*, Doubleday: New York (1981).

de Mello, Anthony, *Wellsprings: A Book of Spiritual Exercises*, Gujarat Sahitya Prakash: Anand, India (1983).

de Mello, Anthony, *One Minute Wisdom*, Gujarat Sahitya Prakash: Anand, India (1987).

de Mello, Anthony, *Awareness*, Harper Collins: London (1990).

de Mello, Anthony, *Call to Love*, Gujaret Sahitya Prakash: Anand, India (1991).

Merton, Thomas, *Thoughts in Solitude*, Burns & Oates: Tunbridge Wells, Kent (1975).

Merton, Thomas, *Conjectures of a Guilty Bystander*, Burns & Oates: Tunbridge Wells, Kent (1995).

Merton, Thomas, *The Way of Chuang Tzu*, Burns & Oates: Tunbridge Wells, Kent (1995).

Mitroff Ian I., Denton, Elizabeth, A., *A Spiritual Audit of Corporate America*, Jossey-Bass Publishers: San Francisco (1999).

287

Moore, Thomas, *Care of the Soul: How to Add Depth and Meaning to Your Everyday Life*, Judy Piatkus: London (1992).

Moore, Thomas, *The Re-Enchantment of Everyday Life*, Hodder & Stoughton: London (1996).

O'Donohue, John, *Anam Cara: Spiritual Wisdom from the Celtic World*, Transworld: London (1997).

Palmer, Martin, *Living Christianity*, Element Books: Longmead, Shaftesbury, Dorset (1993).

Puhl, Louis J., *The Spiritual Exercises of St. Ignatius: A New Translation*, The Newland Press: Westminster, Maryland (1951).

Quotes of Gandhi, UBS: New Delhi.

Raistrick, Arthur, *Quakers in Science & Industry*, William Sessions: York (1950).

Rinpoche, Sogyal, *The Tibetan Book of Living and Dying: A New Spiritual Classic from One of the Foremost Interpreters of Tibetan Buddhism to the West*, Rider: London (1992).

Roddick, Anita, *Business as Unusual: The Journey of Anita Roddick and The Body Shop*, Thorsons: London (2000).

The Rule of St Benedict in English, The Liturgical Press: Collegeville, Minnesota (1981).

Russell, Bertrand, *History of Western Philosophy*, George Allen and Unwin Ltd: London (1948).

The School Is Us: A Practical Guide to Successful Whole School Change, World Wide Fund for Nature UK: Manchester (1993).

Science & Religion: A Symposium, Gerald Howe Ltd: London (1931).

Scott Peck, M., *The Road Less Travelled: A New Psychology of Love, Traditional Values and Spiritual Growth*, Hutchinson & Co.: London (1983).

Scott Peck, M., *The Different Drum: The Creation of True Community – the First Step to World Peace*, Simon & Schuster: USA (1987).

Scott Peck, M., *Further Along the Road Less Travelled: The Unending Journey Towards Spiritual Growth*, Simon & Schuster: London (1993).

Semler, Ricardo, *Maverick! The Success Story Behind the World's Most Unusual Workplace*, Arrow: London (1994).

Shah, Idries, *Tales of the Dervishes: Teaching-Stories of the Sufi Masters Over the Past Thousand Years*, E.P. Dutton & Co. (1970).

Stoller, Tony, *Wrestling with the Angel: Swarthmore Lecture 2001*, Quaker Books: London (2001).

Swimme, Brian, *The Universe Is a Green Dragon: A Cosmic Creation Story*, Bear & Company: Santa Fe, New Mexico (1984).

Thich Nhat Hanh, *The Miracle of Mindfulness: A Manual on Meditation*, Beacon Press: Boston, Massachusetts (1975).

Thich Nhat Hanh, *Being Peace*, Parallax Press: Berkeley, California (1987).

Tolles, Fredrick B., *Meeting House and Counting House: The Quaker Merchants of Colonial Philadelphia 1682–1763*, The University of Carolina Press: New York (1948).

Trevelyan, George, *Magic Casements: The Use of Poetry in the Expanding of Consciousness*, Coventure: London (1980).

Vanstone, W.H., *The Stature of Waiting*, Darton, Longman & Todd: London (1982).

Vernon, Anne, *A Quaker Business Man: The Life of Joseph Rowntree 1836–1925*, George Allen & Unwin: London (1958).

Vest, Norvene, *Friend of the Soul: A Benedictine Spirituality of Work*, Cowley Publications: Boston, Massachusetts (1997).

de Waal, Esther, *Seeking God: The Way of St Benedict*, Fount Paperbacks: London (1984).

Watts, Alan W., *The Way of Zen*, Pantheon Books: New York (1957).

Wheatley, Margaret, J., *Leadership and the New Science*, Berrett-Koehler: San Francisco (1992).

Whyte, David, *The Heart Aroused: Poetry and the Preservation of the Soul in Corporate America*, Currency Doubleday: New York (1994).

Wilber, Ken, *Grace and Gift: Spirituality and Healing in the Life and Death of Treya Killam Wilber*, Shambhala Publications: Boston, Massachusetts (1991).

Wilber, Ken, *A Brief History of Everything*, Shambhala Publications: Boston, Massachusetts (1996).

Wilber, Ken, *One Taste: Daily Reflections on Integral Spirituality*, Shambhala Publications: Boston, Massachusetts (2000).

Wright, Lesley and Smye, Marti, *Corporate Abuse: How 'Lean and Mean' Robs People and Profits*, Macmillan: USA (1996).

The Yearly Meeting of the Religious Society of Friends (Quakers) in Britain, *Quaker Faith and Practice* (1994).

Yungblut, John R., *Discovering the Christ*, Element Books: Longmead, Shaftesbury, Dorset (1991).

Zeldin, Theodore, *Conversation: How Talk Can Change Your Life*, The Harvill Press: London (1998).

Zohar, Danah and Marshall, Ian, *Spiritual Intelligence: The Ultimate Intelligence*, Bloomsbury Publishing: London (2000).

ABOUT THE AUTHOR

AND SPIRITWORKS

GEORGEANNE LAMONT is the founder of SpiritWorks, a training consultancy dedicated to spiritual awareness in the workplace. Our mission is to inspire and encourage people to create soul-friendly work environments in order to achieve high performance and positive transformation.

If you would like to receive the **SpiritWorks** newsletter or details of our seminars, workshops, mentoring and training programmes, contact us at:

SpiritWorks
3 Kinross Avenue
Ascot SL5 9EP, UK

For general information, email: info@spiritworks.ltd.uk
To contact the author, email: georgeanne@spiritworks.ltd.uk
    or telephone 01344 628329
Website: www.spiritworks.ltd.uk

Georgeanne Lamont has worked on spiritual awareness in organisations since 1989. She has twenty years' experience of training and working with educational, local government and voluntary organisations, and with business. She co-authored *Values and Visions*, published by Hodder & Stoughton in 1995. She brings to her work the Quaker belief in people's inherent goodness and her experience that the sacred is found in the everyday.